Chaste Passions

CHASTE PASSIONS

*Medieval English
Virgin Martyr Legends*

Edited and Translated by

KAREN A. WINSTEAD

Cornell University Press

ITHACA AND LONDON

First published 2000 by Cornell University Press
First printing, Cornell Paperbacks, 2000

Printed in the United States of America

Library of Congress Cataloging-in-Publication Data

Chaste passions : medieval English virgin martyr legends / edited and translated by
Karen A. Winstead.
    p. cm.
Includes bibliographical references.
ISBN 0-8014-3569-2 (cloth) — ISBN 0-8014-8557-6 (pbk.)
    1. Christian women saints—Legends.   2. Christian women martyrs—Legends.   3.
Virginity—Religious aspects—Christianity—Legends.   4. Legends, Christian—England. I.
Winstead, Karen A. (Karen Anne), 1960–

BX4656 .C43 2000
270'.092'2—dc21
[B]

99-059377

Cornell University Press strives to use environmentally responsible
suppliers and materials to the fullest extent possible in the publishing
of its books. Such materials include vegetable-based, low-VOC inks
and acid-free papers that are recycled, totally chlorine-free, or partly
composed of nonwood fibers. Books that bear the logo of the FSC
(Forest Stewardship Council) use paper taken from forests that have
been inspected and certified as meeting the highest standards for
environmental and social responsibility. For further information,
visit our website at www.cornellpress.cornell.edu.

Cloth printing   10 9 8 7 6 5 4 3 2 1

Paperback printing   10 9 8 7 6 5 4 3 2 1

For my parents
Elizabeth J. and Arthur T. Welborn

Contents

Figures

Acknowledgments

I must first thank the colleagues and students at The Ohio State University—especially the non-medievalists—whose interest in "those crazy saints" inspired me to pursue these translations, as well as Cornell University Press, which suggested the project to me. A grant from the Center for Medieval and Renaissance Studies at Ohio State enabled me to purchase microfilms of unedited legends, and a Grant-in-Aid for study abroad enabled me to check my transcriptions against the original manuscripts. The department of English funded graduate assistants in summer and autumn 1998, and I am grateful to those assistants, Wendy Matlock and Christopher Manion, for their diligence. Both the anonymous reader for the press and my friend Phil Neal suggested many improvements, especially in tailoring the texts to non-specialists, and I thank them for their careful readings. Finally, I thank my husband, Carl Winstead, an invaluable consultant and my best friend.

This book is dedicated to my parents, Arthur T. and Elizabeth J. Welborn, in recognition of love and support that cannot be repaid.

Introduction

Uncle Pa Keating says he can't think of a single saint in heaven he'd want to sit down and have a pint with. The saints in these books are different. There are stories about virgins, martyrs, virgin martyrs and they're worse than any horror film at the Lyric Cinema.

—FRANK McCOURT, *Angela's Ashes*

Many readers of this book no doubt grew up hearing stories about the saints. To me, the most arresting were those of the girls, some scarcely older than I was, who became virgin martyrs by suffering excruciating tortures to safeguard their "purity." I can still recall the Saint Lucy of my *Picture Book of Saints,* her yellow hair rippling down her sky-blue dress as she gazes toward heaven, the palm of martyrdom in one hand and a chalice containing two eyeballs in the other.[1] Studying the medieval prototypes of these legends in college, I learned that, for about a thousand years, virgin martyrs were among the most popular subjects of art and literature; during late antiquity and the early Middle Ages, hundreds of different legends were generated and were thereafter continually revised for new audiences. I also learned that Father Lawrence Lovasik, carrying this tradition into our times, had doctored his material considerably to suit it to the *Picture Book*—excising the grisliest mutilations, euphemizing the ubiquitous references to sex,

[1] Father Lawrence G. Lovasik, S. V. D., *Picture Book of Saints* (New York: Catholic Book Publishing Company, 1966), 113.

and only hinting at the incestuous desires that drove fathers to prey on their teenage daughters.

Though replete with vivid, not to say gory, detail, virgin martyr legends are notoriously unreliable as historical sources.[2] Most of them originated long after the great persecutions of the third and early fourth centuries in which their subjects were supposed to have died. Lucy's death in 304, for instance, is first described in a vita (life story) dating from the late fifth century, while the infamous plucking out of her eyes is a still later accretion. An even greater gap lies between Katherine of Alexandria's death in the early fourth century and the composition of her life in the ninth century. To be sure, early and reliable references to a few virgin martyrs do exist. Saint Agnes, who died in 350, is listed in a martyrology dating from 354. Even so, it is not at all clear that the historical Agnes has much to do with the Agnes who, according to her fifth-century vita, was protected by an angel when consigned to a brothel by her rejected suitor's father. The repetition of more or less the same plot in the legends of hundreds of different women is a clear sign that most are ahistorical.

That many saints are now considered fictive even by the Catholic Church should not lead us to conclude that the early medieval Church was perpetrating a fraud on a gullible populace. Medieval hagiographers (writers of saints' legends) simply did not share our strict equation of truth with historical accuracy. Indeed, the creators of saints' lives were, for the most part, deeply concerned with truth—but with spiritual rather than literal truth. Their purpose was not to record what had happened, but rather to celebrate the patterns of holiness that gave shape to history and would endure *in saecula saeculorum*. Those patterns are not obviously propitious to women's earthly well-being. Many feminists have argued that virgin martyr legends participate in a system of myths that has sustained women's subjugation through the ages.[3] An extreme expression

---

[2] The classic study of the genesis of saints' legends is Hippolyte Delehaye, *The Legends of the Saints: An Introduction to Hagiography*, trans. V. M. Crawford (Notre Dame: University of Notre Dame Press, 1961).

[3] For examples of very different feminist critiques of virgin martyr legends, see the introductory essays in Brigitte Cazelles, *The Lady as Saint: A Collection of French Hagiographical Romances of the Thirteenth Century* (Philadelphia: University of Pennsylvania Press, 1991); Susan Brownmiller, *Against Our Will: Men, Women and Rape* (New York: Simon and Schuster, 1975), 364–70; and Lynda Van Devanter, *Home before Morning: The Story of an Army Nurse in Vietnam* (New York: Warner Books, 1983), 19.

of the argument goes something like this: virgin martyr legends insist that the only good woman is a chaste woman; a woman's chastity is guaranteed only by her death; therefore, the only good woman is a dead woman. Others have complained that virgin martyr legends convey to girls the pernicious messages that suffering is heroic and that dying young is glamorous. Still others have observed that male martyrs die directly for an ideal, their faith, whereas women's ideals are mediated through a bodily function: the typical virgin martyr is initially persecuted because she will not have sex, and her faith becomes an issue only because it gives her rejected lover an excuse for retaliation. Many critics have viewed the virgin martyr legend, with its graphic description of violence against a vulnerable and naked female body, as a genre of thinly disguised pornography that provides men an acceptable outlet for their hostility toward women. Completely different readings, however, have also emerged from feminist perspectives. Focusing on the saints' defiance of their persecutors rather than on their victimization, some have heralded the saints as valiant rebels against an oppressive patriarchy.[4] Many feminists have noted that no other medieval literary genre portrays women in such a wide variety of "empowering" roles: as preachers, teachers, sovereigns, scholars, and social activists.

My own view is that it is a reductive error to pursue "the" meaning of the virgin martyr legend. Saints' legends as a genre indubitably affirm certain universal paradigms of holiness; virgin martyr legends, in particular, do purvey an ideology of gender and sexuality that many modern readers find repugnant, and feminist criticism has done a valuable service in elucidating that function. What is more interesting, however, is that, alongside these generalities and within the fixed plots, we can find a host of individual interpretations, messages, and slants. The aims and interests of writers of virgin martyr legends varied enormously, and readers' responses, which were not under the authors' control, varied even more.

This volume samples interpretations of the virgin martyr legend by

---

[4] See, for example, Jocelyn Wogan-Browne, "Saints' Lives and the Female Reader," *Forum for Modern Language Studies* 27 (1991): 314–32. Bertha Harris introduces sections of her lesbian novel *Lover* (originally published in 1976) with extracts from legends of female saints, mostly virgin martyrs. In the introduction to the 1993 edition, Harris notes that she was attracted to the saints' "acumen at ecstasy" and their determination "to escape the destiny of their gender." Bertha Harris, *Lover* (New York: New York University Press, 1993), xxiii.

Middle English writers during a crucial period in the development of saints' lives, circa 1200–1485.[5] Before 1200, most vitae were composed in Latin by and for people pursuing religious vocations, including monks, nuns, and recluses. In the thirteenth century, the Church became more committed to teaching the laity, even as the laity began to seek a more active piety. One result of these movements was that more religious literature, including hagiography (biographies and other writings about the saints), was translated into the native languages of these new lay audiences. Vernacular lives did not render the Latin vitae literally, but rather tailored them to appeal to lay readers and listeners, subsequently retailoring them as the tastes and interests of the laity shifted—and they shifted markedly. Generally speaking, virgin martyr legends of the fourteenth century focus on conflict and emphasize the saint's antisocial behavior, while legends of the fifteenth century portray a less confrontational, more prayerful, and therefore more socially acceptable heroine. Within these broad thematic trends we find enormous variety in style. Whereas some hagiographers tell their stories simply, others filter their legends through obtrusive narrators. The personalities of such narrators vary tremendously. William Paris's narrator delights in Christine's cartoonlike resilience, while John Lydgate's wallows in Margaret's sufferings. The narrator of the anonymous *Scottish Legendary* peppers his account of Eugenia's life with misogynist asides to the reader, while Bokenham's narrator expounds on the art of translation.

I have tried to preserve the multifarious voices heard in these legends by translating them into accurate but idiomatic modern English. My choices as a translator have been guided by the recognition that unfamiliar syntax and vocabulary can bury a story's tone and nuances, leaving only the bare sense intelligible. I have sought to provide the modern reader the experience that the original text provided its readers, insofar as that can be done without departing from its meaning. As part of this policy, I have translated verse legends into prose, since a prose rendering not only facilitates accuracy but also sounds more natural to modern readers, who are much less used to verse narration than were their medieval counterparts. I have also simplified the ponderous sentence

---

[5] For a detailed study of the developments of virgin martyr legends in England during this period, see Karen A. Winstead, *Virgin Martyrs: Legends of Sainthood in Late Medieval England* (Ithaca: Cornell University Press, 1997).

structure of the fifteenth-century prose legends, which would not have bothered a fifteenth-century audience but would seem excessively convoluted to the modern ear. To preserve the raunchiness of certain stories, I have used roughly equivalent expletives and obscenities. In doing all this I have of course been guided by my own judgment and by my understanding of style and tone. Readers may question some of my interpretations. Those wishing to know *exactly* what the originals say can, in most cases, work their way through the Middle English with no more than a glossary—and I do hope that these translations will entice many readers to the originals.

The legends gathered here reveal facets of medieval piety that will seem alien to most readers. Few today associate shockingly graphic violence with edifying religious literature. Indeed, the violence is edited out of most modern retellings of saints' legends, for adults as well as for children. Miracles, likewise, are mostly omitted or downplayed to suit our more skeptical—or less credulous—age. Some readers may be offended at the glib tone and coarse language that characterize so many of the texts; few will expect saints—especially female saints—to swear like sailors. One of the principal lessons that those who consider the sacred and the profane dichotomous can learn from these stories is how integral the profane was to medieval sacred culture.[6]

This anthology comprises sixteen legends, each of a different saint. The most common and most typical virgin martyrs in Middle English literature—Margaret, Agnes, Agatha, Lucy, and so on—are represented, but so are some quirky characters. Winifred is part virgin martyr and part holy nun: beheaded by an irate suitor, she is restored to life and resumes her religious vocation. Eugenia, part virgin martyr and part transvestite saint, lives disguised as a monk until accused of attempted rape by a vindictive woman. Justine's martyrdom is almost an afterthought in a

---

[6] The intersection of sacred and profane is especially striking in medieval prayer books, whose margins often feature scenes from secular life that many today might consider outright pornography. See Michael Camille's studies *Mirror in Parchment: The Luttrell Psalter and the Making of Medieval England* (Chicago: University of Chicago Press, 1998) and *Image on the Edge: The Margins of Medieval Art* (Cambridge: Harvard University Press, 1992). Another fascinating study of the surprising character of medieval religion is Kathleen Ashley and Pamela Sheingorn, *Writing Faith: Text, Sign, and History in the Miracles of Sainte Foy* (Chicago: University of Chicago Press, 1999). Eleventh-century accounts of miracles performed at her shrine in Conques represent the virgin martyr Foy as a prankster with a love for trinkets and even as a "serial killer" (37)!

tale dealing primarily with the machinations of an evil magician and his fiendish cohorts. I have also included some unusual renderings of popular legends. The prose life of Saint Katherine translated here recounts not only Katherine's spectacular martyrdom but also her upbringing, her conversion, and her marriage to Christ in an elaborate ceremony witnessed by the Virgin Mary, the apostles, and all the saints and martyrs.[7] Two of the narratives have never been edited ("Justine" and "Barbara" from the *South English Legendary*), and a third is available only in a rare nineteenth-century edition (the conversion portion of the prose *Katherine*). For these three texts I have provided both translations and, in appendices to this volume, transcriptions of the source manuscripts. The proportion of legends with unusual plots is higher in this collection than it was in medieval English anthologies. Most Middle English virgin martyr legends compactly narrate the universal story of the saint's suffering and martyrdom. There is certainly a scholarly rationale for my selection, in that a wide variety of legends gives the reader a sense of the genre's range. I am also catering, however, to the modern reader's taste for diversity. In doing so, I am participating in the enterprise of the medieval writers I am translating—that of making old stories accessible to new readers, who are attracted to them for reasons perhaps very different from those of the earliest audiences.

FURTHER READING

Translations of Related Primary Sources

Cazelles, Brigitte. *The Lady as Saint: A Collection of French Hagiographic Romances of the Thirteenth Century.* Philadelphia: University of Pennsylvania Press, 1991. These French legends, which feature heroines in the tradition of courtly romance, are a fascinating contrast with the contemporary Middle English texts in this volume.

The Plays of Hrotsvit of Gandersheim. Trans. Katharina Wilson. New York: Garland, 1989. This anthology of plays by a tenth-century canoness includes two virgin martyr plays.

Jacobus de Voragine. *The Golden Legend: Readings on the Saints.* 2 vols. Trans. William Granger Ryan. Princeton: Princeton University Press, 1993. A translation of Jacobus's *Legenda aurea*, the most influential and widely disseminated collection of

[7] For a discussion of Katherine's mystical marriage to Christ, a popular subject in late medieval art and literature, see Millard Meiss, *Painting in Florence and Siena after the Black Death: The Arts, Religion, and Society in the Mid-Fourteenth Century* (Princeton: Princeton University Press, 1951), 107–13.

legends in the Middle Ages, source for many of the fourteenth- and fifteenth-century legends in this volume.

Kempe, Margery. *The Book of Margery Kempe.* Trans. B. A. Windeatt. New York: Penguin Books, 1985. Autobiography of a fifteenth-century wife, businesswoman, mother of fourteen, and aspiring saint, whose understanding of virgin martyr legends affected her pursuit of holiness.

Sheingorn, Pamela. *The Book of Sainte Foy.* Philadelphia: University of Pennsylvania Press, 1995. Consists largely of accounts compiled in eleventh-century France of colorful posthumous miracles performed by the "trickster" virgin martyr, Saint Foy.

Wogan-Browne, Jocelyn, and Glyn S. Burgess. *Virgin Lives and Holy Deaths: Two Exemplary Biographies for Anglo-Norman Women.* London: Dent, 1996. Includes the legend of Saint Katherine in Anglo-Norman verse by the nun Clemence of Barking Abbey. This twelfth-century text is the only virgin martyr legend that is known to have been written by an English woman.

Edition

Reames, Sherry. *Middle English Lives of Female Saints.* Kalamazoo, Mich.: Medieval Institute Publications, forthcoming. This anthology, in a series tailored to students, is highly recommended for those wishing to read some saints' lives in the original Middle English.

References

D'Evelyn, Charlotte. "Saints' Legends." In *A Manual of the Writings in Middle English, 1050–1500.* Vol. 2. Ed. J. Burke Severs, 413–39, 556–635. Hamden, Conn.: Archon, 1970.

Farmer, David Hugh. *The Oxford Dictionary of the Saints.* Oxford: Oxford University Press, 1987.

Pelikan, Jaroslav. *The Christian Tradition: A History of the Development of Dogma.* 5 vols. Chicago: University of Chicago Press, 1984. Useful for readers wishing to pursue the theological allusions and discussions in the saints' lives.

Selected Studies

Ashley, Kathleen M., and Pamela Sheingorn. Introduction to *Interpreting Cultural Symbols: Saint Anne in Late Medieval Society.* Ed. Kathleen M. Ashley and Pamela Sheingorn, 1–68. Athens: University of Georgia Press, 1990. Important discussion of cultural and feminist approaches to saints' legends.

Duffy, Eamon. *The Stripping of the Altars: Traditional Religion in England, c. 1400–1580.* New Haven: Yale University Press, 1992.

Görlach, Manfred. *Studies in Middle English Saints' Legends.* Heidelberg: C. Winter, 1998.

Heffernan, Thomas J. *Sacred Biography: Saints and Their Biographers in the Middle Ages.* Oxford: Oxford University Press, 1988.

Schulenburg, Jane Tibbetts. *Forgetful of Their Sex: Female Sanctity and Society, ca. 500–1100.* Chicago: University of Chicago Press, 1998. See especially chap. 3, "At What Cost Virginity? Sanctity and the Heroics of Virginity," which suggests that virgin martyr legends may have inspired medieval nuns to mutilate themselves to avoid rape.

Winstead, Karen A. *Virgin Martyrs: Legends of Sainthood in Late Medieval England.* Ithaca: Cornell University Press, 1997.

Wogan-Browne, Jocelyn, Nicholas Watson, Andrew Taylor, and Ruth Evans, eds. *The Idea of the Vernacular: An Anthology of Middle English Literary Theory, 1280–1520.* University Park: Pennsylvania State University Press, 1999.

Saint Juliana

Anonymous, ca. 1200

The Juliana legend translated here is part of a significant body of Middle English literature that was composed in the West Midlands during the early 1200s. That corpus, which includes a guide for anchoresses, a virginity treatise, and the lives of two other virgin martyrs, Margaret and Katherine, was probably written by male clergy primarily for the guidance of the growing number of women following religious vocations. Early thirteenth-century women, benefiting from a rapid expansion of opportunities in the preceding century, could either join one of the dozens of religious houses that had been recently founded or pursue the more independent vocation of anchoress, leading a life of prayer and contemplation in a cell adjoining a church.

It is not surprising that the writer of *Juliana* considered his heroine—beautiful, self-confident, and determined to remain chaste at any cost—a fitting model for nuns and recluses. Although the legend ostensibly addressed a broader audience of "all those who cannot understand Latin," none of the surviving manuscripts appears to have been produced for a lay audience. Indeed, the legend seems very ill suited to such an audience, for in retelling the traditional Latin passion of Juliana, the Middle English writer celebrates the saint's refusal to submit to a marriage arranged by her father. Although there is no evidence that early thirteenth-century pastors had any desire to foment trouble within families, the Church was then asserting its control over the institution of marriage, insisting that marriage was a sacrament requiring the consent of the couple rather than a civil arrangement that could be imposed by the parents. If the writer of *Juliana* did have a message for the laity, it was probably not that children should rebel against their parents, but that parents arranging marriages should attend to ecclesiastical mandates.

Juliana is written in prose, but its alliteration and regular pattern of stresses give it a distinct rhythm, which is one of the hallmarks of the West Midlands literature of the period. In an attempt to convey an impression of the original language, I have imitated its heavy alliteration in my translation. I have also imitated the legend's inconsistency of tone, at times high-spoken, at times colloquial, as well as the internal rhymes and echoes of the same or similar words (e.g., "strengthens you with his strength against the strong devil") that may irritate many a modern reader.

Edition: Pe *Liflade and te Passiun of Seinte Iuliene.* Ed. S. R. T. O. d'Ardenne. EETS.OS 248. London: Oxford University Press, 1961.

Translation: *Anchoritic Spirituality: Ancrene Wisse and Associated Works.* Trans. Anne Savage and Nicholas Watson. New York: Paulist Press, 1991.

Elkins, Sharon K. *Holy Women of Twelfth-Century England.* Chapel Hill: University of North Carolina Press, 1988.
Innes-Parker, Catherine. "Fragmentation and Reconstruction: Images of the Female Body in *Ancrene Wisse* and the Katherine Group." *Comitatus* 26 (1995): 27–52.
———. "Sexual Violence and the Female Reader: Symbolic 'Rape' in the Saints' Lives of the Katherine Group." *Women's Studies* 24 (1994): 205–71.
Margherita, Gayle. "Body and Metaphor in the Middle English *Juliana.*" In *The Romance of Origins: Language and Sexual Difference in Middle English Literature,* 43–61. Philadelphia: University of Pennsylvania Press, 1994.
Millett, Bella. "Women in No Man's Land: English Recluses and the Development of Vernacular Literature in the Twelfth and Thirteenth Centuries." In *Women and Literature in Britain, 1150–1500,* ed. Carol M. Meale, 86–103. Cambridge: Cambridge University Press, 1993.
———. "The Audience of the Saints' Lives of the Katherine Group." *Reading Medieval Studies* 16 (1990): 127–55.
Millett, Bella, ed. *Ancrene Wisse, the Katherine Group, and the Wooing Group.* Annotated Bibliographies of Old and Middle English Literature. Vol. 2. Woodbridge, Suffolk: D. S. Brewer, 1996.
Noonan, John T., Jr. "Power to Choose." *Viator* 4 (1973): 419–34.
Robertson, Elizabeth. *Early English Devotional Prose and the Female Audience.* Knoxville: University of Tennessee Press, 1990.
Warren, Ann K. *Anchorites and Their Patrons in Medieval England.* Berkeley: University of California Press, 1985.
Winstead, Karen A. *Virgin Martyrs: Legends of Sainthood in Late Medieval England,* 19–63. Ithaca: Cornell University Press, 1997.
Wogan-Browne, Jocelyn. "Saints' Lives and the Female Reader." *Forum for Modern Language Studies* 27 (1991): 314–32.

Fig. 1. Scenes from the life of Saint Juliana: Jacobus de Voragine, *Legenda aurea.* (Courtesy of the Huntington Library. MS HM 3027, fol. 34.)

Saint Juliana

In the name of the father, and of the son, and of the holy spirit: here begins the life and passion of Saint Juliana.

For the love of our lord father, the creator, and the glorious worship of his precious son, and the glorification of the holy spirit who proceeds from them both, one God without beginning, each person fully divine, let all those who cannot understand Latin hear and heed the life of a maiden that has been translated from Latin into English, so that this holy lady who lives in heaven should love us all the more and, through her blessed intercession, lead us from this false life to the everlasting life so pleasing to Christ.

The maiden and martyr to whom I refer was named Juliana and was born to a heathen family in the city of Nicomedia.[1] Her earthly father, Africanus, pursued and oppressed Christians, driving them to death with terrible torments. But Juliana, being one whom the high heavenly lord favored, forsook the faith of her fathers and began to love only the living God, the loving lord who created all creatures, and who governs and guides all creation according to his will.

At that time, our source says, the proud Roman emperor Maximian, with his huge retinue and noble retainers, acclaimed and adored the heathen gods and condemned all who believed in the one God. More than many of his other men, this mighty Maximian loved a certain Eleusius, a man of noble blood, rich in revenues and young in years. This young man Eleusius, the royal darling, favored Africanus with his friendship and made a habit of coming home with him and seeing his daughter. Appreciating Juliana's stunning and exquisite youth, Eleusius felt as if his heart were struck with bolts shot from love's bow, and he would not live without her healing love. After a while, he went to her father, Africanus, begging him to bestow her on him and promising to honor her with all his might as his most prized possession. Africanus, knowing that such a wellborn man was a worthy match for a wellborn lady, granted his boon. Juliana was soon betrothed to him, though it was against her will. But she believed in the God who never deceived anyone who truly trusted in him, and she went to church every single day, entreating him with tender tears to teach her how to save her virginity from shameful intimacies.

[1] A city on the Sea of Marmara, east of Constantinople, in present-day Turkey.

Now, lovelorn Eleusius thought it was taking too long to get his bride wedded and bedded. To stall him a while longer, Juliana informed him that she would not deign to love him—nor could anyone make her go near him—until he was made second in command to Maximian, that is, high reeve of Rome.[2] As soon as Eleusius heard this, he got the emperor to grant him all he wished. Then, following custom, he was driven in a four-wheeled chariot from street to street throughout the city. His chariot was canopied with costly purple cloth, with gold-embroidered fabric and silk and other expensive materials, as befitted a man with pressing duties to discharge and the high reeveship of Rome to govern and to guide. Then he informed Juliana that, since he had done her will, she should do his. The blessed Juliana, Jesus Christ's lover, emboldened by Christ's blessed love, sent a messenger with these words for Eleusius: "You've wasted your time. No matter how you rave or what you do, I must reveal my resolution. If you abandon your pagan practices and believe in God the father and his precious son and the holy spirit, the people's comforter—one God made great with every goodness—I'll happily have you; and if you won't, you're free to find another love." Upon receiving this message, the high reeve seethed. He sent for her father and proceeded to tell him what she said after he thought he'd met all her demands. Astounded, her father, Africanus, swore, "By the gods I'd hate to offend, if what you say is true, she'll be sorry. I'll hand her over to you and you can do what you want with her." Eleusius thanked him.

Juliana was then summoned. Her father, Africanus, first tried being pleasant to see if love would get him anywhere. "Juliana," he said, "my darling daughter, tell me why you rebuff the benefits and bounties, the providence and the pleasures that would result from the marriage I'm promoting. The reeveship of Rome is nothing to scoff at. You have the chance to be first lady of the city and of all its lands."

The blessed Juliana replied, "If he will love and believe in almighty God, then his suit will succeed swiftly enough. If he refuses, I assure you, he won't wed me. So now what?"

---

[2] The writer has translated the Latin *prefectus* (prefect, a high Roman official) as "reeve," a term for a magistrate or official that would have sounded distinctly English. The somewhat later thirteenth-century translation of the *South English Legendary* employs the Latinate term "justice."

Seething, Africanus solemnly swore, "By the gods I adore—the noble god Apollo, my lord, and my beloved lady, dear Diana—if you persist in this lunacy, I'll let wild beasts rip you to bits and chuck your carcass to the birds!"

Juliana answered him softly, saying, "Don't think, father dear, that you can scare me like that. I can swear too—and I swear by Jesus Christ, God's son, whom I believe in and love as the most loving and lovable lord, that even if you burn my living body to ashes in a blazing fire, I won't give an inch on this matter. I don't care what threats you make!"

At that, Africanus changed his tune and tried again to win her with wheedling and flattery. He promised her that, if only she would change her mind, there was no pleasure she should not enjoy.

"Nonsense!" she said. "Do you think that any profits or pleasures could persuade me to marry a man committed to the devil and con-demned to eternal death, so that I can rot with him in hell forever? I as-sure you, your promises are worthless! I want both Eleusius and you to know that I have given myself to someone whom I shall have and hold forever, one unlike Eleusius or any other man. No profit, pleasure, or punishment will make me deceive or desert him."

Incensed, her father sneered, "Who is this husband of yours, whom you've presumed to love without my permission, who's made you disdain everything you ought to hold dear? I don't believe I've met him!"

"Then shame on you," said the maiden. "It's not as if you haven't heard of him before—he's Jesus, God's son, who died on the cross to re-deem mankind. I've never seen him—much to my chagrin—but I love him and always will, and I believe him to be the one lord. No devil or man will wrest me from him."

"By my life," said her father, "you shall forswear his love, for you'll be whipped so soundly with sharp switches that you'll be sorry you were born a woman with women's breasts!"

The maiden said, "I'm so dear to him that I would suffer worse things for his love. Do as you please!"

"By all means," he said. "Gladly!"

And he angrily ordered her stripped stark naked and beaten until her fair body frothed with blood. She was seized, the blows fell, and she be-gan to cry, "Beat away, beat away, you lackeys of Belial.[3] You can lessen neither my love for nor my belief in the living God, my dear lover,

---

[3] Belial was foremost among the angels who joined Lucifer in his revolt against God.

the precious lord. I reject your ruinous advice, and I will never honor or worship those filthy idols, the fiend's vessels, no matter what you do to me!"

"You won't, eh?" said Africanus. "We'll soon see, for I'll heave your hide over to wealthy Eleusius, reeve of Rome, and he'll bring you to whatever wretched end he wishes."

"That's for God to decide!" said this maiden. "You can't do anything to me except what he permits you to do to increase the reward and glory of my virginity. After all, the more you hurt me, the brighter and lovelier my crown will be. Therefore, I'll gladly—and with a happy heart—suffer scourges for the love of my lover, the lovable lord, and I'll savor every pang I suffer for his sake. You say you'll turn me over to odious Eleusius. Go ahead! I couldn't care less about either of you. You two can only hurt me here on earth—and instead of harming me, you'll advance and enhance and increase my heavenly happiness. Killing me will only please God and send me straight to eternal ecstasy. As for you scoundrels—how sad that you were ever born to be brought to such an evil end!—you will sink into suffering and endless sorrow, bitterness and misery in the depths of hell."

Africanus, her father, angrily turned her over to Eleusius, the heinous reeve of Rome, and had her brought before his throne as he sat and passed judgments in the city court. When Eleusius gazed on her lovely body, her finely formed features, and her skin clear as lilies and ruddy as a rose, he sighed like a man sorely wounded. His heart began to burn, his marrow melted; love's pangs shot through each limb of his body—inside he burned and shivered so much that he thought that he wanted no joy in the world other than to do as he wished with her body. He began to say softly and sweetly, "My life, my love, and my lady, if you would only consider that I am the richest and noblest man in Rome! Why do you so foolishly and perversely put us both through so much grief? I don't want to harm you any more than you do. I only want you to renounce your reprehensible religion. If you do, you will live in joy and have whatever you want. Consider, too, the customs and commitments of your family, your forebears. Why do you abandon them to embrace what they detest? You surely don't suppose that you surpass them all in your wisdom!"

"Hush!" she said. "Stop babbling, Eleusius. If you knew and were known by the king of all kings who reigns in heaven, you would care little for lawless customs that teach you to honor manmade gods instead of the lord and thereby anger your creator. Living devils inhabit your gods. When you honor them you honor the fiend, worshipping him as if he were your savior, and he is going to repay you dreadfully, for he will never tire of afflicting you with woe and misery, world without end. Do as you please! I will give you no other answer unless you hear and believe my teachings and love almighty God and abandon your current customs."

"But darling," Eleusius said, "if I did that, the emperor would soon learn of it—the king would find out—and he'd cast me from my office and condemn me to death!"

She replied, "If you're so afraid of a lawless mortal who insults his creator by giving all his love to lifeless objects, if you're so afraid of losing his friendship, how do you expect me to forsake Jesus Christ, God's son, who is the beginning and end of everything good, and who loves me so much that he will let me live with him in heavenly triumph and happiness after this wretched life? Talk all you want, but you won't gain anything. Since I'm your prisoner, you can beat me to a pulp, you can torture me to death, you can skin me alive, you bastard, but no amount of flaying will lessen my love or shake my faith in the living God of all men."

Eleusius reddened with rage, his heart full of fury. He ordered his heathens to strip her stark naked and pin her to the ground, and he ordered six men to beat her bare body for as long as they could, until her flesh was covered with blood. They did as he commanded, and as they beat her they cried, "This is only the beginning of the pain and shame that you will suffer if you don't bow and bend to our will. But you can, if you wish, save yourself; and if you continue to refuse, whoever doesn't do his utmost to harm you deserves the greatest contempt."

"Go ahead, devil's drudges," she said, "and do everything your infernal taskmaster tells you to do. I care little for your love, less for your hatred, and nothing at all for these threats. So there!"

"No?" they said, "Then woe to him who doesn't work his worst on you today!"

It was a shame to see what they did to her lovely flesh. But she endured it all patiently for the lord, and when she felt worst, she cried, "Keep it up! Don't stop! Nothing will make me forsake the one I believe in."

When Eleusius heard that, his face reddened and became inflamed with anger; he quickly ordered her yanked up by her hair. She was then pulled until she dangled well off the ground by her tresses. And they set upon her so viciously from both sides that each blow pierced her lovely body, drenching the rods with gore. "Almighty lord God," she said, "take care of your maiden. You tested Abraham and found him true. Let me truly love you. Keep me, my savior, Jesus Christ, God's son, as you have done, for I have no strength without you and all my trust is in you, not in myself. And I beseech you, confident of your help, gentle almighty God, that my love and faith neither diminish nor die, no matter what pain and death I endure."

When Eleusius saw that she was only becoming more committed to the true faith, he thought he would kill her immediately, and he ordered molten brass poured over her head so that it ran down her beautiful body to her heels. His commands were carried out, but the world's ruler, who preserved Saint John the Evangelist unscathed when he was thrown in a vat of boiling oil, that same lord of life also preserved his bride from the molten brass, making the brass feel like warm water. Eleusius was so furious he didn't know what to say; so he ordered her removed from his sight and taken to a dismal dungeon to endure the plight of imprisonment. So it was done.

When she was alone in the darkness, she began to call upon Christ with this request: "Lord, God almighty, my joy and my reward, my victory and my complete happiness, you see how sorely I am oppressed. Strengthen my faith. Direct and advise me, for all my trust is in you. Guide me and support me, for all my strength is in you. Because I would not forsake you, my father and mother have forsaken me, and my closest relatives, who should be my best friends, are my greatest foes; and my servants are like strangers. Praiseworthy savior, I am happy to rely on your help. Don't forsake me, living lord! As you protected Daniel, left so wickedly among the wild lions, and as you saved the lives of the three children who would not leave you—Ananias, Azarias, and Misael were their names—as you, all-powerful, preserved them unharmed from the frightful fire in the furnace, so you, joy of the world, protect and defend me, and through your wisdom teach me and inform me to save me from sin. Lord, life's guide, lead me through this deceptive and transitory life to the harbor of health, as you led the Israelites from Egypt, without a ship, without wetting their feet, through the Red Sea, and drowned the foes who followed them. Oh lord and father of humanity, overthrow my foe and drive off the devil that torments me, for no one's strength can withstand him without you. Allow me, all-powerful lord, to see him shamed—the one who thinks to lead me astray or scare me from the narrow path that leads me to eternal life; keep me from his evil, living lord. Alert me to his crafty wiles, so that he may not trap me; defend me against the enemy, oh helper of the helpless, so that you will be honored and praised forever on earth as in heaven. Blessed be you forever, lord, as you were and are and shall be throughout eternity."

When she had made this request, a champion of hell disguised as an angel appeared and addressed the maiden: "Juliana, darling, you have suffered so much for my love! The fearsome foes fighting against you are, in their anger, preparing all kinds of torments for you. I can't allow them to afflict you any longer! You've been tested enough and have truly earned my friendship. Your pain grieves me. Now listen to my advice! Do as Eleusius wishes, for I permit you to."

Wondering at his words, the maiden anxiously asked, "What being are you, who tells me such things?"

"I am God's archangel," said the demon, "sent down from heaven to deliver this message."

She wondered greatly, and, not being gullible, she silently and softly called to Christ in her heart. "Jesus," she said, "God's son, who are your father's wisdom, tell me, your woman, what I should do; and if you will, make me understand what this being says to me, if he is your messenger."

Then a gentle voice descending from heaven said, "Blessed Juliana, blessed be the time you were born; your lover will not allow a lying lout to mislead you for long. It is the powerful devil of hell that assails you. Approach him now and with those bonds over there bind him tightly. Almighty God gives you the strength to do it, and then you can lead him around as you please, and he'll tell you all you want to know, willy-nilly, and he'll reveal whatever you wish."

Upon receiving this revelation, the blessed maiden sprang on the "angel" and seized him and said, "Tell me right now who you are, where you came from, and who sent you!"

At that, he began to change his appearance and became what he was, the devil of hell. "Lady," he said, "release me and I'll tell you."

"Tell me now! I'll decide when to let you go."

"Dear lady," he said then, "I am the devil Belial, the worst and most accursed of all evil demons, for I am never satisfied except when I make mankind behave shamelessly. I'm the one who drove Adam and Eve from the pleasures of paradise; and I'm the one who made accursed Cain kill his brother Abel. I'm the one who made Nebuchadnezzar, the bold king of Chaldea, make solid gold idols. I'm also the one who had the three children, chosen above others, flung into the fierce flames of the great furnace. And I'm the one who had the most wise prophet Isaiah sawed in two. I'm the one who made Jerusalem burn and turned God's treasured temple to dust. And I'm the one who enticed the Israelites to leave the lord who released them from Pharaoh's servitude and to make molten gods to praise and worship. And I'm the one who robbed rich Job of his wealth, leaving him to languish on the dungheap. I'm the one whom wise Solomon once restrained. I brought about the beheading of John the Baptist and the stoning of Saint Stephen. And I spoke through Simon the sorcerer, who always warred against Peter and Paul. I advised Nero, the rich Roman emperor, to crucify Peter and behead Paul, and I had the soldier pierce God's side with the sharp point of his spear. If I talked all day I still wouldn't finish reciting my deeds, for I've wrought more wonders than I can remember, and I've ruined more men than any of my brothers."

"Who sent you to me?" the maiden asked. "Who's your master?"

"Lady," he said, "Beelzebub, the bold devil of hell."

"What does he do?" she asked.

"Lady, if you want to know, he discovers and devises all evil, dispatching us where he wishes. And if we don't succeed in misleading some righteous person, we cower and dare not come before him. And he angrily commands those who *have* done his will to beat us and bind us wherever they find us, and make us suffer more sorrow than any man can stand. That's why we must bow to our dear father and obey his every command, lady."

"Say more plainly how you operate and how you deceive God's children."

"Lady Juliana," he said, "I found you and followed you, much to my misfortune. I fully expected to return you to your fathers' faith and make you leave your lord's love. I began to test you, but I'm vanquished. I'll tell you what you want to know. Wherever we see well-intentioned men or women, we set out against them. We make them forsake whatever might change their hearts for the better and make them wish for what will harm them. And we make them lose their desire to pray eagerly that God remove the cravings we planted within them.

And with that they weaken, and when they least expect it, we strengthen our assault. And if we see them heading eagerly to church to confess their sins privately and to hear the teaching of holy scripture, we swarm about them to stop them, if we can, and turn their thoughts to vain things. But those who are valiant enough to perceive what is happening to them cast out the evil desires that I put in their hearts and eagerly beseech the help and healing of God's grace, especially when the priest at Mass partakes of the body God received from that innocent maiden, Mary. Then their faith and prayers are so pleasing to God that we flee and fly away. This is what we do to torture Christians and egg them on to evil."

"But how dare you odious things touch Christ's chosen?" the blessed lady asked.

"How, indeed!" he replied. "Tell me, blessed fool, how *you* dare hold and handle me so roughly? You trust in your lord, of course! Well, I trust in mine, master of mischief, and I work his will insofar as I can. And if I could do even more harm I would be so much the happier. I don't know what possessed me to come here, but my great misfortune made me seek to see you. Damn the sight; it's caused me nothing but grief! I never saw anything so hateful or painful! Alas! Why didn't I know what wretchedness awaited me? Why couldn't my royal father warn his child of this woe? Release me now, lady, and I'll leave you alone and pursue someone else. Otherwise I'll denounce you to my mighty father—and I'm warning you, that wouldn't be in your interest."

"So," said Juliana, Jesus Christ's lover, "you're threatening me, wretch? God knows, you'll be the worse for it!" With that, she seized her shackles and bound both his hands behind his back so hard that his fingernails ached and blackened with blood; and she flung him backwards right down on the ground, and standing on the pest, she took her own bonds and began to beat Belial of hell. And he began to howl piteously, to bawl and to wail, and she fell on him so fiercely that he was sorry to be alive.

"Oh my lady Juliana," he said, "peer of apostles and patriarchs alike, martyrs' darling, angels' companion, and archangels' friend, spare me awhile! I beg you in the name of God and of the cross of his son, whom we fear so much, and of the torment and death he suffered for man's sake, have mercy on my misery."

"Shut up, you infernal shit!" said the blessed maiden. "You don't have mercy on anyone, so don't expect to find any yourself. Tell me more about the woe that you've wrongfully wrought on the world."

"Whoa, lady—hold your holy hands! I've blinded people and broken their shoulders and shanks. I've thrown them in fire and water and made them spit and spew their own blood. I've made one man kill another and hang himself. Indeed, wise woman, how do you expect me to conclude a tale that only grows as I tell it? No one can reckon the people I've ruined who weren't as well blessed as they should have been. Of all the evil on earth, what worse do you want? I am the source of most misdoing, but I've never been handled as I have today. Oh, mighty maidenhood, how you're armed to wage war against us! As ever, you do more damage than any of our other adversaries. We'll seek revenge on all who protect you—they'll never be free from our assaults. We'll hound and humiliate maidens more than ever, and though many may resist us, some will succumb. Oh Jesus, God's son! You reign in maidens' might, much to their honor and our grief. You're all too protective of those who hold you truly in their hearts, if they're mild and meek as maidens ought to be." When he had finished speaking, he began to howl so loudly that people wondered what the racket was.

Eleusius, the reeve, sent servants to see if she were still alive and, if so, to bring her before him. They went and found her, and, though terrified by the demon, they led her forth. And she dragged along the detestable devil, who wheedled and beseeched and besought, "My dear lady Juliana, don't make me the laughingstock of men! You've done me enough harm already. Alas! I've lost my dear father's friendship; from here on, I don't dare come before him. Mighty maiden, free me for God's sake, I beseech you. If I'm told truly, Christians are merciful and mild! Well, you're nothing but grief. Have mercy on me for the lord's love, your lovable lover: lady, I beg you."

But she led him along for market merchants to mock. And they set on him, some with stones, some with bones, and they sicced hounds on him and punched him. And as he was being made the most miserable of all beings, and howling all the while like a foul wretch, the crowds flocked to see. And the blessed woman became a little weary and, yanking him violently with the chain, she pitched him into a pit of shit. She came boldly before the reeve as he sat on his judgment seat, her face shining like the sun. When he saw her, the reeve marveled and said, "Juliana, tell me truly where you learned such sorcery that you heed no torments and fear neither death nor living devils."

"Listen here, heathen hound!" the blessed maiden said. "I praise and worship God the father and his only son, Jesus Christ, and the holy spirit, as much God as the others. Three persons, but not three gods, everywhere undivided. King of champions, he overcame hell's bull Belial, boldest of all, and your lord, Satan, whom you believe in. Do your father's bidding, as befits the son of such a sire. Damn you, colt of such a stud! May the mighty, merciful God, whom I always keep in mind, send me might and strength from heaven to help me and hurt him and shame all who praise and honor such devils. Alas! You were born at a bad time, wretch, that your sorry soul and sorrowful spirit will sport with such playmates in hell. Do yourself a favor, wretched reeve: take stock of yourself, praise God, and pay attention to me. Jesus is so merciful that he longs to save everyone, but he who does no penance will receive no pity."

"So you're still singing that same song?" said Eleusius. "How stupid do you suppose we are? Soon we'll see how well your sorcery will save you!"

And he madly commanded a wonderful wheel to be made, and he had it fitted with spokes and rims, thick and threefold, and with goads sharp as razor blades to slice whatever they touched. And the wheel's axle was attached on both sides to two stone pillars, so that as it turned it would at no point touch the ground. Whoever saw it grind whatever it ran over might well wince.

She was brought forth, as Belial's man commanded, and they fiercely fastened her to the wheel. Eleusius had four knights turn handles on either side of her to rotate the wheel over the blessed maiden as quickly as they could. He ordered them, if they valued their lives and limbs, to spin it swiftly, and they, as the devil urged, did so mercilessly. And she began to break as the sharpened iron struck her all over, from head to toe, as it turned, dismembering her and pulling body and flesh. Her bones broke and the marrow burst out mingled with blood. Those who stood about could see the greatest grief.

As she cried to God, and wanted to commend her spirit into his hands, an angel flew down from heaven and dashed the wheel to pieces and broke her bonds and destroyed everything; and she, feeling as hale and whole as if she were never hurt, raised her hands to heaven and thanked God with these words: "Immortal lord, one God almighty, unlike all others, maker of heaven and earth and all creation, I thank you for all you have done. You made man from clay and gave him a living spirit like your own, and you made everything in the world for his sake. But he sinned straightaway through Eve's urging and was soon cast from the pleasures of paradise. His progeny multiplied beyond reckoning but sinned so greatly that you drowned all but eight in Noah's flood. You then chose under the old law Abraham and Isaac and Jacob and his children. You gave Joseph, Jacob's youngest, happiness in Pharaoh's hall. Long afterward, you led your much-loved Moses, along with his kindred, across the Red Sea without boat or bridge (there Pharaoh's host all drowned), and you fed them for forty years in the wilderness with heavenly food, and crushed under their feet all their foes, and brought them through Joshua to the promised land of Jerusalem. There, in Samuel's day, Saul was the first king, champion of champions. In battle, you blessed little David so that he struck and slew strong Goliath with a stone; then you raised David to rule Saul's realm. Thus, gentle God, you make the meek mighty and humble the haughty. Then, when you thought you ought to—thanks be to you for doing it—you descended to us from heavenly light and took blood and bones in the noble maiden and were born in Bethlehem to save humanity. And you showed yourself to the shepherds, whom the angels led to you, and you were royally worshipped by the three kings. You grew and worked wonders. But first you were presented with gifts at the temple and baptized in the Jordan River by Saint John. You healed the sick and raised the dead. At last, by your will, you allowed one of your chosen twelve to trade you—sell you—and you suffered pain and passion on the cross through the Jews' plot. You died, and after being set in a stone coffin, you descended and spoiled and harrowed hell. You rose and made your resurrection known to your chosen, and you ascended above the stars to highest heaven, and you will come, king, on doomsday to judge the living and the dead. You are the hope of salvation. You are the joy of the righteous and the savior of sinners. You can do anything, but you desire nothing but right. Blessed be you forever! All things should praise and worship you; and I do, dear lord, your own maiden, and I love you as my lover, lovable lord, who has done so much for unworthy me. Be with me, blessed God, and protect me from the devil's drudges and from their wiles. Work such wonders that the reeve will blush and be ashamed with his devil, and you will always be honored as you are worthy of worship forever and ever. Amen."

When she stopped, the executioners stood and cried in a loud voice, "Mighty is the lord that Juliana believes in; we know now there is no other God but he. Reeve, we regret having followed your lead for so long." And they turned together, about five hundred bystanders, and cried in a single voice, "Dear woman, we are all turning to the God that you believe in. You're damned, reeve, with your false beliefs; blessed be Christ and all his chosen. Do your worst with deadly cruelty; do what you want to us—set the fire, fetch the wheel; prepare whatever you can grimly devise to further the will of your father, the fiend of hell. He held us too long as he now holds you. But we shall henceforth adhere to Jesus, God's royal son, savior of mankind." The reeve gnashed his teeth in fury. The madman madly sent for advice to Maximian, the mighty emperor of Rome. He commanded the head of every last convert chopped off.[4] Five hundred men and one hundred thirty women rushed forward to be beheaded and, all martyrs, went happily to heaven.

Meanwhile, Eleusius had his men make a great fire and ordered Juliana bound, foot and hand, and cast into the flames to be burned alive. As she looked up and saw the blaze, she looked to heaven and with hands outstretched she cried to Christ: "Do not abandon me in this need, lord of life! Merciful God, have mercy on me, your maiden, and with your gentle grace heal my sins. Jesus, my joy, don't turn your eyes from me. Behold me and help me, and rescue me from this flame so that the ungodly cannot say, 'The lord you believe in—your supposed shield—where is he now?' I don't ask this, lord, for dread of death, but to prove false their law and strengthen the faith of your chosen. Show, all-powerful God, your mighty power and quickly hear me, glory and praise to you forever."

No sooner had she spoken than an angel bright as fire came down and doused the ferocious flames—each and every one of them. And Juliana stood unharmed in the middle, praising our savior with the loudest voice. Seeing the fire quenched, the reeve was so angry that he began to quake. Sitting like a bristly boar grinding his tusks, the wild beast began to drool and gnash his teeth terribly at the maiden. After considering how to hurt her most, he ordered a vat fetched and filled with pitch and heated until it boiled. And he ordered her thrown into it when it was hottest and bubbling most furiously.

As she was being thrown in, she called to the lord, and the liquid immediately cooled to the temperature of a warm bath—but warm enough for only her to bathe in. Indeed, it bubbled over, boiling hot, onto those who prepared it and scalded them to death, seventy-five in all. When the reeve saw this, he tore his clothes and pulled his hair and cursed his

---

[4] It is not clear in the original whether "he" refers to Maximian or Eleusius.

idols and reviled his lord. "Away with her!" he said, "I don't want to see her again until she lies lifeless, head hewed from her body."

As soon as she heard that, she happily praised God of heaven, for that was just what she wanted. She was led forth—and she was easily dragged. As she stopped at the spot where the condemned were executed, that same Belial that she had beaten showed up a ways behind her and began to cry, "Oh brave men, don't have any mercy on her! She's shamed us all. Destroy her! Give her what she deserves! Oh brave men, don't delay—kill her right away!"

As he spoke, the blessed Juliana glanced up and spotted him. And Belial blenched and ducked behind the guards' shoulders as if dodging an arrow. "Alas that I live!" he said. "I'm trapped! If she seizes me again, I'll never find relief. She caught me once; I'll never go free." As he jerked himself backwards, the very devil fell into a devil of a ditch that he could not escape.

Before she stooped and stretched out her neck, she prayed, and she taught the bystanders with these words: "Hear me, dear people, and listen awhile. Repent your sins and save yourselves through true confession and penance. Abandon your wicked ways and build your homes on firm ground, so that you won't have to worry about the wind and weather. Make sure that the heavenly lord is the foundation of whatever you do, so that it will endure no matter what happens. Entreat God earnestly in Holy Church, so that he gives you the wisdom to act well and strengthens you with his strength against the strong devil, who is always looking for the chance to devour you. Listen eagerly to the teachings of holy scripture and live by them. Happy are those who are watchful and know themselves and sincerely and constantly bemoan their sins. This world passes away like flowing water, and like the joy of a dream dreamed it fades away. The life we live in this world is just a fickle breeze. Forsake the false and seek the true, everlasting life. For you will leave this life— you don't know when—and reap the ripened seed you have sown: that is, you will receive a yield of woe or joy according to your works. I beseech you, brothers and sisters, to pray for me."

And as she stood, she gave them the kiss of peace and, gazing upward, she lifted her voice: "Lord, God almighty, thank you for your gifts. Look after me now. You value true faith over all; do not abandon to your enemy one made in your image, one whom you saved from death through your death on the cross. Don't let me die the eternal death of hell. Welcome me into the court of angels and maidens! I give you my spirit, dear lord, asking, blessed God, in your blessed name, that you give it peace and rest." With that, she bowed and was beheaded, and singing angels accompanied her soul to heaven.

Afterward, a pious and wellborn woman called Sophie passed through the city of Nicomedia on her way to Rome and bore this maiden's body away with her on her boat, wrapped richly in expensive cloth. When they were afloat, there came such a violent storm that no one could steer the ship, and it was driven ashore in Campania.[5] There Sophie had a church built a mile from the sea, and she interred Juliana's body in a stone coffin with all the honor befitting a saint.

As soon as the reeve realized that Juliana's remains had been removed, he leaped in a boat, accompanied by some men, and rowed in hot pursuit, seeking to seize the body and sink it in the sea. But storms arose so furious and strong that the planks of the boat broke and drowned him and thirty-four others and drove their bloated bodies onto the land, where wild animals tore them limb from limb, dismembering them completely. And their wicked souls sank to hell to burn in pain and sorrow forever.

Thus the blessed Juliana passed through torments from worldly woe to heavenly joy in the renowned city of Nicomedia on the sixteenth of February, fourteen days before the first of March.

Through her intercession, she obtained for us the grace of God, who rules in three persons and is nonetheless undivided. Praised be he alone, as he was and ever is, in eternity.

> When the lord on Judgment Day winnows his wheat
> And sends the dusty chaff to hell's heat,
> May he who translated this from Latin to English
> Be a grain on God's golden threshing floor.
> And also he who copied it here as best he could.
>   Amen.

[5] An Italian province southeast of the Tiber.

Saints Agatha, Lucy, Justine, and Barbara

The South English Legendary

As the Church continued to promote religious awareness among ordinary people during the thirteenth century, more and more saints' legends were written with a predominantly lay audience in mind. The outstanding product of this trend was a voluminous anthology known as the *South English Legendary*. Composed in the second half of the thirteenth century and comprising almost one hundred narratives, the *South English Legendary* proclaimed the exploits of "Christ's knights," the apostles and martyrs, to "people eager to hear tell of battles between kings and of doughty knights." Fifty-one manuscripts attest to the collection's popularity; indeed, only three Middle English texts, the *Prick of Conscience,* the *Canterbury Tales,* and *Piers Plowman,* survive in more copies. The worn condition of so many of these manuscripts suggests that they were very well read.

The interlocking stories of Agatha and Lucy are representative of the collection's style and tone. The language is bold and crude. The narrator inveighs against sin with the passion of a street-corner preacher. His world is one of stark contrasts between good and evil, virgins and whores. Combative saints confound their hapless enemies with their resilience and their impertinence. When the persecutors eventually do manage to kill their victims, their comeuppance is prompt. Though the Juliana of our previous selection was equally vituperative and combative, she was also prayerful and didactic. Omitting the passages of prayer and instruction typical of such earlier martyr legends helps to distill the lives in the *South English Legendary* into brutal narratives of action. As we will see in later selections (from the *North English Legendary* through William Paris's "Christine"), this treatment became typical of saints' legends composed during the fourteenth century.

As the *South English Legendary* was copied and disseminated during the fourteenth and fifteenth centuries, it underwent many changes; old stories were revised and new ones added. Justine's legend, for example, is not found in the earliest manuscripts of the legendary, while (surprisingly, given her seeming ubiquity in art) Barbara's is found only in one fifteenth-century manuscript.

Neither the Justine nor the Barbara legend has been edited. My translations are, respectively, of MS Egerton 1993, British Library, London (fols. 203v.–206r), and MS Rawl. Poet. 225, Bodleian Library, Oxford (fols. 2r–5r). For transcriptions of these texts, see appendix A.

Edition: *South English Legendary.* Ed. Charlotte D'Evelyn and Anna J. Mill. 3 vols. EETS.OS 235, 236, 244. London: Oxford University Press, 1956, 1959.

Görlach, Manfred. *Studies in Middle English Saints' Legends,* 25–57. Heidelberg: C. Winter, 1998.
———. *The Textual Tradition of the "South English Legendary."* Leeds: University of Leeds School of English, 1974.
Jankofsky, Klaus P., ed. *The "South English Legendary": A Critical Assessment.* Tübingen: Francke Verlag, 1992.
Samson, Annie. "The *South English Legendary:* Constructing a Context." In *Thirteenth-Century England.* Vol. 1. Proceedings of the Newcastle-upon-Tyne Conference, 1985. Ed. P. R. Coss and D. S. Lloyd, 185–95. Wolfeboro, N.H.: Boydell, 1986.
Winstead, Karen A. *Virgin Martyrs: Legends of Sainthood in Late Medieval England,* 71–78. Ithaca: Cornell University Press, 1997.

Saint Agatha

Saint Agatha, the maiden, was born in Sicily. She became a Christian at an early age and rejected sin and fornication. She was well behaved and stable in Christ's teachings—much to the chagrin of the duke who governed that land. He hesitated to hurt her, but because she was young, he thought he could lead her from her faith.

An old harlot lived nearby, a downright whore and madam who had nine daughters, all downright whores. The duke promised her a reward if she would teach this maid and mislead her, and misguide her, and tempt her to foul thoughts and deeds. The maiden was brought to the whore, who was called Aphrodisia. Thinking they could influence

Agatha, Aphrodisia and all her daughters flattered her and promised her fancy things of silver and gold, riches, and plenty of other delights. "How," they asked, "can such a courteous, generous, pretty, mild—and oh so sweet—creature live without pleasure? Your young blood won't stand it! Why should you be deprived of joy, when there isn't a prince in this land who wouldn't have you?"

Despite her youth, this maid replied, "Shut up, bitches! You won't get anywhere with me! I've given my heart to the highest prince of all. I'll always cherish him as my mate. He's so sweet and mild and kind that he's always in my thoughts. I'm so attached to him that you can never drag me away."

Day and night, this foul woman and her whores tried to excite evil thoughts in this young maiden. She was with them thirty days, and all the while they tried to teach her the devil's lessons, but to no avail. This witch went to the duke, Quintian, and said, "I can't do anything with this woman! It would be easier to make hard rock soft as wool than to trick that girl into changing her mind." (What a shameful advisor she was. I tell you, that wicked whore caused great unhappiness in this world!)

The duke sent for the maiden and asked who she was. "I'm God's handmaid," she said. He asked about her family, and she said that they were of noble blood. "How can you be both a gentlewoman and a handmaid?" he asked.

The maiden replied, "It is nobler to be God's handmaid or servant than to be a king or a judge."

"Enough talk of him!" said the duke. "Honor our gods, or you'll suffer so much you'll be sorry!"

The maiden replied, "No pain can harm me so long as I keep my mind on God in heaven. You can throw me in a fire, but just thinking of how he suffered for me will extinguish the flames."

The duke had the maiden taken to prison. Agatha was as happy as if she were being led to a feast. For a long time she was confined to a strong cell. Then one day the duke ordered her brought before him. "Agatha," he said, "reconsider. Abandon your false beliefs and believe in the gods, who may help you before it's too late!"

The maiden said, "You're wasting your breath with empty words! Let me give *you* some advice: honor the one who bought you at great price,[1] and abandon your false, impotent gods carved from wood or stone."

---

[1] I.e., Christ, by dying on the cross.

"You won't give up your nonsense?" said the duke. "I'll torture you so much that you'll writhe in agony before the day is done!" He had hooks and willow twists bound to her breasts and torturers twisted them off.

"Asshole!" said the maiden to Duke Quintian. "Aren't your sins great enough? Why do you hurt the very part you suckled on your own mother? To hell with you: you can't scare me!"

That pure thing suffered great torments before they were through, but her heart was so firmly fixed on God that she felt nothing at all. When they were done, she was put in prison. The duke ordered that no one should visit her to treat her wounds or relieve her pain. But our sweet lord didn't forget her in her need.

While she was alone in prison, an old man came. He brought containers full of ointment and said he would heal her. "No you won't," the maiden said. "I'll have dealings with no one but God."

The old man replied, "I've come here in his name, for I'm his apostle.[2] He sent me to heal the wounds you suffered for his sake. Heavenly joy awaits you." As soon as he rubbed her wounds, they were healed. The maiden did not know what became of him when he had finished.

After three days, the duke had her brought before him. "Have you changed your mind?" he asked.

"No!" she said. "Your words are just polluting the air. Only a madman would ask sticks and stones for help instead of the God who healed all my injuries."

"How dare you speak of your false God," said the duke. "If you're fool enough to mention him again, I'll sentence you to an awful death!"

"Asshole!" the maiden said. "As long as I live, I'll never stop talking or thinking about him!"

The duke had a great fire prepared to burn her. But when she was brought to the fire, the ground started shaking throughout the city. The judgment hall fell, crushing two men who had condemned her to death. The people of the city were frightened and said to the duke, "This girl is good, and we're being terrorized for her sake! You've made her suffer greatly, and you're going to stop!" When the duke heard this, he was terrified. He had the maiden returned to prison. Then he sneaked away, unnoticed, though a back door.

When the maiden was back in prison, she knelt down. "Lord," she said, "you've saved me from many torments. You've rescued me from

---

[2] Most other versions specifically identify him as Saint Peter.

fire and from awful wounds. You know that I've been faithful to you since childhood. Let me rest, lord, for I've been here long enough. It's time for you to end my life and take my soul." With those words she died, right there before the people.

There were many mourners and few dry eyes. Those who loved her followed her faithfully. They took her body with great honor and buried it. As they were doing so, a company of more than three hundred of the fairest children—young ones of the same age in rich white clothing—came carrying a marble slab, which they placed on Agatha's tomb. When they had finished, they went sweetly away. They were angels who had come to earth for Agatha's sake. Scholars diligently examined the slab and found this inscription: "This maiden had holy thoughts and honored God. On her account, the entire country was saved from distress."

Only later did people understand what this last statement meant. A year after Agatha's death, fire spilled out of a hill as water overflows a well. It burned everything around, killing living things and devouring solid rock as if it were coal. It spread so widely that everyone was terrified. Not daring to stay in any town, people ran like madmen, never stopping until they reached the tomb of Saint Agatha. As it happened, it was her feast day. The fire was quenched throughout the land, as if it had never been. But first it had burned six days and six nights and ran like water, destroying everything it touched. Thus our lord showed how the maiden Saint Agatha saved the entire country.

May she deliver us to the joys of heaven as surely as she delivered her country from the flames!

Saint Lucy

Saint Lucy, the holy maiden, was born in Sicily. She began serving God at an early age and renounced sin and fornication. Her mother, who raised her, was called Dame Euthicia. She was proud to have such a child, as she certainly should have been!

Lucy's mother was stricken with a severe and lingering illness. For four years, she suffered from dysentery.[3] Though she spent much on doctors, no one could heal her; no one could stop the bleeding.

Throughout the land, there was talk of Saint Agatha and of the mir-

---

[3] Dysentery was endemic in medieval Europe, and often fatal.

acles that occurred through God's grace at her shrine. Night and day, people from all over flocked by the thousands to the city of Athens, where the holy woman was buried.

When Saint Lucy saw such crowds passing through every day, she said, "Mother, you're very sick, and we're always hearing about the miracles of Saint Agatha. Let's go with the others to visit her; you'll be healed there through our lord's grace."

Now, Lucy had privately converted to Christianity, but her mother was heathen, as were all her forebears. Lucy had been married at an early age to a heathen, but she was still a virgin, not having committed that filthy act. She quietly took her mother and set out with the others to Saint Agatha's tomb, expecting to improve her mother's life. When they arrived, they stayed there awhile and heard Mass with the others who were there. The gospel for the day, as Lucy understood it, was about a woman who had dysentery for some time and was immediately cured when she touched the hem of our lord's garment as he walked in a crowd.

"Dear mother," said Lucy, "if you believe in Holy Church and in the words of the gospel, and if you will act accordingly, you will be cured by touching Saint Agatha's tomb, just as the woman who followed Christ was cured by him." When the others had gone away, Lucy took her mother to Saint Agatha's holy tomb. They stayed there praying—they wouldn't leave—and the maiden Lucy fell asleep. The holy maiden Saint Agatha descended from heaven with a bright shining crown and a company of angels. "Lucy," she said, "dear sister, why are you so agitated? Why do you ask me so anxiously for something you can do yourself? *Your* good faith helps your mother; through you and your goodness, she is cured. Furthermore, just as this city is famous on my account, so your country will be famous on yours."

Lucy awoke, shaking violently. "Mother, don't be afraid: you're well again!" she said. "For love of the holy maiden who restored your health, don't ever force me from my pure intention. Don't let my husband in his wantonness deprive me of my virginity. Don't make me exchange eternal life for transient thrills! Instead, mother, please let me give to the poor everything you promised my husband as part of the marriage settlement."

After she was cured, Lucy's mother became a devout woman and allowed her daughter to distribute her goods among the poor, while they lasted.

When the news reached Lucy's husband, he went to her nurse and asked what possessed Lucy to give away her goods, and to whom she was giving them. The nurse ingeniously told him that Lucy had found a precious thing, worth a thousand times more than all her possessions put together. It was the best merchandise you could buy, for if you had some, you'd be plenty rich. The merchandise the maiden bought was heavenly. The man thought that answer over, and when he realized that Lucy was a Christian, he angrily informed the judge, Paschasius.

Lucy was brought before the judge, who said, "What have you been thinking, girl? Stop this foolishness, I tell you, and make the proper sacrifice to our gods."

The holy maiden replied, "I have, for the past three years, made my sacrifice to Jesus Christ. I've sold all I have and committed myself to his teaching, and now I'm ready to give up my body, sir judge, yielding each limb to his service. Do what you want with me!"

"Now I see!" said the judge. "You've spent all your goods in fornication and lechery. Now that you have no more to spend, you say you'll spend your body. You talk like a whore—abandoning your lord, your husband, and taking up with lechers."

"I was married to Jesus Christ," the holy maiden said, "and I will be true to my marriage. It's you who want to make me a whore when you try to make me forsake my sweet spouse Jesus Christ for another."

"No matter what you vowed," the judge said, "you'll forsake him or be taken to a public brothel. There anyone who wants to can lie with you in lechery and shame."

The maiden said, "No woman can be deprived of her virginity—no matter what is done to her body—unless her heart consents. If you defile my body against my will, my virginity is all the purer and my reward all the greater."

The judge issued a proclamation throughout the land, inviting everyone who wanted to fool around with a very pretty woman to come to the brothel, one and all, for she would be there, and she wouldn't be turning anyone away. He ordered his men to seize her and take her to the brothel immediately. They all came and pulled her. They shoved and pulled as hard as they could, but they couldn't stir her one foot from the spot where she stood. Then they took sturdy ropes, bound her feet and hands, and everyone yanked and tugged at her. A thousand men tried with all their might to move her, but she remained solid as a rock. They couldn't budge her.

"What's going on?" said the judge. "Why can't a thousand men move her from this spot?"

"Sir judge," said the maiden, "you miss the point. Even if you had ten thousand more men, I'd stay right here. I feel within myself the holy verse that Saint David said in the psalter, that a thousand men should fall to the ground at my side and that ten thousand should not draw near me on my right side. Therefore, your efforts are wasted: God is stronger than you; don't doubt it!"

"You're a witch!" said the judge. "My scholars and enchanters will remove your hex!" He summoned his scholars and enchanters, and they put their charms on her. When they had done all they could, the people started pulling at Lucy again, but she still stood as firm as a hill and didn't stir a bit. When the judge saw that, he raved with anger. "Certainly," he said, "witching will do her no good!" He ordered strong teams of oxen brought to the maiden and tied to her. He had them goaded and dragged. They began to pull and tug, but the maiden stood still; they couldn't budge her an inch. (I wonder whether a woman today could be brought to shame with less force. Some women—just a few—must take less pulling, since not all men have so many oxen.)

"We'll just have to overcome her some other way," the judge said. "Make the most ferocious fire you can, and burn that whore to ashes where she stands!"

The great fire was made, but the flames didn't burn her or harm her in the least. Then they took boiling pitch and brimstone and cast it, bubbling, over her tender, naked body. The maiden didn't flinch; she felt no pain at all, but happily preached of Jesus, heaven's king. The wicked judge didn't know what else he could do to overcome the pure thing, so he had a sharp sword thrust through her throat, intending to quench her speech and her holy life with a single blow. Though stabbed through the throat, she spoke all the better. She preached eagerly of Jesus Christ and laughed scornfully. She said, "You who are Christians, rejoice and be afraid of nothing, for I see great joy and will bring you joyful news. Right now, Holy Church is brought into God's peace, for our two old and bitter enemies have been defeated. You have nothing to fear from either of them. Wicked Diocletian, who caused such harm, has been expelled from his kingdom forever, and evil Maximian has just died a wicked death.[4] You'll see him no more. I bring this news from God, whom I will see this day. Now bring me our lord's body, for my life is at an end." Priests went forth immediately, as did the people that stood by. They brought this holy maiden God's flesh and blood. When she had taken it and received the rites, and when the appropriate prayers had all been said—at the final word, "Amen"—she gave up her spirit. Angels were at hand to conduct her soul to heaven, where she lives with Jesus Christ, in endless joy. For her sake, may God let us go there, too. Amen.

Saint Justine

Saint Justine came from a noble family of Antioch.[5] She loved Jesus Christ from an early age and became a Christian. A nobleman's son named Cyprian lived nearby. Before he was seven years old, he became the devil's man. Just as we bind ourselves to Jesus Christ when we're christened, he bound himself to the devil and forsook our lord. When he grew older and more knowledgeable, he could work wonders through the devil—in words and deeds. In fact, he was so powerful that he could change people into animals—they were powerless to resist him!

This wicked man lusted after Saint Justine; he couldn't think of anything besides gaining her love. He pursued her, but she was so full of God's grace that he could get nowhere. Seeing that he couldn't succeed through his own devices, he summoned the devil, promising his soul in exchange for Justine's love. The devil said, "I overcame Adam in paradise, bereft that fool of joy through sin. I made Cain slay his brother Abel, Adam's eldest son. Why shouldn't I win you an ordinary wench? I certainly have the power!"

At night the devil set out to tempt that holy maiden. He beset her with wanton thoughts, but when she realized she was being tempted by the devil, she made the sign of the cross. The devil lost all his power; the toad was overcome.

---

[4] The Roman emperors Diocletian (d. 313) and Maximian (d. 310) were notorious for their persecution of Christians; see also the life of Saint Katherine in this volume.

[5] An ancient city of the eastern Mediterranean, now in Turkey.

"I'm telling you," he said to Cyprian, "my power was taken from me! I was overcome by a sign of the cross!"

"If you can't get her for me," Cyprian said, "I'll conjure a more powerful devil!"

The mightier devil came and promised to do his will. He went to tempt this holy maiden, but his efforts were completely useless, for he received the same treatment as his brother. So he told Cyprian that his power didn't amount to anything. "You're worthless!" said Cyprian. "I'll conjure our highest master; he'll put an end to this nonsense!"

When the chief devil appeared, Cyprian asked, "What's going on? Are we really going to succumb to a wench? Is there no alternative?"

"Leave it to me," said the devil. "By midnight she'll be here—no matter how coy she is!"

The devil went to her in the form of a lovely maiden. "Justine," he said, "God sent me to you. I've vowed to live chastely, and since you're a chaste maiden, I've come to join my soul with yours in purity. But tell me: What will be our reward?"

"Truly," said this maiden, "we'll join the angels. Therefore there's nothing worthier than to be a pure maiden on earth."

"Ah yes," the devil said. "But one thing our lord said often comes to mind. When he made Adam and Eve—just after he gave them life—he joined them together as man and wife and told them to multiply here on earth. This command bothers me whenever I think of it, for either God didn't mean what he said, or those who aren't following his order are living in deadly sin. Since you know very well that the first thing God did after he created Adam and Eve was to institute marriage between man and wife, let's figure out how we can fulfill our lord's command without sinning." That damned scoundrel thought he'd betray the innocent girl through his false argument! That reasoning leads fools astray every day! We can see here whose follower they are, and who teaches them to play! They say it's God's command to increase our kind on earth; they'll follow their master's teaching and seek the depths of hell. This devil brought the maiden so close to sin that she set out with him, her mind completely changed. But as soon as God gave her the grace to see that her companion was the devil, she stopped and raised God's banner: she made the sign of the cross and blew on her companion, whose woman's form melted away like snow. When her companion mysteriously vanished, this maiden realized that the devil had come to ruin her. Another time, as this maiden lay alone in her bedroom, the devil came in the form of a good-looking young man. But when she made the sign of the cross, he disappeared into thin air. When at last the damned rogue realized that his caginess was getting him nowhere, he was thoroughly humiliated. He used his power to afflict her with a debilitating illness—she nearly died of it! But her pure thoughts remained fixed on Jesus.

So the devil took his wicked power and went off to spread a plague among cattle. Far and near, cattle throughout the land were dropping dead. The plague depleted the livestock, causing sorrow and care throughout the land. The devil then went to the governors of the land and said that God had inflicted the plague on the land on account of Cyprian's love for that silly woman Justine. Until they were married, the plague would continue, and the cattle and eventually they themselves would die.

That evil situation caused great sorrow in Antioch. The land that was once so rich was nearly ruined. Now, you can see how the devil can use richness and poverty to drive people to sin. Many people went to Justine's guardians and told them to marry her to Cyprian—or else. They weren't about to let the land be ruined on account of her stupidity. Her guardians were willing, but she wouldn't hear of it; she swore she'd rather die. Nonetheless, she was very sorry to see the land reduced to nothing, so she persistently asked our lord to send relief and crush the devil's power. In his grace, God answered the maiden's prayer and saved the land from the plague. But the hateful pestilence had already ravaged the country for five whole years.

The devil was humiliated, for he'd promised to win Justine for Cyprian. To save face, he took Justine's form and went to Cyprian, asking what he'd like. He called to her and kissed her, but all in vain: as soon as he said, "Welcome, Justine!" the phantom disappeared. The devil couldn't stand to hear Saint Justine named! What better proof of this maiden's purity than that her very name made him flee?

The devil's incompetence infuriated Cyprian. He decided to win her through his own enchantments. He turned himself into a maiden through his craft and went, meek and lovely, to Saint Justine. When the maiden laid eyes on him, though, he turned right back into Cyprian. Her power was great indeed, since she could overcome the black arts with just a glance. "You fool!" the maiden said. "Stop wasting your time! Your power is worthless compared with God's!"

A while later, Cyprian came up with a new plan: he turned himself into a sparrow. He flew up and alighted on a high branch outside Justine's bedroom. She spotted him, though, and he immediately became Cyprian again. He was a sorry ape[6] clinging to the branches, for, despite all his magic, he couldn't get down without breaking his neck. "Have mercy, Justine," he cried. What did the sparrow want? What became of all its feathers? What did that ape think he was doing there—where did he expect to go? A feeble cock he was, and cold. Why didn't he fly down? Let him sit there and contemplate his shame!

"What are you doing there? Why are you such a big ape? People are going to gape at your shame," the maiden said. Being a good person, she got a ladder and let him down, and told him not to come around and make a fool of himself again. The idiot sneaked away, sorely ashamed.

Then he summoned the devil and asked what happened to his learning: "Where is your wit? Your power is gone! You should be ashamed at being bested by a wench!"

The devil said, "I *am* stronger than her. But her master is stronger than me or you. We've been overcome through his strength, not hers."

"Explain," said Cyprian.

"Swear that you'll stay with me, and I'll tell you the whole story," said the devil. When Cyprian swore the oath, the devil said, "Okay, I'll tell you. He can overcome us—and all of hell—with just a little thing. The sign of the cross that she had in her thoughts and the power of the one who died on it have brought us down."

"It seems, then," said Cyprian, "that her God is stronger than you."

"Right you are," said the devil. "It hurts me to think about it, for he brings us and all ours into great torment."

"It follows, then," said Cyprian, "that I should become his man so that he doesn't torment *me!*"

"That's not an option for you now, Cyprian," the devil said. "Remember your oath."

"To hell with my oath! I commit myself to the high God—he'll save me. The sign of the holy cross will rid me of you!" As soon as he made the sign of the cross, the devil couldn't stay. Unable to chide Cyprian further, he went sadly on his evil way. May he not have the chance to tempt fools for a good long time!

---

[6] Apes, whose antics were frequently featured in the margins of illustrated prayer books, were considered the embodiment of lust and depravity.

Cyprian went to a local bishop, confessed his sins, and accepted Christianity. He served our lord so well and was such a holy man that he was soon made bishop. He loved Justine purely, where he had once loved her foully. He made her a nun, and soon afterward an abbess of her house. She and Cyprian loved each other deeply and purely—a much better love than the love that made Cyprian fly to her as a wretched sparrow and end up an ape!

The prince of the land heard about them. He summoned them before him to break them of their Christianity, ordering them to sacrifice to the gods. "Never!" they replied. The prince got angry and had a huge, sturdy kettle set on a fire, full of pitch and wax and grease. These holy things were thrown in. The more the kettle boiled, the less pain they felt. They scorned the torturers for being so slow; they told them to pile on more wood and fan the fire with bellows. They'd need to know how to make a proper bath for themselves down in hell. A wicked heathen priest jumped forward to increase their torment, but he accomplished little: the fire turned against him and burned him to a coal. After that, the bystanders retreated, afraid to approach. These holy things thought it was taking these people a long time to kill them! Seeing no other way, the prince then had their heads chopped off and their bodies thrown in a foul place for beasts to devour, but no bird or beast would come near. They were martyred exactly two hundred and eighteen years after our sweet lord's incarnation. Christians later came and found their bodies whole. They conducted them to Rome and buried them properly and with honor.

Now, Jesus, for the sweet love of the maid Justine and for the love of Saint Cyprian, shield us from the pains of hell.

Saint Barbara

When Maximian in all his tyranny governed the empire, he had a citizen of high standing and well versed in folly named Dioscurus. He was a rich man with many worldly possessions and a large income from land and various other sources. He was a pagan, though. He didn't believe in God almighty but practiced idolatry day and night. He hadn't an inkling of the Christian faith. Whoever tried to preach it to him, he prosecuted to the full extent of the law.

He had a daughter, an only child. Her name was Barbara, and she was

Fig. 2. Execution of Saint Barbara. (Courtesy of the Bodleian Library, Oxford. MS Douce 219, fol. 41r.)

very beautiful. In fact, she was so much lovelier than anyone else that in his love he built a tower for her. Broad and tall and fair to look at, it was meant to hide her and keep her from ravishers all the summer days and the winter nights. When the tower was built, he enclosed his daughter in it. She might be personable and pretty, but no man was going to win her love!

The gentlemen of the country weren't put off. They went to her father, asking that they be allowed to court her, so that one of them might marry her. Upon reflection, her father went to the tower and asked her what she wanted to do. She meekly answered, "Father, I'm happy living just like this; please don't make me do otherwise." Then her father told the citizens, "I suppose it won't happen. She wants to live alone for the time being."

When he'd given the citizens that answer, he decided to make a worthy tower to reside in himself. He summoned a multitude of workers to complete the building—some to do the foundations, some to do the walls. He told them, "Perform this assignment for me and receive your payment here. I must travel to another land."

After her father had gone, Barbara came down to look at the work. She greeted each workman. "Welcome, lady," they said. When she saw the noble house with two windows set at the north, she summoned the workers and asked them why only two windows had been put there. They replied, "Because your father commanded us to do it that way." She then asked them once or twice to put another window in and say it was her idea. The builders all said, "We're afraid that your father will punish us if we carry out your request. For your sake he'll immediately sentence us to a bitter death." Barbara said boldly, "Do as I say, for my aim is to please my father. I'll speak such fair words to him that he'll do you no harm." They all agreed and added another window, just like the two others.

Later that year, when the construction was completed, Barbara's father returned from his journey and summoned all the builders into his presence. He asked the man in charge of the work why they added a third window in defiance of his instructions. "Sir, I tell you, it was for the best reason. Your daughter talked to me about it. It was her idea—she said you wouldn't punish us."

Then the father called his daughter and said, "What have you done? Why have you changed my plans?"

"Lord father," said Barbara, "don't be upset, for I was only thinking of your benefit. I ordered three windows to represent the blessed Trinity, so that one God and no more shall be wholeheartedly worshipped above all creatures; the God who gives light to all creatures, and who came to dwell in this world. I assure you, this is the only reason I did this thing."

When her father heard these words, he was so consumed with anger that he lost his wits. He wanted to stab her to death—and he was going to, too—but God, who always preserves his true servants, graciously protected her from danger by this means: he enclosed her in a building stone and transported her to a hill. Two shepherds saw the miracle. Her father said to one of them, "Did you see such a thing?" "No," said the herdsman and denied it stoutly, hoping to save her from danger, "even if I should die or have your realm for that news!" Then his cruel companion contradicted him and revealed where she was. Her father said, "She'll have her comeuppance!" and threatened her without mercy. Then the blessed virgin cursed the shepherd, and suddenly all his sheep turned into flies, which can be seen at her tomb, where her blessed body lies enshrined. Her father was infuriated. He dragged her by her hair and beat her soundly and said that she'd never get out of prison.

The judge had her brought before him and said, "Why would someone so gracious and beautiful throw away everything she has? You're going to be taken from your comfortable life and stripped of all earthly pleasures and tortured and, at last, cruelly killed! I advise you to sacrifice to our gods without delay! If you don't, you'll be brought to a painful end."

The blessed virgin answered, "I sacrifice only to Jesus Christ, who descended from heaven and became man and died on a cross to save us. He made the skies, the earth, and the seas. Truly, there is no other God; may he be forever blessed! Your gods are just hell hounds!"

The judge was furious. He ordered her stripped and her flesh ripped to pieces with a hideous instrument. When she was so torn and bloodied that she no longer looked like a living creature, she was cast into a dark prison until he could think of something worse to do with her.

At midnight, our lord came to comfort her. He showed her a wonderful sight and assured her that she would win great grace, that heaven and earth rejoiced in her glorious palm of martyrdom, and that her crown was all ready for her to receive very soon.

But the judge had her brought forth again and had both her sides cruelly seared with burning lamps. Then he had her tender head beaten with various instruments. Even in this pain, she fell down and prayed to almighty God with all her heart: "Almighty lord, you who know all hearts, you know very well that I suffer bitter and cruel pains in your name. Shield me with your cloak, and don't abandon me in my persecution, but grant me, your servant, this grace. Give your grace and mercy generously to those who call on me in their time of need. And, only lord, on the day of my martyrdom, help humble petitioners and assure them of your mercy and have them led to bliss."

Suddenly a voice replied, "Come to me, my chosen spouse, and rest in heavenly bliss forever. A gracious feast has been prepared for you. Our benevolent lord, who governs all things, has heard your request, and the entire company of heaven affirms it. So don't be afraid to die."

Her father beheaded her right there. Her body fell meekly to the ground, while her soul went off to God in heaven. And as her father descended the hill, fire came down from heaven and devoured him completely; not a bone remained. Then a nobleman of good faith took that virgin's body and made a royal tomb for it. At that honorable sepulchre, God's mighty power continually confirms Barbara's excellence through miracles done on her behalf.

Lord, enhance the devotion of whoever reads this brief translation, and pray for me, who wrote it in English. I ask this favor of your charity. May God confound our enemies and bless us forever with mercy and grace. Amen.

Saint Anastasia

The North English Legendary

While the *South English Legendary* continued to be read and copied in southwestern England during the late fourteenth century, a new collection was being produced in the North. This anthology, naturally enough known as the *North English Legendary*, was also designed for a broad lay audience, and its rhymed couplets employ simple, direct language. The eventful narratives abound with racy incidents and are often, despite the saints' gruesome ordeals, frankly humorous. The Anastasia legend, for example, includes a scene wherein a prince cavorts with some dirty kitchen utensils, mistaking them for the saint and her companions. (This episode will be known to many modern readers through the tenth-century German canoness Hrotsvitha of Gandersheim's lively rendition of it in her Latin play *Dulcitius.*)

Though addressed to a similar audience, the *North English Legendary* differs in many respects from the *South English Legendary*, especially in its six virgin martyr legends. Although these legends feature the same battles of the sexes, their conflicts are less grisly, and their heroines evade male authority through stealth rather than through defiance. Thus, for example, Anastasia studies Christianity secretly, feigns illness to avoid consummating her marriage, and slips out at night to share her husband's wealth with the needy. Despite the saints' refusal to conform to certain social norms, the *North English Legendary* is suffused with the bourgeois values that pervade many religious texts of the late Middle Ages, including the mystery plays, Books of Hours, and the *Book of Margery Kempe.* In the *North English Legendary*, the virgins' persecutors are more often attracted to their riches than to their beauty, while the saints themselves practice a restrained charity that would have appealed to prosperous merchants in late medieval England. Again, the Anastasia legend is a case in point: once married, the saint gives generously "because she had riches to spare," and she waits until her death is imminent to distribute all her possessions among the poor.

The development of Anastasia's legend demonstrates the increased association of sanctity with virginity as the Middle Ages progressed. In early medieval accounts of her life, Anastasia was a holy matron; only later was she transformed into a woman who managed to avoid paying the "marriage debt." Anastasia was never one of the most popular virgin martyrs. There are few paintings or statues of her, and in England, at least, no freestanding legends were written about her. Her story is, nonetheless, well represented in Middle English legendaries, which preserve four distinct versions of her martyrdom.

Edition: *Altenglischer Legenden: Neue Folge*, 25–28. Heilbronn: Henninger, 1881.

Thompson, Anne B. "Audacious Fictions: Anastasia and the Triumph of Narrative." *Assays* 8 (1995): 1–28.
Winstead, Karen A. *Virgin Martyrs: Legends of Sainthood in Late Medieval England*, 78–82. Ithaca: Cornell University Press, 1997.

Saint Anastasia

Saint Anastasia was born in Rome to one of the best families. As scholars report, her father and mother were pagans, but when Anastasia grew up, she converted to Christianity. The noble Saint Chrysogonus, who was then living in Rome, taught her the tenets of the faith, and she obeyed him in everything.[1] She learned all she wanted from him, but so discreetly that no one knew it.

Anastasia's powerful and strong-willed guardians married her with a large dowry to a man called Pupillus. But when she was married, she said she was too sick to go near him; she pretended to be in no state to visit any man's bed. But secretly, both day and night, she went out to visit the poor and relieve their misery—especially those she knew to be Chris-

---

[1] The relationship between Anastasia and Chrysogonus and the latter's martyrdom are described in Jacobus de Voragine's *Golden Legend* 2:333–34.

tians—because she had riches to spare. She gave with a free hand until at last she was caught: her husband spied her as she went out mornings and evenings accompanied by a single maiden, both women dressed simply, like Christians, to avoid recognition, and helping all who suffered in poverty or in prison. When her husband realized that she was giving away his wealth, he said she wouldn't be doing that anymore, and he commanded that she be shut up in a stone building without food. He'd rather she starve than squander his wealth as she'd been doing. So she was imprisoned, but her friends slipped food to her. She wrote to Saint Chrysogonus, telling him about her confinement and asking his advice. He comforted her, telling her to remain faithful and promising that she would survive her troubles. So it happened: an illness struck her husband, and he languished and died. When he was out of the way, Anastasia was released from prison and returned home, much to her friends' delight.

Anastasia then lived as a widow. For her servants, she had three sisters, who were good-looking and sweet-natured, and these she converted to Christianity. Thus lived the beautiful Anastasia and her beautiful servants, all Christians, and all giving their love to God alone.

The beauty of these women turned the head of a powerful heathen prince, and he began to woo them. He sent for them with fair words, looking to corrupt them. He revealed his intentions to them but quickly realized that they wanted nothing to do with him. Determined to have his way with or without their consent, he confined them to a building where kitchenwares were kept: cauldrons, pots, pans, kettles, cressets, and other such things. One day the randy prince wanted to take a stab at the ladies. He went into the building, telling his men to wait outside. Once inside, he lost his mind: thinking the pots and pans were fair damsels, he hugged and kissed them. He carried on with them as he pleased until his face and clothing were black as coal, while the maidens stood by and watched, untouched by the foul proceedings. His vision was so clouded that he didn't know what a mess he was making. When he had satisfied his wicked desires, he went out, all black and grimy. His men thought he looked more or less like a devil; some spat on him in scorn, some beat him briskly, and those that dared not touch him ran off and left him.

Baffled by his men's actions, the prince set out to complain to the emperor about them. But as he went along, other men struck him with rods and staves, crying loudly, "My, how he raves!" When he arrived, all the emperor's men ridiculed him and threw filth in his face, so the bewildered prince ran on without stopping. Not being able to see himself, he thought he was dressed in nice, clean clothing; he couldn't understand why neither his men nor his family recognized him, nor could he understand why those who used to respect him no longer did.

Finally he saw how foully he'd fared and realized that he'd done things with the cookware that he'd thought he was doing with the damsels. Then he complained to the emperor that these sly and knowing women had blinded him by witchcraft and made him act as he'd done, adding that they believed in Christ's law and would recognize no other god. The angry emperor had Anastasia and her three maidservants brought before him at the bar. At the prince's request, he ordered all four stripped, saying that they should be humiliated just as they'd humiliated the prince—but that wasn't the only reason, for he also wanted to see them naked. However, God arranged that no one could remove their clothing, howsoever he tried. The emperor marveled at that, and the prince swooned in astonishment.

Anastasia was then handed over to an eminent knight who was close to the emperor, with this understanding: if he could get her to renounce Christianity and live by their law, he should marry her. The knight was happy with this bargain, for he knew she was very wealthy. He brought her to his bedroom, where he thought he'd have his way with her, but when he took her in his arms, he was struck stone blind. Fearful at what he'd done, he had himself led before his gods. He told them what had happened and asked whether they could cure him. His gods replied, "Your affliction comes from offending Anastasia. You will not recover; instead, you will dwell with us forever." His men led him home again, where he died in agony.

When the knight was dead, the emperor turned Anastasia over to another knight, saying that they would soon decide what to do with her. Having heard much about Anastasia's great wealth, this knight was filled with greed and spoke to her as follows: "Anastasia, as you can see, you've been placed in my power, to rescue or ruin as I wish. I'll give you a chance to save yourself. If you want to be taken seriously as a Christian, you'll do as Christ advises, and you know very well that he says, 'Qui non renunciaverit omnibus que possidet, etc.'—that is, 'Whoever will adhere to my law must forsake his worldly goods, else he cannot be my servant.'

Here's my advice: Turn your riches over to me, and I'll let you go on your way. Then you can call yourself a true Christian."

Saint Anastasia answered, "You misunderstood. My lord Christ does not command me to give my wealth to the wealthy; he tells me to give to the poor and feed the feeble. Since I know you have plenty, giving my riches to you would violate God's commandment, and I'll never do that."

At that, she was cast in a strong prison without food or drink. Yet for somewhat over two months, heaven provided for her. She then had her goods distributed to the poor and lame, while they lasted, and through her, many maidens and wives were converted to Christianity. Something more than a month later, she was condemned to be burned. Her body was bound to a stake, and she died for Christ's sake, along with many others of her persuasion, who were tortured to death in diverse ways. Christians buried her body with the honor it deserved, and her soul was summoned to heaven forever. May God summon us there too!

Saint Cecilia

Geoffrey Chaucer

Chaucer's legend of Saint Cecilia is probably the best-known saint's legend written in English. Although most readers encounter it as the story told by the Second Nun in his *Canterbury Tales*, Chaucer wrote the piece in the 1370s or early 1380s, as much as a decade before he began work on that famous collection. It is found both in manuscripts of the *Canterbury Tales* and also in two fifteenth-century anthologies of religious writings.

Chaucer has been credited with transforming the saint's legend into a "literary" genre, providing a model for self-proclaimed disciples such as John Lydgate and Osbern Bokenham, whose works appear later in this volume. The rich vocabulary and complex syntax, especially of the prologue, do set Chaucer's narrative apart from earlier English saints' legends, as do the many biblical, liturgical, and literary allusions. For example, Chaucer opens his legend with an allusion to "idleness," the alluring gatekeeper of the garden of love in Guillaume de Lorris's allegorical *Romance of the Rose* (ca. 1237). Similarly, his invocation to Mary begins with a reference to the writings of Bernard of Clairvaux, the twelfth-century theologian known for his intense devotion to the Virgin, and in part paraphrases a passage from the last canto of Dante's *Divine Comedy*. Yet the conscious literariness of Chaucer's work should not distract us from its thorough grounding in the tradition of popular hagiography. Though introduced by the lessons, prayers, and meditations that will become hallmarks of fifteenth-century hagiography, the story itself is a taut drama of conflict and defiance in the style of the *South English Legendary.*

Cecilia's rebelliousness, which Chaucer captures so powerfully, had made her something of a cultural icon by his day. Cecilia offered a prototype for wives who wished to abstain from sex—to have a "spiritual marriage," as Dyan Elliott terms it—and many holy women of the later Middle Ages imitated her (with varying success) in discouraging their bridegrooms from exacting the "conjugal debt." Chaucer's adaptation suggests, however, that Cecilia's insubordinate spirit appealed to men as well as women. Indeed, Lynn Staley has persuasively argued that Chaucer's legend furnished a safe means of voicing his dissatisfactions with contemporary politics.

Edition: Chaucer, Geoffrey. *The Riverside Chaucer.* 3d ed. Ed. Larry D. Benson, 262–69. Boston: Houghton Mifflin, 1987.

Arthur, Karen. "Equivocal Subjectivity in Chaucer's *Second Nun's Prologue* and *Tale.*" *Chaucer Review* 32 (1998): 217–31.
Connolly, Thomas. *Mourning into Joy: Music, Raphael, and Saint Cecilia.* New Haven: Yale University Press, 1994.
Cooper, Helen. *The Oxford Guides to Chaucer: The Canterbury Tales,* 358–67. Oxford: Oxford University Press, 1989.
Elliott, Dyan. *Spiritual Marriage: Sexual Abstinence in Medieval Wedlock.* Princeton: Princeton University Press, 1993.
Kolve, V. A. "Chaucer's *Second Nun's Tale* and the Iconography of St. Cecilia." In *New Perspectives in Chaucer Criticism,* ed. Donald M. Rose, 137–58. Norman, Okla.: Pilgrim Books, 1981.
Raybin, David. "Chaucer's Creation and Recreation of the 'Lyf of Seynt Cecile.' " *Chaucer Review* 32 (1997): 196–212.
Reames, Sherry L. "Artistry, Decorum, and Purpose in Three Middle English Retellings of the Cecilia Legend." In *The Endless Knot: Essays in Old and Middle English in Honor of Marie Borroff,* ed. M. Teresa Tavormina and R. F. Yeager, 177–99. Cambridge: D. S. Brewer, 1995.
———. "The Cecilia Legend as Chaucer Inherited It and Retold It: The Disappearance of an Augustinian Ideal." *Speculum* 55 (1980): 38–57.
———. "A Recent Discovery concerning the Sources of Chaucer's 'Second Nun's Tale.' " *Modern Philology* 87 (1990): 337–61.
Staley, Lynn. "Chaucer and the Postures of Sanctity." In David Aers and Lynn Staley, *The Powers of the Holy: Religion, Politics, and Gender in Late Medieval English Culture,* 179–259. University Park: Pennsylvania State University Press, 1996.
Strohm, Paul. "*Passioun, Lyf, Miracle, Legende:* Some Generic Terms in Middle English Hagiographical Narrative." *Chaucer Review* 10 (1974–75): 62–75, 154–71.
Weise, Judith A. "Chaucer's Tell-Tale Lexicon: Romancing Seinte Cecyle." *Style* 31 (1997): 440–79.

Fig. 3. Saint Cecilia of Rome and her husband Valerian being crowned by an angel: Master of the Pesaro Altarpiece. (Courtesy of the Philadelphia Museum of Art; bequest of John D. McIlhenny.)

Saint Cecilia

Prologue

The servant and nurse of the vices, called "idleness" in English, who is the porter at the gate of delights, we should do all we can to avoid and defeat through her opposite, that is, gainful activity, lest the devil seize us through idleness. For he who with his thousand crafty snares waits to entrap us can so handily catch an idle person that the idler won't know the devil's got him until he's seized by the hem of his shirt! We therefore have every reason to resist idleness.

Even if people weren't afraid of death, reason would surely show them that idleness is no more than rotten laziness, which brings neither good nor profit. Sloth has idleness on a leash, allowing her only to sleep, eat, drink, and devour everything others earn. To stay away from such confounding idleness, I have labored most industriously to translate your glorious life and passion, you with your garland made of roses and lilies—"you" meaning the maiden and martyr Saint Cecilia.

Invocation to Mary

Oh flower of virgins, of whom Saint Bernard so eagerly writes, I call upon you first. Solace of us wretches, help me relate the death of your maiden, who earned eternal life and victory over the devil, as people may soon read in her story. Oh maiden and mother, daughter of your son; oh well of mercy, healer of sinful souls, whom God in his goodness chose to inhabit; oh humble queen of all creatures, you so ennobled our humanity that the Creator did not scorn to clothe his son in flesh and blood.

Within the happy cloister of your womb, eternal love and peace assumed the form of a man, lord and guide of the threefold world: earth, sea, and heaven. And you, spotless virgin, bore—while remaining a pure maiden—the creator of all creatures. Magnificence, mercy, goodness, and compassion are so united within you, oh sun of excellence, that you not only help those who seek your assistance but, in your benevolence, dearest doctor, you treat those who have not yet called upon you.

Oh meek and happy, lovely maiden, help me, an exiled wretch in this desert of bitterness. Think of the Canaanite woman who said that even dogs eat crumbs that fall from their lord's table.[1] Accept my faith, though I am sinful, an unworthy son of Eve. And since faith without works is dead, give me the time and understanding to be free from this utter darkness. You who are so fair and full of grace, Christ's mother, dear Anne's daughter, be my advocate in that high place where "Hosanna" is forever sung. Illuminate my imprisoned soul, afflicted by my body's contagion and weighed down by earthly lust and false love. Oh haven of refuges, savior of those who suffer distress, help me now, as I turn to my work.

Before beginning, though, I ask my readers to forgive me for not writing this story more ingeniously, for I must adhere to the words and the meaning of him who wrote the story in the saint's honor. I ask you to amend my work.[2]

Interpretation of the name Cecilia that Brother Jacob of Genoa put in the Legend[3]

First I will explicate Saint Cecilia's name, as readers may find in her legend. In English, it means "heaven's lily," referring to the pure chastity of her virginity. Or, because she had the whiteness of chastity, the verdure of conscience, and the sweet savor of a good reputation, "lily" was her name. Or, Cecilia means "way of the blind," for she was an example through her good teaching. Alternatively, I read, Cecilia is a conjunction of "heaven" and "lia," the "heaven" referring to her holy thoughts and the "lia" to her constant industriousness.

Cecilia can also be translated as "lacking blindness," on account of her illuminating wisdom and her shining morals. Or else—wait—this maiden's clear name derives from "heaven" and "leos," enabling people

---

[1] Matthew 15:22–28.

[2] Requests that more knowledgeable readers correct and improve a writer's translation are common in all genres of medieval literature.

[3] Around 1360, the Dominican friar Jacobus de Voragine compiled a collection of saints' legends in Latin known as the *Golden Legend (Legenda aurea)*. Each legend begins with an etymology of the saint's name. The *Golden Legend* was the most widely circulated and influential legendary of the Middle Ages.

to rightly call her "people's heaven," example of all good and prudent behavior. For "leos" means "people" in English, and just as people may see the sun and moon and stars in the heavens, they may spiritually see the brightness of her wisdom and the glowing excellence of her various deeds. And just as philosophers write that heaven is swift and round and burning, so was Cecilia ever swift and busy in her good deeds, round and whole in her perseverance, and burning ever bright in her charity. Now I have told you what she was called.

The life of Saint Cecilia

This bright maiden Cecilia, as her life tells, was descended from noble Romans and was from infancy fostered in Christ's faith, ever bearing his gospel in mind. I read that she never ceased praying, loving and fearing God, and beseeching him to preserve her virginity.

On the day when this virgin was to be married to a young man called Valerian, she humbly and devoutly wore a hair shirt beneath her golden robes, right next to her flesh. And while the organs played, she sang to God, privately in her heart, "Oh lord, to you I entrust my soul and my undefiled body, lest I be ruined." For the love of him who died on a tree, she fasted every second and third day, remaining ever steadfast in her prayers.

When night fell, and she had to go to bed with her husband—in the usual manner—she confided to him, "O sweet and precious darling husband, I want to tell you a secret, if you swear you won't betray it." Valerian vehemently swore that he would never betray her, under any circumstances. Then she said, "I have an angel who loves me so much that, whether I'm awake or asleep, he's always ready to protect my body. Believe me, if he sees you touching me, or loving me shamefully, he'll slay you in the act, and so you'll die a young man. But if you love me purely, he'll love you for your purity, just as he loves me, and he'll show you his joy and his splendor."

Checked by God's will, Valerian replied, "If you want me to believe you, let me see that angel. If he's a real angel, I'll do as you ask. But if you love another man, I swear I'll slay you both with this very sword!"

Cecilia answered, "You'll see the angel, if you wish, provided that you believe in Christ and receive baptism. Go to the Appian Way," she said, "just three miles out of town. Tell the paupers who live there that I, Ce-

cilia, sent you to them to take you to the venerable Urban.[4] Tell him
what I told you, and when he's purged your sins, you'll see that angel before you leave."

Valerian went there and found this holy old Urban, just as he was told,
hiding among the graves of the saints. He immediately delivered his
message and Urban threw up his hands in joy. He let the tears fall from
his eyes. "Almighty lord, oh Jesus Christ," he said, "sower of chaste wisdom and shepherd of us all, receive the fruit of that seed of chastity you
sowed in Cecilia! As honest as a busy bee, your own thrall Cecilia serves
you! Look! The man she just married, once ferocious as a lion, she sends
you meek as a lamb!"

After he spoke, an old man in shining white clothes appeared before
Valerian, carrying a book inscribed with golden letters. Valerian
swooned in dread at the sight, but the old man called him over and he
read in the book, "One lord, one faith, one God, and no others, one
Christendom, and the father of everything, above all and over all."
These words were written in gold. When they were read, the old man
said, "Do you believe this? Yes or no?"

"I believe it all," said Valerian, "for I dare say there is no surer truth
under heaven." Then the old man vanished—Valerian didn't know
where—and Pope Urban baptized him on the spot.

Valerian goes home and finds Cecilia in the bedroom with an angel.
The angel held two garlands of roses and lilies. He first gave one to Cecilia, as I understand, then brought the other over to Valerian, her mate.
"Guard these crowns well with purity of body and thought," he said. "I
brought them for you from paradise. Believe me, they'll never rot or lose
their sweet scent. And only people who are chaste and hate shame will
be able to see them. As for you, Valerian, because you listened to good
advice so readily, ask for what you want and you'll have your request."

"I have a brother," Valerian replied, "whom I love more than any man
on earth. I ask that my brother may have the grace to know the truth, as
I do here."

The angel said, "God likes your request. You'll both come to his
blessed feast carrying the palm of martyrdom."

Just as he finished speaking, Tiburtius, Valerian's brother, arrived.
When he smelled the roses and the lilies, he was amazed and said,

---

[4] Urban I, pope from 222 until his martyrdom in 230.

"Where, at this time of year, does that sweet scent of roses and lilies come from? They couldn't smell stronger if I held them in my hands! Their scent has infused my heart and utterly transformed me!"

Valerian said, "We have two garlands, snow white and rose red; though they shine clearly, you cannot see them. Just as my prayers have allowed you to smell them, you shall see them, dear brother, if you will believe properly and receive the truth."

Tiburtius replied, "Are you really saying this to me, or am I dreaming?"

"My brother," Valerian said, "we've been dreaming up until now. At last, we live in truth."

"How do you know?" asked Tiburtius. "And how did you find out?"

Valerian said, "I'll tell you. God's angel has taught me the truth, and you'll see him too, but only if you'll renounce idols and be pure."

The noble theologian Saint Ambrose solemnly commended the miracle of these two garlands in his preface to the canon of the Mass, saying, "To receive the palm of martyrdom, Saint Cecilia, filled with God's grace, gave up the world as well as her bridal chamber. Consider the conversion of Tiburtius and Valerian, for which God, in his goodness, provided two garlands of sweet-smelling flowers, which he had his angel bring them. The virgin brought these men to heavenly bliss. The world has indeed seen what chaste devotion to love is worth."[5]

Then Cecilia clearly demonstrated to Tiburtius that idols are dumb, deaf, and therefore completely useless, and she told him to abandon them. "Whoever doesn't believe this is a beast, for sure!" Tiburtius said. When she heard this, she kissed his breast, delighted that he could perceive the truth. "This day I take you as my colleague," said the dear, happy, lovely maiden. Then she said this: "Just as Christ's love made me your brother's wife," she said, "just so I take you as my partner, since you will despise your idols. Go with your brother now, and be baptized and be purified so that you can see the face of the angel your brother has told you about."

Tiburtius said, "Brother dear, where shall I go? And to whom?"

"To whom?" he said. "Come right along and I'll take you to Pope Urban!"

---

[5] Ambrose, a fourth-century Church Father, wrote extensively on virginity and related some of the first Latin virgin martyr legends. This aside is found in Chaucer's source.

"To Urban? Valerian, brother, you want to take me there? You can't be serious! Do you mean the Urban who's been condemned to death multiple times? The one who scurries from one shelter to another, not daring to show his face? If he were found, he'd be burned in a red-hot fire—and so would we, if we were caught with him! So while we were looking for divine secrets hidden in heaven, we'd be burned here on earth!"

"My own dear brother," Cecilia replied, "it would be reasonable to fear losing this life, if it were our only life. But don't be afraid, for there's a better life in another place that God's son revealed through his grace. The father's son judiciously created all people; the ghost, who proceeded from the father, gave them souls. While he lived here on earth, the son of the most high God showed, through words and miracles, that there is another life for people to live."

Tiburtius replied, "Dear sister—didn't you just say that there's only one true God? How can you now speak of three?"

"I'll tell you," she said. "Just as one person has three faculties—memory, imagination, and intellect—so three persons may reside within one divinity." Then she busily preached about Christ's coming, about his suffering and passion. She told how God's son was kept in the world to win full forgiveness for a humanity bound in sin and care. She said all this to Tiburtius. Then Tiburtius happily accompanied Valerian to Pope Urban, who thanked God with a joyful heart and baptized him and completed his education, thus making him God's knight. Then Tiburtius grew so full of grace that he saw God's angel every day. And every favor he asked of God, he promptly received.

It would be hard to list the many wonders Jesus did for Tiburtius and Valerian. But to make a long story short, Roman officers tracked them down and brought them before the prefect Almachius, who questioned them and, learning their disposition, sent them off to the statue of Jupiter, saying, "Whoever won't sacrifice, lop off his head; that's my decree!"

A certain Maximus, the prefect's officer and subordinate, summoned the saints and wept for pity as he led them forth. When Maximus heard the saints' teaching, he got the torturers to let him take them home. By evening, Valerian and Tiburtius had persuaded the torturers, Maximus, and all his people to renounce their false faith and believe in the one God!

When night fell, Cecilia brought priests to baptize the whole company. At daybreak, she exhorted them stoutly, "Now Christ's own knights, beloved and dear, cast off the works of darkness and arm yourselves in the armor of light. You've engaged in a great battle. Your course is run; you've kept your faith. Go receive the crown of everlasting life. The righteous judge you've served will give it to you—just as you deserve!"

After she'd spoken, Valerian and Tiburtius were led forth to do sacrifice. But when they arrived at the place, to put it briefly, they wouldn't offer incense or sacrifice a thing. Instead, they got down on their knees and, humbly and with dignity, lost their heads. Their souls joined the king of grace. Maximus, who saw everything, wept, saying that he'd seen their souls glide into heaven, accompanied by brightly shining angels. His words converted many people, causing Almachius to beat him to death with a lead-weighted whip. Cecilia buried him in the same tomb as Tiburtius and Valerian.

Thereupon Almachius immediately had his officers fetch Cecilia publicly so that she might sacrifice and give incense to Jupiter in his presence. They, however, converted by her wisdom, believed her words. Weeping profusely, they exclaimed, "We believe that Christ, God's son—who is served by such a good servant—is truly God. We all believe this and declare it unanimously, even if we die for it!"

When he heard of these doings, Almachius had Cecilia brought before him. His first question was, "What kind of woman are you?"

"I am a gentlewoman by birth," she said.

"You may not like this, but I'm going to ask about your religion and faith."

"You've started your interrogation foolishly, stupidly expecting two answers from one question."

Almachius said, "Where do you come by such rude answers?"

"Why, from my conscience and convictions!" she replied.

Almachius said, "Don't you give a thought to my power?"

She answered, "Your power is nothing to be afraid of. Every mortal man's power is like a bladder filled with air: one prick of a pin and—pop!—it's completely deflated."

"You've gotten off to a bad start," he said. "You're clinging to an error. Don't you know that our noble and mighty princes have ordained that every Christian shall be punished unless he renounce his Christianity?"

"Your princes err, as do your nobles!" Cecilia replied. "With a crazy verdict you make us out to be guilty when in fact we're not. You know perfectly well that we're innocent. Just because we honor Christ and call ourselves Christians, you label us criminals and condemn us! But we know our virtue and cannot deny it!"

Almachius answered, "Save yourself by one of these two means: sacrifice to the gods or renounce Christianity."

Then the lovely, holy, blessed maiden began to laugh. "You befuddled judge!" she said. "You want me to deny being innocent and thereby make myself guilty? See how he dissembles, right here in court! He rants and raves like a lunatic!"

Almachius replied, "Silly fool, don't you realize the extent of my power? Haven't our mighty princes given me the power and authority over life and death? Why do you answer me so proudly?"

"I'm speaking steadfastly, not proudly," she said, "for we Christians hate the deadly sin of pride! And if you're not afraid to hear the truth, I'll expose your lies right here and now. You say your princes have given you power over life and death—but you can only take life; that's all! You can say your princes have made you an executioner, but to claim any more is to lie! Your power amounts to nothing!"

"Enough of your impudence!" Almachius said. "Sacrifice to our gods right now, before you leave! As a philosopher, I can tolerate the wrongs you do me, but I can't tolerate your lies about our gods!"

"You fool!" Cecilia answered. "You haven't said one word to me that doesn't reveal your stupidity. In every way, you show that you're a stupid official and a foolish judge. There's nothing wrong with your eyes. Yet this thing that we all see is a stone you want to call a god! Take my advice: touch it and feel it. You'll find that it's a stone, even if your blind eyes don't see it! You dishonor yourself—people will scorn you and laugh at your stupidity, for everyone knows that almighty God is in heaven and these statues can't do you—or themselves, for that matter—any good. They're completely worthless!"

She went on in the same vein. He grew angry and told men to lead her home. "Burn her with red-hot flames right at home in a bath," he said. His command was carried out. They put her in a bath, and day and night they stoked a great fire beneath her. All night long, and all day, too, despite the fire and the heat of the bath, she remained cool and felt no pain. She didn't sweat a drop. Yet she was doomed to die in that bath, for Almachius sent his servant to behead her right there. The executioner struck three times, but he couldn't cut her neck in two. And since the law forbade striking a fourth blow—hard or soft—the executioner dared do no more. Off he went, leaving her there half dead, her neck hacked. The Christians who were around collected her fair blood in cloths. She lived for three days in this torment, and she never stopped teaching people about the faith she'd fostered in them. She preached to them and gave them all she owned, entrusting everything to Pope Urban. To him she said, "I asked heaven's king to let me live for just three days so that I could commend these souls to you before I go and so that I could arrange to have my house made into a church in perpetuity."

Saint Urban and his deacons secretly took her body and buried it honorably among the other saints.[6] Her house is called the Church of Saint Cecilia. Saint Urban consecrated it—as was only proper—and it stands to this day, a place where people nobly serve Christ and his saint.

---

[6] In his brief life of Urban, Jacobus de Voragine writes that, after Cecilia's death, Almachius conducted an intensive manhunt for the pope, who was found hiding in a cave and was charged with "misleading five thousand persons, among them the blasphemer Cecilia and two illustrious men, Tiburtius and Valerian." Urban was tortured and killed after telling Almachius that he couldn't produce Cecilia's wealth for him because it had been distributed among the poor. See *Golden Legend* 1:314.

Saint Christine

William Paris

This legend of Christine is one of two Middle English virgin martyr legends that we know were composed by laymen. (The other is Chaucer's Cecilia legend.) William Paris wrote as a political prisoner. He was a follower of Thomas Beauchamp, Earl of Warwick, who was exiled to the Isle of Man in 1397 for treason against King Richard II. According to his epilogue to "Christine," Paris was the only man to remain loyal to Beauchamp in his disgrace. He followed his lord to prison and wrote the legend in his spare time. As far as we know, "Christine" is all he wrote.

It is easy to imagine that Paris empathized with Christine as a fellow political prisoner. His narrative, briskly told in staccato sentences, is positively gleeful. The frankly partisan narrator cheers for the saint and boos her enemies. He gloats as one judge after another tries and fails to kill the impudent twelve-year-old, two of them dying from their efforts. When Christine seems in particular trouble, he even says a quick prayer for her.

Unlike most thirteenth- and fourteenth-century saints' lives, Paris's "Christine" has been much admired by scholars. Carl Horstmann suggested that it was so well crafted that Paris must have been influenced by Chaucer. Although Paris is indeed a good craftsman, his legend bears few marks of Chaucer's style. All we can say for sure is that Paris shared Chaucer's taste for feisty heroines and action-packed narratives. To judge from the legends that were being written and read at the time, so did most people in the late fourteenth century.

Like his heroine, Paris was a survivor. After Richard II was deposed in 1399, both he and Beauchamp were released, and his loyalty was rewarded with various gifts, including the manor of Great Comberton in Worcestershire, which Beauchamp granted him "for the rent of a rose at Midsummer" (Stouck, "Poet," 114).

Edition: Paris, William. "Cristine." In *Sammlung Altenglischer Legenden,* ed. Carl Horstmann, 183–90. Heilbronn: Henninger, 1878.

Gerould, Gordon Hall. "The Legend of St. Christina by William Paris." *Modern Language Notes* 29 (1914): 129–33.
Salter, Elizabeth. *Fourteenth-Century English Poetry: Contexts and Readings,* 64–65. Oxford: Clarendon, 1983.
Stouck, Mary-Ann. "A Poet in the Household of the Beauchamp Earls of Warwick, c. 1393–1427." *Warwickshire History* 9 (1994): 113–17.
———. "Saints and Rebels: Hagiography and Opposition to the King in Late Fourteenth-Century England." *Medievalia et Humanistica* 24, n.s. (1997): 75–94.
Winstead, Karen A. *Virgin Martyrs: Legends of Sainthood in Late Medieval England,* 83–85. Ithaca: Cornell University Press, 1997.

Saint Christine

Saint Christine was a radiant maiden, as scholars have seen and read in books. She served God both day and night, as a martyr and pure virgin should. She was born in Italy, I think, and came from a powerful family. But she forsook them all and gave her heart entirely to Christ.

That gentle maiden was so lovely that whoever set eyes on her—man, woman, or child—loved her. God endowed her with such grace that she fled all vice and wild deeds, vowing to be God's servant and undefiled maiden.

Her father was called Urban—a wicked tyrant and a madman. As in so many cases, though, a rogue can produce a perfectly good child, and so did Urban, by the cross! For all his wrongdoing, he fathered Christine, who lives with Christ in heavenly bliss.

Many men desired that maid—and would have married her if they could. Just seeing her on one day made them feel better for a full week afterward! Her appearance made them say to one another, "This is the finest person we've ever seen, that's for sure!"

Her family didn't want to marry her to anyone; they planned to dedicate her to the gods. Her father confined her in a stone tower with twelve maidens to attend her. She couldn't trust a single one of them, for they were there to spy on how she lived and prayed.

That maiden had gods of shiny gold and silver in the tower with her, which she was supposed to worship and honor day and night. But suddenly almighty God sent help: he made her yearn to bring her soul to heaven's light. The holy ghost within Christine taught her to forsake every one of her false gods, which are only pallid sticks and stones. She resolved to fear nothing but think only of heaven. See how God can turn non-Christians into his holy martyrs! Some—like good Saint John the Baptist—had grace before they were born; some—like fair Christine— acquired it in their youth; and some—as we can see in Paul's life—got it after youth was gone. Some received it at the hour of their death, like Barabbas, the thief hanged so high.[1]

She had incense, but she hid it in a window, and she did so in good conscience, for she intended never to sacrifice to the false gods of heathendom, no matter who told her to. She asked Christ that she might be martyred before that happened!

One day Urban wanted to see his daughter. Christine's attendants all said, "Lord Urban, we tell you that your daughter and our noble lady scorns our gods and everything that has to do with them. In fact, she says she'll be a Christian if she can!"

Urban said, "Let me see my daughter alone. If she confirms what you say, I'll coax her into changing her mind. Believe me, unless she does sacrifice she'll be sorry—and so will I, for knowing my daughter has come to such a state will break my heart in two!"

With a stern face, Urban went upstairs to Christine's room and said, "Dear daughter, Christine! Look: I've come to visit with you and to watch you sacrifice to all our mighty gods. That's why I'm here."

"Don't call me your daughter, Urban, for I'll never call you father. My thoughts are for Jesus alone; I'm his child, sir. Don't tell me about idols made of metal; talk to me about God in majesty, for he alone made and redeemed me."

"Fair daughter," Urban said, "don't worship only one god—if you do, you'll shortchange all the others. If you give thanks to them all, you won't need to worry. Follow the example of your kin, I entreat you."

"You think you're making sense, but you're really talking like a fool who has no conception of truth and happiness. Listen, Urban: I'll sacri-

---

[1] According to the Gospels, Barabbas was the murderer whom the people chose to have Pilate release instead of Christ. Here he seems to be confused with the "good thief" who was crucified beside Christ and repented before his death. See Luke 23:40–43.

fice with all my heart to God in heaven and to the son and to the holy ghost—these three and no more!"

"Since you're willing to worship three gods, why not honor others as well?"

Christine replied, "I'll tell you why, fool: these three make up exactly one God."

Urban went away, mad as could be. He thought his heart would break in two for love of his noble daughter.

When he had left, Christine threw down every single idol and broke their legs and arms in two. She also removed all the silver and gold plating and got rid of it, giving it to poor Christians, who had nothing.

Urban returned another day to worship his gods and found not a one—they were all gone. He summoned Christine's attendants: "What has my little girl Christine done with all our gods? Tell me!"

They replied, "Your daughter threw them all out the window."

Urban said, "So help me, my daughter is a damned fool! Maidens, how dared she smash such powerful gods?"

They replied, "You can see how she dared! Now they're all in pieces. Fix them, sir! Can you?"

"Take off her clothes," Urban said, "and bring her before me right now. You twelve men—go and beat her, naked as she was born." They beat her until they could do no more and stood helpless. She apparently felt no pain, though, for she said to her father, "You're a shameless abomination to God, devoid of honor, I say! See how exhausted your men are. They don't know where their strength has gone! Ask your gods to help them now—if they can do anything, let them try! For my God's love, I can stand more beating than you can command!"

That sweet maiden Christine was bound with chains and put in a dungeon. When her mother heard where she was, she tore her clothes and fainted away. Then she headed straight for the dungeon, her cheeks wet with tears. When she saw Christine, she fell down at her feet and said, "Christine, my darling daughter, light of my eyes, alas that I should ever see you here, brought to such a pass! You know that you can make your father and me very happy. Take pity on me, gentle girl—and on your father, fair daughter—and restore our joy!"

Saint Christine said to her mother, "Why do you call me your daughter? Don't you know that I'm named after my God in majesty? Christ, God's son, that's his name. He suffered for you and me: therefore I'll be his servant. I won't have it any other way."

Seeing that she would not be able to change Christine's mind with fair speech, her mother left, a sorry soul, and she could not be comforted with food and drink. When Urban asked her how it went, she relayed Christine's answer. He carried on like a madman and demanded to see his daughter.

"Fetch her," said Urban. "I want her brought before the bar and I'll try to make her change her wicked ideas. She said she wasn't my daughter—the bitch I myself begat! She broke my richly crafted gods. No wonder I'm furious!"

Christine now stands before the bar—God grant her the grace to speak well! "Sacrifice to our powerful gods!" Urban demanded. "If you refuse, you'll die in excruciating agony. Unless you sacrifice, I'll never be able to call you my daughter—and I won't want to!"

Then the lovely maiden Christine said to her father, who sat so high, "What an honor you're doing me by no longer calling me the devil's daughter! The child of a devil is a devil himself, and you, father, are the direct descendant of that cursed fiend Satan!"

Urban then commanded that her clear white flesh be scraped from her bones with sharp hooked nails. He ordered all her limbs broken, one by one. By Saint John, it was a shame to see what was done to that maiden!

When Christine saw her flesh, she took a slice and threw it right at Urban's eye; if he hadn't ducked, she would have hit him. Then the witty maiden said to her supposed father, "Have a morsel, tyrant! Go ahead! After all, it's the flesh you produced."

Urban was so enraged that he put the maiden on a wheel and, to change her mind, he had a great fire, fed with oil, lit beneath her. It avoided her, though—she felt nothing but good—and instead burned to death fifteen hundred bystanders. Convinced that she acted through witchcraft or sorcery, her father was so distraught he couldn't sit still. He ordered his men to return her to prison. May Christ (and our lady, too) help that maiden, just as he did when he died for her on the cross!

When day had gone and night had come, they tied an exceedingly heavy stone around her neck, then they threw her into the sea. But once that evil deed had been done, lovely angels came from heaven and, through God's grace and great power, held her up. Then Christ himself came down and baptized Christine in the sea. It is written that he said these very words: "In my father and in myself, Jesus Christ, God's heav-

enly son, and in the holy ghost, us three, I baptize you with this water."
Christ christened Christine with his own hands: he was both godfather
and priest that night. I understand that Christine was named after
Christ; thus she was called after her godfather, Christ, who christened
her in the sea. She must indeed have been a holy person whom Christ
thus baptized in the sea! Christ entrusted her to Saint Michael, who
brought her back to land.

When her father heard what had happened, he was beside himself,
not knowing what to do. Out of sheer frustration, he smacked himself in
the face. When he saw her, he glared at her and said, "What's this witchcraft of yours, that neither land nor sea can kill you?"

She replied, "I received this grace from heaven, scoundrel."

"Put her in a dungeon!" said Urban. "I'll have her head tomorrow, by
my life!" He may have been using a figure of speech, but he was right,
that cursed fellow—for he was dead by daybreak, and Christine lived,
that lovely maiden.

His successor was ruthless Dionysius, who intended to make short
work of the virgin. He ordered an iron cauldron, hot as coal and filled
with oil, pitch, and resin. It boiled so hot it was terrifying! But when they
cast fair Christine in it, she didn't even notice. To increase her suffering—and to burn her more quickly to ashes—four men rocked her back
and forth. She lay like a babe in its cradle, feeling no pain. She thanked
God for not letting her be destroyed by the torments they inflicted, saying, "Thank you, heaven's king, for arranging this for me—to be born
twice and rocked twice in a cradle!" When Dionysius looked over and
saw she felt nothing, he was so angry he thought he'd hang himself.

Then Dionysius said to Christine, "Since these torments don't hurt
you, it's obvious that our gods have helped you because they want you to
be converted. Come with me, Christine, and repent; if you do, they'll
have mercy and pity on you."

She said, "Dionysius, you son of the devil! I'm not at all afraid of your
torments. Why not finish what you've begun? Don't let up until you've
tortured me to death! You and Urban can drink from the same cask,
down in the depths of hell!"

Then Dionysius said, "Cut off her hair—never mind if it's pretty!
Shave her head and strip her! Parade that wretch naked through the city
to Apollo! Let him deal with her! His power is so great that he can
amend her wickedness!"

So they led her through the city. When women saw that maiden—completely naked, with no clothing to conceal her belly and sides—they cried out against Dionysius, "Damn you, Dionysius! You've humiliated all women today!"

When that noble maiden was brought to Apollo, she said, "In Christ's name I command you to fall to pieces!" Apollo was pulverized on the spot, right there for everyone to see. With this miracle, Christine converted three thousand heathens.

When Dionysius heard that Christine had destroyed Apollo, his heart broke from fear. So he died, unrepentant. God sent Christine such grace that she hasn't yet felt any pain, while both her enemies are destroyed—they can do no more to her!

So Urban and Dionysius are out of the picture; they have no more power over Christine. But in came a third rogue; his name, I know, was Julian. The scoundrel started by having his men prepare a red-hot oven for Christine. When it was hot—it shone bright as ever a fire can—cruel Julian said, "Put her in! Let's see what happens." Without pity they threw her in, thinking they'd never see her again. But she felt no more heat than she would have in a bath! She stayed in there for a total of five days, singing like a carefree girl and accompanied by angels. She felt nothing of the torments and pains that Julian inflicted on her: all was angels' play to her. When Julian heard that, far from suffering, she was singing with bright angels, he thought she'd accomplished it by witchcraft. Lacking the grace to perceive the truth, he summoned another person to kill Christine. I hear his name was Marcus and that he came with six snakes.

Marcus was a snake-charmer. His snakes would kill any creature he wanted to harm. Now they're set on Christine. She wasn't at all afraid of them. See them play around her neck! Her neck was drenched with sweat; two snakes licked it all away. Two went down to her feet, licked them clean, and stayed there. Two dangled from her breasts, as if they wanted to suckle the sweet maiden. They couldn't hurt her at all, so Julian saw.

Then Julian said to Marcus, "You said your beasts would kill her right away! Make them bite her, if you can! You know perfectly well they haven't done so." Marcus immediately started chanting to make the snakes bite that blessed woman. But the snakes all left Christine and killed the charmer. Saint Christine saw how Marcus, who was to have made the snakes bite, lay dead. She ordered the snakes to go away to the desert, where they wouldn't bite anyone, and she ordered Marcus to get up. He stood up before the maid, making Julian so furious that he thought his heart would burst that day.

Her breasts were round as apples—they really were! They cut them off—such a shame—when she was just twelve years old. Milk gushed out, as everyone saw, and some were sorry. But Julian was unmoved, and he had no regrets.

Saint Christine said, with heart and soul, "Thank you, God in majesty, for all you've done to show your might through me. In all my ordeals, you've protected me, letting neither fire nor water harm me. Now I think it's time for me to be brought to the fair bliss of heaven."

Amazed that she could prate so in her torment, Julian ordered a rogue, "Cut out her tongue; it's hurting me."

When her tongue lay at her feet, that lovely maiden spoke as well as if it had never been cut out. Everyone saw and heard her. She picked her tongue up and threw it at Julian's eye; from then on, he couldn't see from that side. She smiled a little when she hit him. Not at all amused, Julian said, "Damn you! You're a witch—I know it!"

He looked aside with his one eye and said to the tongue, "While you were in her big fat mouth, you hurt me with your words. Your blow has hurt me even more by taking out my eye! Words flow to and fro like the wind, but blows sting like the dickens!" Beside himself with fury, he shot her with three arrows. Two landed in her heart, the third in her side. When Christine was struck, her soul went to radiant heaven, where she would feel no more pain.

Her body lies in a strong castle—the book calls it Bolsena—where many sick people have recovered their health, and many blind people have recovered their sight. I truly believe that if anyone prays earnestly to that damsel, she will help him with all her might—if what they want is good and right.

Saint Christine, pray that we may fare better, we who have been long imprisoned on the Isle of Man. Sir Thomas Beauchamp was once earl of Warwick; now he's a poor man, with just one squire to attend him. Where are the knights that accompanied him in his prosperity? Where are the squires, now that he needs them, the ones who thought they'd never leave him? Once he fed and clothed many yeomen; not one of them dared remain with their lord. That lord sits alone in prison. He has no men—except William Paris, by Saint John!—who wouldn't part from him. He wrote this life in English as he sat in the prison of stone, when he could spare time from serving his lord.

Jesus Christ, God's mighty son, who came down to amend our ills and settled in a pure virgin, Mary, now your mother, grant that all who have heard this will see you in heaven. Let them see you sitting there in bliss with Christine, your radiant maiden! Amen.

Saint Eugenia

The Scottish Legendary

The legend of Eugenia combines the virgin martyr legend with another genre of hagiography, the legend of the transvestite saint. In the typical transvestite saint's legend, a woman who wishes to escape marriage enters a monastery disguised as a man. Her holiness impresses everyone, until another woman falls in love with the "monk" and, finding her advances spurned, levels a charge of rape. Sometimes, as in the legend of Theodora, the saint acquiesces to punishment by perpetual solitary confinement and is exonerated only when her body is being washed for burial; sometimes, as in the Eugenia legend, she proves her innocence dramatically by disrobing.

This version of the Eugenia legend is part of the *Scottish Legendary*, a large collection of saints' lives in Scots dialect, which was produced in the late fourteenth or early fifteenth century. It probably did not enjoy a wide circulation, for it survives in only one manuscript, MS Gg.2.6, Cambridge University. The collection was once attributed to John Barbour, archdeacon of Aberdeen and author of the Scots epic *The Bruce;* that attribution is now considered erroneous, however.

Although we know nothing about the true author or authors of the *Scottish Legendary*, the narrator of the Eugenia legend is a vivid personality. He opens with a direct address to his readers, in which he connects the Eugenia story to the preceding story of Theodora, another transvestite saint, whose flight to the monastery was motivated by her remorse at having committed adultery. Throughout the narrative, he interjects his opinions in digressions that seem distinctly Chaucerian. He may, indeed, have been one of the several Scots writers who knew and imitated Chaucer's works. If so, his gibes at women suggest that he was more influenced by the *Nun's Priest's Tale* than by the *Second Nun's Tale*. Virgin martyr legends are certainly not exempt from the misogyny that pervades medieval literature, but rarely do we see in them the fully developed antifeminist exempla and diatribes that are found in "Eugenia."

Edition: *Barbour's des Schottischen Nationaldichters Legendensammlung.* 2 vols. Ed. Carl Horstmann, 2:38–50. Heilbronn: Henninger, 1881–82.

Anson, John. "The Female Transvestite in Early Monasticism: The Origin and Development of a Motif." *Viator* 5 (1974): 1–32.
Bullough, Vern L. "Cross Dressing and Gender Role Change in the Middle Ages." In *Handbook of Medieval Sexuality,* ed. Vern L. Bullough and James A. Brundage, 223–42. New York: Garland, 1996.
Bullough, Vern L., and Bonnie Bullough. "Cross Dressing and Social Status in the Middle Ages." In *Cross Dressing, Sex, and Gender,* 45–73. Philadelphia: University of Pennsylvania Press, 1993.
D'Evelyn, Charlotte. "The Scottish Legendary." In *A Manual of the Writings in Middle English, 1050–1500.* Vol. 2. Ed. J. Burke Severs, 419–22. Hamden, Conn.: Archon, 1970.
Hotchkiss, Valerie R. " 'Female Men of God': Cross Dressing in Medieval Hagiography." In *Clothes Make the Man: Female Cross Dressing in Medieval Europe,* 13–31. New York: Garland, 1996.

Saint Eugenia

I have just told you about God's darling Theodora, whose story should move women to love God and to realize that there is no virtue except through God's grace. Her story shows how the devil may be overcome through a contrite heart and true penance and how the sinner may be raised up by paying for the ill he does his neighbor. Taking up the cross drives the devil away, for he cannot stand to be around meekness and virginity. Loyal patience is a good defense against him. We may take example from Eugenia as well, who, with virginity and meekness and sorely tempted patience, overcame the fiend, despite his cunning. She earned the light of heaven, which God gladly gives to those who suffer persecution and death for him here on earth.

Two young lords, Sir Protus and Sir Hyacinth, were sent off to study in Rome along with Eugenia, who also came from a noble family. The two young men were dedicated scholars. Eugenia's father was a powerful senator called Philip, who was given jurisdiction over Alexandria by the full Senate on account of his intelligence and virtue. So he went to the city that was given to him with his wife, Claudia, and his two wise and fair sons. Avitus was the eldest and heir, and Sergius his younger brother. Philip also brought his daughter Eugenia, who had been so well educated that she knew the arts and most of the seven sciences by heart.[1] Protus and Hyacinth, her companions in study, did not want to part from her. Not only was she so wise that she knew more about the sciences than any other woman, but she was also fairer than any other woman. Gracious, serious, and well spoken, she kept herself from all unlawful fleshly lusts.

When, at age fifteen, she was old enough to marry, many would gladly have had her. Among her most zealous suitors was a noble knight named Aquilinus, who sent a distinguished delegation to propose marriage. She answered gravely and wisely, "Good men, you should know that a husband shouldn't be chosen for his riches and relatives but rather for his good morals."

She was then still a pagan. She didn't yet know the true king who made all things but rather believed as her elders did, for our faith was unknown to them. Because she took great pleasure in reading and writing, she happened to read a book containing various epistles of Saint Paul, which taught about spiritual salvation. From that time onward, her heart was drawn to Christ's law, both spiritually and intellectually, for her learning inclined her to think that law best.

Outside Alexandria was a little town where Christians took refuge from persecution by those who then governed the city. One day, when Eugenia was on a pleasure trip there, she heard some Christians singing loudly and clearly, "People are praying to fiends, not gods; the true God is the one who made heaven and earth in seven days!" She asked Protus and Hyacinth, "What do you think?" Because they had studied with her and were discerning men, they were readily persuaded. Then she said to them, "I think we've wasted our time studying philosophy. What good are Aristotle's arguments, or Plato's examples, or Socrates' instructions? In short, all that poets, rhetoricians, or anyone can say is brought to nothing by this Christian teaching. Now I clearly see that there is only

---

[1] A reference to the seven liberal arts—grammar, logic, rhetoric, arithmetic, geometry, music, and astronomy—which formed the basis for a university education in the Middle Ages.

one God to believe in. Usurped power has made me your lady,[2] and wisdom has made me your sister; let's now be brothers and follow Christ alone and his truthful teachings!"

They were satisfied with her advice and happily agreed to do whatever she said. Because she wanted to look like their brother, she dressed in men's clothing and went with them to an abbey.

The abbot, Helenus, wouldn't go near a woman. He had a good reputation, for he wouldn't tolerate females visiting his abbey. To defend our faith through reason, he once got into a dispute with a clever heretic whose arguments left him speechless. The theologian says that there is little merit in believing what man's logic or reason gives one cause to believe. Therefore the abbot, who had no further arguments to present, had a fire made and said, "Whoever goes into this fire and is unburned speaks the truth, and he who is burned lies." Then, taking the initiative, he hopped into the fire and stayed there unharmed in hide, hair, or clothing. When he stepped out of the fire hale and sound, he told the heretic it was his turn. The heretic wouldn't take the test and went away ashamed.

When Eugenia and her companions came to the abbot, Eugenia (who had changed her name to Eugene) asked him to kindly allow them to join his order. The abbot asked, "What are you?" She responded, "A man, just as you see." He said, "You may well call yourself a man, even though you are a woman, because your deeds are manly." He spoke so because God had revealed to him who she was. Then Eugene and the two young men put on monks' habits, and she dealt truthfully with everyone—except that they thought her name was Eugene. From the time they put on their habits, they were obedient to the rule of the monastery, and their behavior endeared them to the abbot. They were humble and pure in every respect. They wanted no possessions, though they were wellborn. Moreover, they were obedient to their superiors, renouncing their free will in order to give better thanks to God. They were more abstinent than their rule required. Thus they were the most perfect monks in the house.

At home, Eugenia's father lamented his daughter greatly, sorrowing for her night and day. He was first alarmed when her chariot came home and when he saw her once richly furnished chamber empty. No one can

[2]Eugenia seems to mean that her father's position as governor made her their social superior.

describe how he and his wife suffered. Eugenia's two brothers, Avitus and Sergius, searched hard for their missing sister. They had no idea where she could have gone with Protus and Hyacinth, who were steadfast men from the best families in Rome. Her father sent men to look for her in faraway lands, but when the searchers had looked an entire year without finding her, they returned and admitted defeat. We need not describe the sorrow of her father, mother, and brothers. Her father had diviners brought who knew about everything. He entreated them to apply their skills to his daughter's case and bring him some good news. They quickly returned and told him that the gods had taken her up into the stars. So her father had a statue made of her and had everyone honor it daily, as they would a god.

Eugenia and her two companions persevered with such devotion that when the abbot died, Eugenia was chosen to take his place. She governed the house so well that both God and man rejoiced.

At the time, a matron named Melancia lived in Alexandria. She was lovely, noble, and exceedingly rich. This Melancia came down with a fever that sapped her strength and kept her in constant agony. When she heard that a man of excellent repute named Eugene lived at a certain abbey, she thought he might cure her of her illness if he would come to her. Though she was a pagan, she implored him nevertheless to rid her of her infirmity, fearing that she might die in sin. Eugenia appeared in her monk's habit, bringing oil, which she blessed and gave to Melancia, telling her to anoint herself with it without delay. She did as she was told and soon was completely cured of the awful fever, which is known as quartan.[3] She sent great presents of gold, silver, wine, and wheat to the abbot, but he refused them all, telling the matron to keep her possessions and to give thanks to God, who had cured her.

This matron sometimes went to the abbey, where she visited the abbot and gave thanks for her health. Being a woman, and believing Eugene to be a man, she fell in love with him and, lacking self-control, was eager to satisfy her lustful cravings. She burned as if she were on fire and looked for an opportunity to fulfill her desires. Accordingly, she pretended to be terribly sick and sent word to the humble abbot, asking him, for God's sake, to visit her, because she was too ill to go to him. Eugene, in his perfect charity, agreed and went in all good faith to help. He was re-

[3]So-called because bouts of fever recur every four days.

ceived with respect and brought to the matron, within the rich curtains that surrounded the bed. Dismissing her attendants, she took the monk in her arms, intending to fulfill her wretched yearning. She let him know how much she loved him and begged him to lie with her in her bed—otherwise she would not recover from her illness. When he understood what she wanted, the abbot got to his feet and moved away from her, greatly distressed at her proposition, saying, "You hussy, you're well named Melancia, meaning 'full of darkest evil.' "

When she saw that she was being rejected, she feared exposure and decided to transfer her wickedness to him by accusing him before he had the chance to accuse her. So she scratched her face, mussed her hair, and bloodied her mouth and nose, then cried out until her attendants rushed in and asked who had dared treat her so. She said, "See how this monk has assaulted me! Believing him loyal, I called him to cure me, as I have done before, but he's a wolf in a sheep's skin—full of hypocrisy! He wanted to sin with me, and he would have overcome me, had I not defended myself vigorously and cried out for help." Then she called her chambermaid and told her to say that she was on hand when the monk assaulted her. Thus she got a false witness against the innocent monk. She wanted him ruined for refusing to give in to her.

Scripture says—so we can believe it's true—that no snake has a head so ugly and venomous and cruel as does the adder. Nor can anyone be more wicked than a woman taking vengeance. Think of Joseph in Genesis: because he wouldn't lie with Potiphar's wife, she falsely accused him and had him imprisoned for a long time. But the lord God pitied him enough to make him lord of Egypt. Consider another example of how women punish those who won't do their will: the wife of Otto, the predecessor of the good emperor Henry, who was first duke of Bavaria. The emperor Otto had a handsome earl whose good looks and valor so enchanted the empress that she asked him to sin with her. Being loyal to his lord, the earl would not agree; and when push came to shove he flatly refused. Thus rejected, she had the earl seized and beheaded without trial, on her own evidence, without giving him any chance to defend himself. She had him beheaded, although he was innocent, as it was known later. Indeed, when he was about to be killed, he told his grieving wife that she should prove his innocence before the law. After he was executed, his wife took his head and kept it until the day the emperor set aside, for God's sake, to right all wrongs concerning either land or goods, especially wrongs done to widows and orphans. Then the widow took the head and showed it to the emperor, asking what should be done to someone who slew an innocent man. Then, as judge, he decreed that whoever did such a thing should die. She said, "It's you, Caesar, who caused my husband's death, and I will prove his innocence by the hot-iron ordeal." Then a sheet of hot iron—more than fifteen feet long—was brought, and the widow walked across it without being harmed. When he saw that, the emperor was displeased, but he turned himself over to the widow to be punished at her will. Everyone around thought he was doomed and offered great lands in exchange for his life—those lands still exist and are known by names that recall this incident. The emperor quickly learned what had actually happened: that his own wife had caused him to be condemned to death! He immediately had her seized and burned—on account of justice, not anger. This took place 984 years after Christ's incarnation. Theodora suffered for the same reason, as people may see in the previous story. But I'll stop giving examples, lest women call me their enemy.

One thing I *will* say, though: if a woman plans to do something—no matter how wicked—she'll burn like fire until she accomplishes her desire. She'll care neither for God's blame, nor for sound advice, nor for dangers to herself or to those she loves. Life, death, health—of soul or body—won't matter until she gets what she's after. Especially when she's after a man: if he doesn't consent once she's told him what she wants, there was never a lynx more eager to catch and kill the people who took her cubs than she will be to punish him who has denied her will.

So it was with Melancia when the abbot rejected her advances. Not daring to do anything directly, she went to court and brought charges against the unsuspecting abbot. She claimed that he had assaulted her in her bed. He had beaten her black and blue—and scratched her, too—and grabbed her so tightly by the neck that he would have had his way with her, had help not arrived, just in time. She had yelled and cried so loudly that the servants came and forced him to flee, leaving her there all battered. If her servants hadn't come running and seen everything, he would surely have accomplished his will before any help arrived. Therefore, she concluded, people shouldn't believe the wicked man who now preaches the law of Jesus Christ, their lord; his words and deeds are at odds, if, as people say, he really does preach righteousness all the time.

When Philip, who was prefect of Alexandria, heard this case, he was furious. He commanded an armed guard to arrest Eugenia and her companions, bind them tight, and bring them into his presence immediately. He was hot as fire, though he was Eugenia's father. He thought that Eugenia was a monk and his daughter long gone. The armed guards went to the abbey without delay. They took and bound the abbot and all the monks they could find. They hustled them to Alexandria and, following the prefect's orders, threw them in prison to await judgment, expecting them to be condemned.

When they had arrived, Philip set up his seat of judgment in the marketplace, ready to enforce the law. He had the monks brought before him, intending to throw the abbot to the wild beasts, so that they could tear and devour him to their hearts' content. Melancia, who was not reluctant to denounce the abbot, appeared and said, "Sir judge, punish this false monk who got into my bedroom under false pretenses and intended to have his way with me!" Sobbing, she rehearsed her charge as you heard before.

The judge said angrily to the abbot, "Say, scoundrel and hypocrite, you who've used your religious clothes to beguile honest people more easily: What would you do if you had power? Tell me, wicked, worthless wretch: Did your God Christ teach you to stoop to foul corruption? Is that his teaching? If you wanted lechery, you should have sent for a whore rather than imposing your foul desires on a gentlewoman. In my opinion, only a madman would believe in your Christ's teachings! You're obviously guilty; why, you can't even answer this charge!"

Eugenia was a little worried that her father would recognize her. Therefore, she bowed her head low as she demurely replied, "Christ, our lord, who should ever be praised, taught his followers to love chastity. He told his servants that if they lived chastely for his sake, they would depart from this life to his everlasting bliss. What he's promised us is too wonderful for the heart to imagine or the tongue to describe. Though we can prove this woman a liar and a felon, it is better to accept this little blame than to have her die with lasting shame—for, if we demonstrate the truth, she knows perfectly well that she can be punished. But we'll be patient in your presence. Nevertheless, if she has witnesses to her falsehoods, let her bring them forth so we can hear their perjury. If she had any shame, she and her witness would have stayed home!"

The wicked woman Melancia had her maid there, ready to give false testimony. She repeated the story flawlessly—word for word—expecting to be suitably thanked. Her fellow servants, one and all, swore falsely, just as they were taught. They said they had found Melancia in bed, battered and bleeding.

Eugenia waited until she saw that the judge was about to pass a cruel sentence on her. Then she made her defense, saying, "As the wise Ecclesiastes says truthfully in the third chapter of his book, there is a time to remain silent and a time to speak forcefully. It's not time to be silent, since I'm compelled to speak, even if I'd rather not. I don't want this woman to malign Christ's servants. I must speak now—not out of pride, but to expose a lie! Falsehood mustn't rejoice in a victory over truth. So that wisdom may overcome malice, I will tell the truth—however reluctantly—to erase all doubt that I am Christ's servant. I have always kept my flesh pure, just as he taught. That's why I took this habit—not out of hypocrisy! With that, she immediately cast off her hood and robe and tore her kirtle to her knees so that everyone could see she was a woman. Having done that, she shielded her body and said to the prefect, who had seen the truth with his own eyes, "Dear father, and Claudia, next to you, who bore me in her own body, look closely at your daughter Eugenia. Avitus and Sergius—don't you recognize your sister? And these two—Protus and Hyacinth—who were my school companions? I'll be amazed if you don't recognize us!"

The judge then looked carefully at the one who had torn her kirtle. He examined her face and knew she was his daughter. Overjoyed, he took her in his arms and kissed her many times and cried. She cried, too, for they still lived in error—just as before. Her mother and two brothers, recognizing Eugenia, embraced her and kissed her a hundred times. They cried with joy, just as her father had, and because no one before had dared teach them Christian truth. They clothed her in garments adorned with fine gold, for she was of a noble line, and fair ermine, just as if she'd been the daughter of a queen. Her father had her companions in learning, Protus and Hyacinth, sit beside him, and he honored them as if they were great men. Then in the presence of everyone, great and small, a blast of fire and brimstone blew down from heaven and burned to powder Melancia, her lying maid, and her entire household. God's vengeance caused it. Seeing such wonders with his own eyes, her father, along with his wife and sons, converted to Christianity. So did everyone in the country who saw or heard what had happened. The new converts built many churches. The unbelievers came and dared accept Christ's faith. Many priests were ordained to baptize them all.

When news traveled from Alexandria to Rome that Philip had become a Christian and had taken the entire country with him, he was declared unfit to hold office. The Senate deprived him of his rank, since he had changed his religion. Then they wrote, informing him of their decision and appointing someone else to his office. He was glad to hear the news, for Christ's sake. For high office and lordship often cause men to do wrong, and rank and humility are rarely found in one person. Therefore, Philip praised God highly for taking him from such a height. Then all the converted made him bishop of the country in God's name.

Philip became a different man: he committed himself to abstinence, and he suffered wrongs patiently; he diligently dedicated himself to chastity and charity, to prayer, vigil, and preaching. He gladly practiced what he preached, so that people should have an example of how to live. He persevered in these habits for the rest of his life and won many people to God through his deeds and teachings. The unbelievers resented him for his virtuous life and for having left their religion to become a Christian. They ambushed him as he was kneeling at prayer and made a martyr of him; he was grateful to serve as a sacrifice to God.

When he was dead, Claudia went to Rome and openly preached the Christian faith. She preached God's word eloquently and expeditiously to those who were not Christian; moreover, she practiced what she preached. Through God's grace, she converted many to Christianity and made a fine end—as you will find written below.

Good Eugenia's reputation spread so far and wide that the emperor heard how diligently she was luring people away from their ancient faith: "She leads people astray, and she forces them to preach a new law and to teach of a certain Jesus of Galilee, whom the Jews hanged on a tree. She says he—and no other—is God. If she's permitted to continue, she'll do our gods such outrageous wrongs that no one will honor or worship them anymore, nor will a temple to them remain standing in the land. Therefore, lord, we advise you to take action according to the lawful judgment of the Roman Senate." The emperor became enraged. He called his council to him and asked what should be done. They answered that killing her would be most effective, "for if she lives, she'll lead many into error, causing them to renounce their gods. It's better that she alone die than that many people be punished." The emperor agreed to do as they advised.

Torturers sought out Eugenia and bound her hand and foot. Then they attached a great millstone to her neck and threw her into the Tiber for her crimes against the gods. But there people could see God's might for themselves, for when she was thrown into the river before the crowd, her bonds were immediately undone, and the millstone fell away. She was able to stand up on the water—just as if it were dry land—and she walked back and forth there for a little while. Then she was seized again and bound hand and foot and cast into a burning oven. But as soon as she was in there, the fierce heat was quenched, and all saw that she was no more harmed than if she'd been in a warm bath. Indeed, it refreshed her, even though it looked as if it were burning hot. Thus God showed his might by keeping her safe and sound when everyone thought she'd surely die.

They took and bound her again, planning to inflict some new pain on her. They cast her into a deep dungeon. To confuse her, they closed it so tightly and skillfully that not a bit of light could penetrate. They left her without food or drink, good or bad, or anything that could be eaten. But God sent a light brighter than the sun's beam, and when she'd been in prison for ten days, according to the book, God appeared to her, accompanied by a multitude of angels. He gave her fair, fresh bread, whiter than snow, and said, "Take this food from my hand, good daughter, for I am God, your savior, whom you served as best you could and loved more than all the things young people value most. I've come to tell you that you'll come to me on the day I came to earth from heaven."

On Christmas Day itself, they sent to see if she was still alive. They found her not only living, but also as fair as if she'd been fed with the best food man could make. The heathen executioner then hauled her out and struck her head off, thus making a martyr of her. God took her to his everlasting bliss. The very hour she was slain, she appeared to her mother and told her that she would join her next Sunday in everlasting and indescribable joy. The next Sunday, as Claudia lay in prayer, she yielded her spirit, and God received it in heaven.

Protus and Hyacinth, who'd stood by Eugenia through thick and thin, were taken to the temple after her death. Through their prayers, they made it crumble and pulverized all the idols there! When those who brought them saw what had happened, they said, "If you'll sacrifice to our gods and renounce your wicked sorcery, your lives will be spared and you'll receive great riches on account of your noble blood. All you have to do is turn from your error." They answered in unison, "We believe in the God who died on the cross; for his sake we'll endure whatever you want to do to us. We will never sacrifice to idols, which are no more than demons!" Then the wicked men took them and struck off their heads. Thus they were martyred, by the reckoning of Rome, two hundred and fifty-six years after God took flesh from our lady.

I ask these saints to pray for us, so that we may end our lives without shame, debt, or deadly sin.

Saint Winifred

John Mirk

To the best of my knowledge, Winifred is the only virgin martyr to have survived a beheading, though several "cephalophoric" (head-carrying) martyrs—Saint Dennis of Paris, for example— were said to have picked up their heads and carried them to suitable burial places. Her resurrection may represent a hagiographical variant of the Celtic beheading motif found in *Sir Gawain and the Green Knight* and in the Old Irish saga *Bricriu's Feast*. Indeed, Winifred's cult originated in early medieval Wales, where she is said to have died circa 650. In 1137 her bones were brought to Shrewsbury Abbey, and shortly thereafter the first account of her life was written.

Dating from the late fourteenth century, the text translated here is part of a cycle of prose sermons by John Mirk, a prolific author of pastoral literature. Perhaps anticipating a Shrewsbury audience, Mirk includes material of local interest: a relatively lengthy account of how Winifred's body came to reside in Shrewsbury and miracle stories that prove her relics' efficacy. Though addressing a broad audience of parishioners, Mirk is far more restrained in tone than the authors of other popular works, such as the *South English Legendary* and the *North English Legendary*. Indeed, with his sober language and less aggressive heroine, he anticipates features that would dominate the writing of saints' legends some decades later.

Edition: *Mirk's Festial.* Ed. Theodor Erbe, 177–82. EETS.ES 96. 1905. Reprint, Millwood, N.Y.: Kraus, 1987.

Saint Winifred

Christian men and women, today is Saint Winifred's day. This day is now designated a holy day, and many people are devoted to this holy maiden. Since you who love this holy saint come to church today to honor God and his holy maiden and martyr, you will now hear how she suffered martyrdom. Though some people know the story, many do not. Besides, a good tale told twice is all the easier to learn and to understand.

There once lived a holy hermit called Beuno, who approached a good and wealthy landowner called Thewit, Winifred's father, asking him for some land on which to build a church, where he might serve God and preach God's word to the people. Happy to oblige, Thewit granted Beuno some land next to his own house, planning to attend services there with other members of his household. While the church was under construction, Beuno often preached God's word to the people, among them Winifred and her father. When Winifred heard Beuno speak of the great reward that virgins would have in heaven—surpassing that of widows and wives—she was so moved by his words that she vowed to shun men's bodies and remain a virgin as long as she lived.

One Sunday after the church had been built, Thewit and his household attended services, while Winifred stayed home sick. As she sat at home alone, a king's son named Caradoc came, intending to lie with the maiden. When he proposed committing that sin, she said she would go to her room to make herself more presentable and then return to him. Once inside her room, she escaped through a back door and ran toward the church as fast as she could, hoping to find help there. But when Caradoc saw her running toward the church, he overtook her and said that if she wouldn't do his will, he'd cut off her head. At that, Winifred knelt down and said, "I'd rather have you kill me than spoil the body I promised to keep pure in chastity for my lord Jesus Christ as long as I live." Then Caradoc drew out his sword and with a single stroke struck off her head, which never stopped tumbling until it reached the church just down the hill. Upon seeing the head, people cried out in terror, making such a racket that Beuno wondered what had happened and went to see what was the matter. When he saw the head, he picked it up, kissed it many times, weeping profusely, and carried it back to the body in time to see Caradoc wiping his bloody sword on the grass. Beuno said,

"You wicked man, ask God's pardon for this horrible deed and he may yet have mercy on you; if you won't, may God take vengeance on you right now, in front of all these people." When Caradoc merely laughed, he dropped dead on the ground, and instantly the earth opened and swallowed him, plunging body and soul into hell.

Beuno then took Winifred's head, set it against her body, covered it with her mantle, and went to say Mass. After singing and preaching at length about this maiden to the congregation, he said that God did not wish her dead yet, for he had intended her to help many people. Therefore, he asked every man and woman to entreat God to bring her back to life. And he did, too. Then she sat up, wiped the dirt from her face, and spoke to them—as healthy and whole as she'd ever been.

God performed three fair miracles there. One was that the earth swallowed her killer's body. Another was that a lovely fountain sprang from the place where her head rested, where there had been none before. The third was that she rose to life after she was killed. Then there was a fourth: a white circle, like a white thread, marked where her neck had been cut. Because of this miracle, her name was changed from Brewafour to Winifred, which means in English a white thread. Winifred took the great miracle that God performed for her very much to heart. She devoted herself to holy living and, day and night, strove to serve God as Beuno taught her. After she had grown perfect in every respect, Beuno moved away. Many years later, a revelation from God instructed Winifred to leave her home, and she joined a large community of virgins. She lived so perfectly there that everyone took her as a model. And because of the white circle that remained a visible token of her martyrdom, all men and women paid attention to her words and deeds, and many left their worldly occupations and came to live with her. When she had lived there many years—fifteen winters—God warned her that her death was drawing near. Therefore, she prepared herself, and when she had taken the sacrament of Holy Church in the sight of all her sisters, she committed her soul to Jesus Christ, whom she loved with all her heart, and she was buried in the churchyard where many saints had been buried before her.

Now you shall hear how this holy saint came to the Abbey of Shrewsbury. When the abbey was newly built, the monks that lived there were most distressed because, unlike other abbeys in the country, they had no patron saint to convey their prayers to God. Having already heard of

Saint Winifred, the abbot of that house sent his prior to Wales to find where she was buried. The prior set forth, and by the grace of God and the revelation of this maiden, he came to the place where she lay. By virtue of his rank and with other help, he brought her bones to the Church of Saint Giles on the outskirts of Shrewsbury; and there she stayed until the day when she was to be brought with great honor and reverence to Shrewsbury Abbey. When that day arrived, a great crowd came, partly because of a great miracle that had taken place in the church—a child was cured of a serious illness—and partly to honor the holy maiden. Thus, accompanied by the abbot of Shrewsbury and the monks and many other clergy, they brought her to the abbey and placed her where she lies today. God promptly performed thirty great miracles in her honor, which have been recorded with many others, both those she performed during her lifetime and the many others she performed at her spring.

Now, to increase your devotion for this saint, I will tell you about a miracle that was performed for a man called Adam from Arkleton. This man had a serious case of epilepsy. Both his hands lay flat against his arms so that his arms were like stumps, and his leg was so bad that he could not walk without pain. Now this Adam, with his three afflictions, dragged himself to church and prayed all night before Winifred's shrine. In the morning he was so exhausted from his vigil that he fell asleep. When he woke up, his limbs felt fine. He saw that his arms were straight and he moved his fingers freely. He tried getting up and found that he could walk without pain. He felt completely cured of his epilepsy. At that, he thanked God and the holy virgin in a loud voice. And he was so grateful for his health that he vowed never to leave Winifred but to remain a servant in that church as long as he lived. And so he did.

Thus, good men and women, you can see how important it is to honor this holy virgin and martyr. Though your bodies may be healthy enough, many of your souls are surely ailing, and it's even more important to pray for healthy souls than healthy bodies. Indeed, God often makes the body sick to heal the soul, for sickness of the soul brings death unless it is promptly treated. Therefore, ask Saint Winifred to grant you health in body and soul so that you may come to the healer of all souls, Jesus Christ, God's heavenly son.

Saints Margaret and Petronilla

John Lydgate

Although Chaucer is said to have inaugurated a "literary" approach to the saint's legend, Lydgate thoroughly transformed the genre. A self-proclaimed admirer and disciple of Chaucer, Lydgate imitates in "Margaret" his predecessor's elaborate preamble, meant to delight an educated audience. He expects his readers to catch his allusions to the red of martyrdom and the white of virginity, as well as his play on Margaret the name, margarite the pearl, and marguerite the daisy. His conventional protestations of authorial unworthiness are cannily disingenuous; indeed, his self-deprecation is a form of self-aggrandizement, for it links him to the saint whose exceptional modesty he straightaway proceeds to laud.

Whereas Chaucer followed his rhetorically elaborate prologue with a straightforward account of Cecilia's martyrdom, Lydgate employs the same lavish rhetoric throughout. His syntax is convoluted, each sentence laden with redundancies and conceits. His verse, thick with adjectives, drips pathos, and the conventions of courtly love literature suffuse speeches, dialogues, and characterizations. Both of Lydgate's legends conclude in a stylized fashion: "Margaret" with an envoi, or formal dedication, and "Petronilla" with a prayer to the saint in ballade royale form.

Lydgate created not only a different kind of hagiography but a different kind of saint as well: a paragon both of social mores and of unremitting faith. In most of the preceding selections in this volume, the virgin martyrs humiliated their adversaries in raucous altercation. Invective is rare in Lydgate's legends. Instead of arguing with Olibrius, Margaret firmly but politely reaffirms her faith, while Petronilla uses diplomacy to avoid confrontation altogether. The saints' physical aggressiveness is also curtailed; contrast Juliana's tussle with the devil to Margaret's oddly dignified encounter. Both Margaret and Petronilla epitomize qualities that conservative middle- or upper-class readers of the day prized—modesty, courtesy, tact, eloquence, grace—and their conduct conforms to prevailing norms of femininity. Moreover, unlike the saints of earlier legends, they suffer, inviting the empathy of the reader. Paris's Christine may laughingly pelt her persecutors with bits of her flesh, but Petronilla suffers "unbearably" during her illness, and Margaret writhes in agony as the torturers beat her.

A Benedictine monk of the wealthy and prestigious abbey at Bury St. Edmunds, Suffolk, Lydgate was one of the most prolific and most admired authors of his day. As we will see when we come to "Agnes," Bokenham places him beside Chaucer and John Gower in a trinity of literary masters. Lydgate's region of England, East Anglia, was rife with writers, bibliophiles, patrons of the arts, and dilettantes. Prominent among the patrons were women. It was one of these, Ann Mortimer, Lady March, who, sometime between 1415 and 1426, asked Lydgate to write "Margaret."

Margaret was a special favorite of women, her miraculous deliverance from the belly of the dragon having earned her the patronage of expectant mothers. That one who died to preserve her virginity should become a patron saint of childbirth might seem odd—especially as "giving birth" to Margaret destroyed the metaphorical mother!—but the association of causes with unlikely saints was common. Margaret is frequently represented emerging triumphantly from the dragon. With Saint Katherine, she was one of the two most widely venerated virgin martyrs. Petronilla's cult, by contrast, was largely an East Anglian phenomenon (see Coss, *Lady in Medieval England*, 64). Several churches and chapels there were dedicated to her, as was the lepers' hospital maintained by the abbey of Bury St. Edmunds, for which Lydgate apparently composed his narrative. The abbey itself boasted Petronilla's skull among its relics. Petronilla is the only virgin martyr I know whose persecutor, Flaccus, plays no direct role in her death. The story of Petronilla's companion Fellicula, whom Flaccus woos and kills in the approved fashion, seems almost an appended counterweight to Petronilla's striking departure from the norm.

Fig. 4. Scenes from the life of Saint Margaret. (Courtesy of the Bodleian Library, Oxford. MS Douce 112, fol. 167r.)

Edition: *The Minor Poems of John Lydgate.* 2 vols. Ed. Henry Noble MacCracken, 1:173–92 (Margaret); 154–59 (Petronilla). EETS.ES 107, EETS.OS 192. London: Oxford University Press, 1911, 1934.

Coss, P. R. *The Lady in Medieval England, 1000–1500.* Mechanicsburg, Penn.: Stackpole Books, 1998.
Ebin, Lois A. *John Lydgate.* Boston: Twayne, 1985.
Gibson, Gail McMurray. *The Theater of Devotion: East Anglian Drama and Society in the Late Middle Ages.* Chicago: University of Chicago Press, 1989.
Lerer, Seth. *Chaucer and His Readers: Imagining the Author in Late-Medieval England.* Princeton: Princeton University Press, 1993.
Lewis, Katherine J. "The Life of St. Margaret of Antioch in Late Medieval England: A Gendered Reading." *Studies in Church History* (1998): 129–41.
McCash, June Hall, ed. *The Cultural Patronage of Medieval Women.* Athens: University of Georgia Press, 1996.
Moore, Samuel. "Patrons of Letters in Norfolk and Suffolk, ca. 1450." Parts 1 and 2. *PMLA* 27 (1912) and 28 (1913): 79–105.
Pearsall, Derek. *John Lydgate.* London: Routledge, 1970.
Schirmer, Walter F. *John Lydgate: A Study in the Culture of the Fifteenth Century.* Trans. Ann E. Keep. Westport, Conn.: Greenwood, 1961.
Winstead, Karen A. *Virgin Martyrs: Legends of Sainthood in Late Medieval England,* 112–46. Ithaca: Cornell University Press, 1997.

Saint Margaret

My purpose is to compile a life in honor of Saint Margaret, even though I am no rhetorician, nor can I embellish my style with colorful flourishes. (Yet, I dare say, plain writing sometimes conceals important information. It often happens that gold and pearls and precious gems are locked in plain black coffers, and well-respected philosophers aver that a flawless royal ruby can be enclosed in a very shabby sack.) And even though I lack the eloquence to describe her perfect holiness, her chaste life, her tender innocence, and her cruel martyrdom. Her heart was so constant that she remained faithful unto death. She so delighted in Christ's faith that she despised all earthly glory, this daisy with red and white petals, colored purple when her triumphant blood was shed, this chaste lily decked with red roses through martyrdom.

As scholars are fond of pointing out in their books, she's called Margaret after the margarite, that most precious of gems. Pearls are by nature white, strong, round, and small; Margaret had all those attributes. First, she was white in her virginity, her virtue tested and proven. She was also small in her humility, and strong in God's love, this glorious maiden. For her triumph over death, she received the martyr's palm in heaven, and she was crowned with laurels above the seven stars.[1]

This stone has the properties of a cordial, offering much relief to the spirit. Just so, Margaret's heart was ever imperial—in virtue, that is—for during her earthly strife she vanquished the devil and the world, and she sacrificed her flesh for the lord, who died on the cross for our redemption. To repay him, this virgin shed her blood freely in her passion.

Oh gem of gems, most illustrious virgin, help me write your life. Graciously pour aureate liquid into my quaking pen. I tremble for dread: I have no muse of rhetoric. In fact, I would decline to write this martyrdom were it not for one thing: that you are too gracious to refuse to guide me and my pen, oh blessed lodestar, when I err. Let your light, shining in the darkness, illuminate my undertaking. And remember, oh virgin, the one who, for your sake, had me compile and write your holy life—Lady March, I mean, who first commanded me to make a compilation from the French and Latin versions of your holy passion. Trusting that my readers will support my effort and correct my errors, I will proceed to the story.

Here the prologue of Saint Margaret ends, and the story of her life begins

This blessed maiden and glorious martyr was born in the illustrious city of Antioch.[2] As you find in her legend, her father was Theodosius, a pagan patriarch, who followed the religious practices of the day.

Gracious in both figure and face, this maiden was sent to a nurse. At an early age, she had forsaken paganism and was baptized, thus incurring her father's wrath. He loathed her as soon as he knew of her christening.

By age fifteen, her beauty made her a sovereign among maidens. Glowing with kindness, blossoming with virtue, humble in her bearing, this gracious creature tended her nurse's sheep in the pasture. Devoid of pride, rancor, and anger, she was called a paragon of meekness. The holy spirit so inspired her heart that her thoughts and intentions were fixed on perfection. Thinking of Christ was her only joy. She was kind to

---

[1] I.e., in heaven. "The seven stars" (or septentrion) refers to either of the northern constellations Ursa Major (the Great Bear/Big Dipper) or Ursa Minor.

[2] An ancient city of the eastern Mediterranean, now in Turkey.

everyone, and though she rarely spoke, her speech was gentle. Her virtue inspired everyone to love her, for God's grace was always with her, and she always shunned vice.

Then one day the prefect Olibrius happened to see Margaret tending her sheep as he was out riding. He was immediately ravished by her beauty, her great fairness, and her fresh face. Her heavenly eyes pierced his heart, searing it with an unbearable pain. Hungry for love, this cruel wolf set out to devour this holy innocent. He spoke at first to himself: "Who is this beauty and where does she live? Whoever saw such a lovely maiden—she's far lovelier than any other. Indeed, she is the very font of womanhood, for her two eyes have completely pierced my heart." Then he addressed his servants, telling them to go to the innocent maid, find out who she was, and report back to him about her lineage. He wanted to know whether she came of gentle blood, "for if she's of noble birth, I want her as my wife, to love and cherish all my life for her great beauty, as is only fitting. If she's from a lowly line, I'll take her for my concubine."

When she was brought before him, he asked about her faith, her family, her occupation, and her name, admonishing her to answer truthfully on all counts. Not being reckless or hasty, but rather demure and serious, she studied him carefully and commended herself to God. Her face not changing its color or expression, her heart ever constant, she gave him this answer: "Regarding my lineage, I come from most noble blood. My name is Margaret. As for my faith, I am a devout Christian. In life and death, I will remain constant to that religion."

Taken aback, the judge replied, "Margaret, it is most appropriate for you to have noble lineage and great beauty. These qualities make you worthy to be called a margarite, fair in shape and complexion, a choice gem among white pearls. These qualities delight me. But you had better take my advice and change your faith. It would be such a shame, given your beauty and youth and virginity, for you to believe in him who died on a cross. It's madness! Therefore, do as I say and forsake his faith. Deny that God who was hanged on a tree and crucified."

"It is certain," she said, "no matter what you say, that he willingly suffered and humbly died for humanity, shedding his blood for our redemption, to free us and ransom us so that we should not miss his joy in heaven, where he reigns eternally in bliss."

Furious, the judge locked her in prison until the next day, when he summoned her promptly so that she could tell him what she had decided on the matter of her faith. He said, "Margaret, consider your youth and your great beauty. Don't waste your thoughts on madness, but turn your heart and mind to our gods. Do your duty by honoring them, if you know what's good for you!"

She replied, "With heart and will and mind, I worship him who made man and then redeemed him, whom heaven and earth and sea dread. He governs all the elements, for nothing—wind, weather, creature—can endure without his mercy."

The judge said, "If you don't agree to my demands, you'll be sorry! Believe me, I'll torture your body and carve your flesh into little bits!"

Margaret replied, "As long as I live, I will persist in my convictions. Since Christ suffered pain and death for me, shed his blood for my redemption, rest assured I'm not afraid to die and shed my blood for him. Indeed, I'll do so gladly."

The judge then suspended the virgin from a gallows. In his rage, he tore her flesh, and her blood flowed straight down. In her agony, this tender maiden, her veins torn, poured out her blood until all the liquid in her body was gone.

Alas! Bystanders wept greatly out of compassion. Alas! For sorrow, they could scarcely stand to see her blood gush out and flow down. The suffering she endured for Christ was so intolerable that people cried out in pity, "Alas, Margaret! You were once the fairest of women and now—alas!—your body is stained red with blood. We're so sorry for you! Alas, alas, how can such a young, fresh maiden stand such hideous torment? Why have you given up your beauty and your fair figure? Your anguish is caused by your stubborn beliefs! Chase these fantasies from your heart and end this agony!"

She said, "Go away, you false counselors, you worldly people, frivolous, fickle, fleshly, and always looking for something new! If only you knew that the mortal torments to my flesh are the salve and salvation of my soul." Then she said to the judge, "Greedy hound and insatiable lion! You can certainly make a wreck of my body, but my soul will remain stable in Christ's faith. The lord Jesus Christ, whom I serve, will preserve my spirit from all harm."

The bewildered judge could not bear to see the red blood flow down her face like a river running through a field. When he saw her sides bleed, he covered his face with his cloak. Amid her cruel and terrible pain, he ordered her taken down and returned to prison.

Back in prison, she asked God if she might see her mortal enemy, odious and terrible, the cause of her adversity, the one who brought about humanity's ruin. Suddenly, as she lay bound in prison, the old serpent Satan appeared in the form of an evil dragon and quickly began to attack her. Mouth open to devour her, he first swallowed her head. To save herself, the terrified maiden crossed herself. Before she knew what had happened, he'd burst apart, ending her suffering. Then he began to attack her again—this time, the story says, disguised as a man. Devoutly, she raised her clear eyes to God and prayed. As she prayed, the dragon lying beneath her feet, the devil, vanquished, took her by the hand and said these words: "Binding me with invisible bonds ought to satisfy you! Withdraw your power and let me rise; I can't stand being constrained by you—you've so debilitated me in this battle!"

She fearlessly arose, this innocent maiden, this tender creature, and by God's grace she seized him by the head and threw him to her feet, despite all his evil armor; he couldn't get up again. To injure the serpent even further, she set her right foot on his back. "Oh fiend of serpentine malice," she said, "remember how I, a pure maiden, vanquished you, to my greater glory, through feminine power. Never forget how I trampled Satan, root and fruit of sin."

With that, the serpent cried loudly, "I'm vanquished; I can't deny it. I have no power against you. Your innocence has brought me down. A young maiden has crushed me with her slender limbs! I could accept being vanquished by a man, who at least has power and strength. But now, alas, against everything that's right and proper, an innocent virgin, a pure maiden, has overthrown me in my malice. And this, alas, is the greatest cause of my unending, deadly sorrow—this increases my pain greatly—that both your father and mother were my friends. You alone, through your virginity, your chaste life, and your perfect holiness, have vanquished me and crushed me!"

Then she demanded that the serpent reveal, without concealing anything, the methods and means—the malice, envy, and pride—he used to assail people: "Tell mankind everything, at once, and be sure you don't lie!"

"Truly," he said, "I have no choice but to tell the truth. My nature is to lie. I am devoid of truth and virtue, always ready to work against the welfare of good people, always envious of those who are perfect and virtuous. I am their enemy, of course, though they often repel me with virtue.

When they gain the upper hand, I am so bereft of charity that I can only regret my loss of grace, that mankind should occupy my place in heaven. I know very well that I can never recover my place but will remain forever in hell, enduring pain and sorrow. I was cast out of heaven because of pride; that foul vice became my guide. Still, my malice makes me resent those who took my place. This, too, is the truth: once Solomon, as ancient books record, trapped many deceptive demons in a vessel. But after that wise king's death, they emitted sparks from the vessel. Believing that there was a great treasure within, men intentionally broke the vessel, and the fiends escaped, polluting the air wherever they went. They harm people much with their malice and temptation. Young and old are deceived by their illusions. But all their collusion and all their violence cannot prevail over resolute resistance."

When the old malicious serpent spoke thus to the maiden, who pinned him with her foot, she declined to harm him further. The dragon arose and disappeared. Confronted by her spiritual enemy, Margaret vanquished the prince of darkness. And since she had overcome the prince, she must necessarily triumph over his cruel minister. Therefore, she had no further need to worry.

The next day, this flower of goodness, with no refuge but the lord, was brought before the judge. There were many spectators. Because she would not sacrifice to the false gods, she was violently and cruelly stripped, and left standing naked, for people to despise. After that, this jewel of maidenhood was burned with red-hot brands. Her sides, once white as milk, were scorched. The cruel torturers had no pity. For Christ's sake, her body, soft as silk, stood naked and bare. To increase her agony, she was bound and cast into boiling water. The bystanders wept and lamented for pity, marveling, in their compassion, that a tender creature could withstand and endure such torment. To vary her suffering, the tyrant tortured her alternately with fire and water.

Suddenly there was an earthquake. Fearing vengeance, five thousand people whom God wished to save were converted from their error. See how a maiden can magnify Christ's faith in her torment! The blind judge, bereft of all mercy and afraid of still more conversions, immediately commanded this noble maiden, blossoming in youth and virginity, to be beheaded right there as she knelt in prayer. She meekly begged the judge to let her live just a little longer to pray. Devoutly, with a whole and full heart, just as she was about to die, this maiden prayed. First, in perfect charity, she prayed for her enemies and tormentors, for those who caused her such distress and pursued her with such cruel attacks. Gathering the flowers of perfect love, she asked God to help all those who called on him in her name. And for all those who remember her and trust her to help them in their need, she asked that God, sitting in glory, be gracious enough to let them prosper and not be misled. "And lord," she said, "help all those who honor me for your sake, especially women laboring in childbirth. For my sake, oh lord, be their doctor. Let my prayers help them. Let nothing harm those women, lord, who call on me in their agony, but for my sake save them from harm. Let them not perish in childbirth, lord. Be their comfort and consolation. Deliver them through the grace of your aid. Help them, lord, in their tribulation. And be especially gracious to all people who ask my help anywhere."

From the heavenly mansion on high, a voice resounded, saying that God heard and granted her petition. Then this most excellent maiden arose devoutly and fearlessly and said to the man holding the sword, "Draw near, my own dear brother. Strike with your sword, and don't hold back. My body shall remain here, but my soul shall be conducted to heaven." She bowed her head humbly. The executioner, with all his might, lifted his sword and severed her neck. The people who had witnessed her bitter passion began to cry and lament for pity. She thus achieved the crown of martyrdom willingly for Christ's sake. The book says this maiden, a mirror of steadfastness, earned her laurels through perfect suffering on July thirteenth.

A holy saint writes of this maiden: "This Margaret was perfect in her credence, God-fearing, and most stable in her faith. Her entire heart was set on God up to the moment of her death. Her heart ever contrite, she was so virtuous she eschewed all wrong. Her blessed life and habits epitomized perfect patience, resolute purity and faith, and prudent chastity. God granted her the supreme reward of being the paragon of virginity to everyone in her time. She forsook her father, mother, and kin—her holy living repelled them—and committed herself entirely to Christ's law. This blessed maiden, this glorious virgin, triumphed over all her enemies, until at last, in complete virtue, she shed her chaste blood for Christ's sake."

So ends the life of Saint Margaret.

Envoi

Noble princesses, ladies, and lesser gentlewomen, lift up your hearts. Call upon your advocate Saint Margaret, jewel of chastity. And all women in need, ask this maiden to protect you from sickness and disease and to ease your labor. And all people who languish in misfortune and adversity, all who need help, with devout heart, and with humility and complete trust, kneeling on your knees, beg this maiden to relieve and comfort you in all your travails.

Blessed virgin, exalted in heaven on high with all the other martyrs in the celestial see, stop the war, the awful conflict that comes from the three enemies[3] whose assault we cannot flee. Chaste gem, grant your servants peace, and be their shield in mischief and distress.

Petronilla

This is to commemorate the perfect life of a most gracious and upstanding virgin, a virgin crowned with every virtue: Petronilla, the apostle Peter's daughter. With her gentle demeanor and demure visage, she was the loveliest of maidens. Moreover, as her legend clearly tells, though her beauty was great, her meekness was greater still.

According to her story, Peter's teaching so firmly established her in Christ's doctrine and faith that she was called the clear mirror of perfection—a perfection proved, by God's providence, through sickness. Indeed, her life says that throughout her illness she had perfect patience.

Though a burning fever kept her quaking in unbearable agony, oscillating between hot and cold, that virtuous innocent never complained. Ever steadfast, she gave thanks to God. So perfect was her charity that she never wavered from her sacred vow of chastity. Indeed, she was so perfect that the lord ranked her among the five maidens who bore their lamps before Jesus, unquenched by the darkness of night.[4]

Notable miracles are recorded of this virgin. Once when Peter was having dinner with his most virtuous disciples, compassion moved one

---

[3] The flesh, the devil, and the world—a well-known formula (even today, as in the Litany from the Anglican Book of Common Prayer); cf. Chaucer's *Tale of Melibee:* "the three enemies of mankind—that is to say, the flesh, the devil, and the world" (l. 1421).

[4] An allusion to the five wise virgins of Matthew 25:1–13.

of them, Titus, to ask this reasonable question: "With all due respect, given your power and holiness, why do you cure every sick person except your own daughter, Petronilla, who quakes piteously in her fever? Not once have you been inclined to bid her rise, to assuage her suffering." Then, moved by a father's compassion, Peter told Petronilla to arise and wait upon their table. Cured of her infirmity, she was told to serve the guests. Bearing herself like a most gracious virgin, she humbly and diligently hastened to accomplish whatever he commanded. After the meek virgin had done his bidding without complaint, Peter told her to return to bed, burning with fever, just as before. For Christ's sake, she deemed it just. Humble and grounded in all virtue, she considered it a joy to suffer for Jesus Christ's love.

She gave her heart to Christ completely, without change or duplicity. She prayed steadfastly for the relief of the sick. As her life attests, her inner heart burned with charity. Though God and nature gave her great beauty, her humility was greater still. She remained a pure virgin all her life, both on account of her circumstances and out of propriety.

Earl Flaccus, desiring her for his wife, came to court her. He wanted her for her bearing and feminine nobility, her conduct and lovely face. Though he had great riches, he was anxious to acquire her in marriage. She did not answer him recklessly. Heart and mind ever constant, she took him aside, away from the crowd. Gently and demurely, and much to her benefit, she asked him to bring maidens, wives, and girls with him on the wedding day to escort her to his dwelling. Flaccus was delighted. The earl, that proud knight, arranged everything as she wished. Meanwhile, the virtuous virgin spent her time praying with Fellicula, the confidante of her illness, who had been summoned within the hour.

Thus ends Petronilla's story, for those who want a plain account of her life. Flaccus was foiled. Petronilla made her confession to a holy priest called Nichomedes, who was summoned to her sickbed. After receiving the Eucharist, she yielded up her spirit, a pure virgin, as certified by Holy Church.

Fellicula was determined to remain a virgin despite Flaccus. Disdaining his love and hate, she went seven days without food. That tyrant killed her, making her chaste blood flow red as roses. Then, out of spite, he slew Nichomedes in the Tiber.

And so they achieved martyrdom. Their passions were crowned with the reddest roses and Petronilla's chaste love with white lilies. According to her life, Saint Peter's daughter was a paragon of patience when she lay ill. Decked in purple, her soul ascended to the heavenly mansion on the last day of May. That's the time of year when all the birds sing, and the nightingales, in their harmony, salute Esperus with clear, amorous notes. Pricked by a sharp thorn, their hearts are too alert to be vulnerable to cuckoos or to owls.[5] By analogy, Petronilla's glad and carefree heart was always watching for the chance to serve Jesus. Like the nightingale with its bright, heavenly feathers, she was sluggish neither day nor night. Thanking God in suffering and illness, she vanquished three enemies[6] through God's might and died in virginal purity.

Ballade

Most virtuous virgin, Petronilla, blossoming with spiritual freshness, Peter's daughter, you lived in prayer and purity for the love of Jesus Christ. Your story attests that in your sickness, your heart was ever meek, eager to do your father's will. For your virtue, you are called the mirror of patience. God and nature made you so lovely that you excelled all others in bearing and beauty. Afflicted with fever, you gave thanks to God. Whoever wishes can see in your legend that your virtue was proven through your illness.

Therefore, we pray with humble respect that you help those who seek you and grant them virtuous patience in their illness. Ask, on behalf of those of us in trouble, that Jesus mercifully alleviate our sickness. And to prove your virtues even further, let him help your servants, whether they sleep or wake. Oh blessed Petronilla! For your father's sake, send health and virtuous patience to all devout petitioners afflicted with fever and pestilence.

Devout pilgrims to her shrine[7] can be confident of having their petitions granted.

---

[5] Esperus is the evening star. Nightingales were associated with both earthly and spiritual love; Lydgate, however, wrote a poem ("A Seying of the Nightingale") in which an angel reveals that those who believe that the nightingale sings of earthly delights are misinterpreting its song. In contrast to nightingales, which were generally represented as idealists, cuckoos and owls were often portrayed as ruthless pragmatists.

[6] The world, the flesh, and the devil.

[7] Perhaps at Lydgate's abbey at Bury, which had among its relics the saint's skull.

Saints Agnes and Dorothy

Osbern Bokenham

O sbern Bokenham was an Augustinian friar from Stoke-Clare, Suffolk, who during the 1430s and 1440s wrote thirteen lives of female saints in Middle English verse for his friends and acquaintances among the East Anglian gentry. Ten of those legends were of virgin martyrs, and eight of the twelve patrons he mentions were women. All but one of his patrons were laypeople. In 1447, his friend and fellow friar Thomas Burgh had the legends gathered into a single volume for presentation to a convent. That neatly written and finely decorated manuscript, British Library Arundel 327, is the only surviving copy of Bokenham's collected works.

A younger contemporary of Lydgate, Bokenham seems to have written in his famous neighbor's shadow. He knows that a saint's life should be a rhetorical masterpiece, but he despairs of being able to achieve the standard established by Chaucer, Gower, and Lydgate, who are to him, as I noted earlier, a sort of literary trinity. As with Lydgate, though, we should beware of taking Bokenham's professions of inadequacy at face value. Indeed, it is tempting to see his introduction to "Agnes" as an attempt to outmatch the slavish humility of Lydgate. He, too, benefits from his modesty; after paying duty to the masters and essaying an eminently Lydgatean prologue, with convoluted sentences and learned references to the classical rhetorician Cicero (Tullius) and the goddess of wisdom Athena (Pallas), he declares defeat and, with it, license to write as he pleases.

Bokenham's legends attest to the continuing popularity of Jacobus de

Voragine's *Golden Legend* in late medieval England. His etymologies of Agnes and Dorothy are both taken from Jacobus, and indeed his entire life of Dorothy is closely based on the *Golden Legend*. For "Agnes," however, Bokenham does what many of his contemporaries were doing: he turns to a longer version of the saint's life as a source for his narrative, in this case, a fifth-century Latin life of Saint Agnes once mistakenly attributed to Ambrose, bishop of Milan (d. 397).

Edition: *Legendys of Hooly Wummen.* Ed. Mary S. Serjeantson, 110–36. EETS.OS 206. 1938. Reprint, Millwood, N.Y.: Kraus, 1987.

Translation: Bokenham, Osbern. *A Legend of Holy Women.* Trans. Sheila Delany, 81–99. Notre Dame: University of Notre Dame Press, 1992.

Delany, Sheila. *Impolitic Bodies: Poetry, Saints, and Society in Fifteenth-Century England: The Work of Osbern Bokenham.* New York: Oxford University Press, 1998.
Edwards, A. S. G. "The Transmission and Audience of Osbern Bokenham's *Legendys of Hooly Wummen.*" In *Late-Medieval Religious Texts and Their Transmission: Essays in Honour of A. I. Doyle,* ed. A. J. Minnis, 157–67. Cambridge: D. S. Brewer, 1994.
Gibson, Gail McMurray. *The Theater of Devotion: East Anglian Drama and Society in the Late Middle Ages.* Chicago: University of Chicago Press, 1989.
Johnson, Ian. "Tales of a True Translator: Medieval Literary Theory, Anecdote, and Autobiography in Osbern Bokenham's *Legendys of Hooly Wummen.*" In *The Medieval Translator.* Vol. 4. Ed. Roger Ellis and Ruth Evans, 104–24. Binghamton, N.Y.: Medieval and Renaissance Texts and Studies, 1994.
McCash, June Hall, ed. *The Cultural Patronage of Medieval Women.* Athens: University of Georgia Press, 1996.
Moore, Samuel. "Patrons of Letters in Norfolk and Suffolk, ca. 1450." Parts 1 and 2. *PMLA* 27 (1912) and 28 (1913): 79–105.
Winstead, Karen A. *Virgin Martyrs: Legends of Sainthood in Late Medieval England,* 112–46. Ithaca: Cornell University Press, 1997.
Wolf, Kirsten. "The Legend of Saint Dorothy: Medieval Vernacular Renderings and Their Latin Sources." *Analecta Bollandiana* 114 (1996): 41–72.

Saint Agnes

Prologue

> May holy Agnes enrich her writer's pen
> And allow the work undertaken to be completed.

I propose to translate the life of Saint Agnes into English as best I can, following Saint Ambrose, who recorded it so eloquently in Latin. Blessed virgin, ask God to let me acquit myself well enough to fulfill my promise!

Fig. 5. Saint Agnes. (Courtesy of the Bodleian Library, Oxford. MS Tanner 17, fol. 7r.)

With utmost humility, I beseech readers not to despise the roughness of my writing, for Pallas would not deign to conduct me into Tullius's mottled meadow of rhetoric to gather the flowers of crafty eloquence. Indeed, whenever I ventured there, she drove me away with great disdain. When I asked her, most respectfully, to show me some favor, she replied, "You've come too late. The freshest flowers have already been gathered by three persons: Gower, Chaucer, and John Lydgate. Though the first two have met their end, the third lingers on." Since Pallas dismissed me so derisively, I've stopped arguing with her. I've given up hoping even to approach Tullius's meadow. Therefore, I'll speak and write plainly in my Suffolk language; whoever doesn't like it can find something better.

Agnes was derived from "agna," Jacobus says. "Agna" is a lamb, a very meek animal, and a simple one, too. Agnes had both of these qualities; indeed, the greatest adversities could diminish neither her meekness nor her simplicity. Agnes, as the cleric further says, is also derived from "knowledge"—a most appropriate derivation, for since her youth she knew the way of truth! Truth, according to Augustine, is the enemy of three vices Agnes vanquished during her life: falsehood, duplicity, and vanity.[1] She overcame falsehood through her faith, vanity through her hope, and duplicity through her perfect charity. We find ample evidence of these virtues in her life—but enough for now. Prolixity merely tires the reader.

Oh holy lamb of God, oh blessed Agnes, so inflamed in your tender youth with the love of God that raging pains could not quench your devotion, inspire my wit and language so that I can complete the legend I've begun.

Here begins the life of Saint Agnes

I, Christ's servant, Bishop Ambrose, greet you holy virgins, and I exhort you to honor the feast day of a young maiden. On that feast, all people should rejoice, singing sweet psalms. Christ's poor should be happy.

Let us now all rejoice in our lord. For the edification of virgins, we will relate how Agnes was martyred when she was only thirteen years old. At that time she lost death and found life, for her only love was the Creator.

---

[1] Augustine (354–430) was bishop of Hippo and author of influential works on theology and doctrine. One of his many sermons deals with Saint Agnes.

Though she was young in years, her soul was mature; indeed, her soul was as mature as her body was young. And though her body was lovely, her soul was even lovelier.

One day when this gem of virginity was coming home from school, the prefect's son fell in love with her. He importuned her family. He offered her many things and promised her even more. He'd brought precious jewelry with him, which Agnes valued like so much dung.

Goaded on by an even greater love, this handsome young man, believing she was holding out for better jewelry, brought shining precious stones and many rings. He conveyed his affection both in person and through his friends, offering many riches—palaces, great possessions, many servants—if only she would become his wife.

This wise Agnes replied, "Get away from me, you who feed sin and thwart goodness! I'll have you know that I'm engaged to someone who's given me better jewels. His family is more distinguished than yours. He's bound me with the ring of his faith. He's adorned my right hand with a precious golden bracelet and has encircled my neck with a necklace of incomparably precious stones. He's given me innumerable pearls and surrounded me with shining gems on every side. He's marked my face with a special sign, indicating that I should be loved by no one but him. He's clothed me in a garment woven with gold and set with precious clasps. He's shown me incomparable treasures, which he's said will be mine if I only persevere in his love. Therefore, I can't take up with you and spurn the lover to whom I'm bound, whose lineage is more distinguished than yours, whose power is greater, whose love is sweeter, whose face is fairer, and who offers a much more blessed happiness. This lover has prepared my bridal chamber; his organs are playing, and his maidens are singing a song of pure bliss. I've accepted many of his kisses, sweeter than milk and honey; and he has often embraced me without blemishing my virginity. His body is now joined with mine. He's anointed my cheeks with his blood. His mother is a virgin—his father, too. Angels serve him humbly, and the sun and moon wonder at his beauty. His breath makes the dead rise. Fickle fortune will never diminish his wealth. Therefore, I keep faith with him and always will, with all my heart. So listen to me, and accept this plain answer: I'll never love anyone but him."

This young man was so depressed by these words that he took to bed, anguished in spirit and sick in body. But by his heavy sighs the doctors guessed what was wrong and told his father. When the father learned how devoted his son was to Agnes, he iterated the boy's offer—and then some. His efforts were wasted, though. She plainly said that nothing would entice her to repudiate her first spouse's offer.

Being the prefect, the boy's father couldn't imagine a more eligible suitor than his son. He wondered whom Agnes could be so impressed with, and who could offer such treasures. As he wondered, one of those who is always ready to deceive and mislead stood by, who said, "Sir, this girl has been a Christian since childhood. She's so deluded by witchcraft and Christian lore that she believes Christ is her husband!" The prefect was glad to hear this and sent a large band of deputies to conduct Agnes to his palace. When she arrived, he flattered her and made many great promises. Then he threatened her. But neither flattery nor fear could deceive Christ's maiden. She stood firm, without changing her expression. So rooted was she in Christ's love that she wholeheartedly despised both his promises and his threats. Seeing such strength and resolve in the girl, the prefect took the matter up with her father and mother. Because of their nobility, he could not attack them openly, so instead he charged them with being Christians.

The next day, he ordered Agnes brought before him. He spoke of his son's love, and how he was pining away for her sake, but Agnes merely scoffed. Seeing this, the prefect brought her before his judgment seat and said, "In my opinion, if this Christian witchcraft isn't somehow driven from you, no one will be able to coax you from your madness, and your ears will be deaf to any words of wisdom! This, therefore, is my judgment: I'll send you to the goddess Vesta.[2] If virginity is so important to you, you can keep it respectably by humbly serving her day and night."

She said, "If for Christ's sake I reject your son—who, though smitten with foul love, is at least a living, thinking human being—how can you expect me to worship dumb idols, insulting divine grace by bowing to powerless stones?"

"I was trying to indulge your tender youth by not punishing your blasphemy!" the prefect said. "Assuming you haven't completely lost your senses, I advise you to stop provoking our gods so brazenly."

Agnes replied, "Don't suppose that I need or want your indulgence just because I'm young in years! Virtuous faith isn't measured in years but rather in the intelligence of the soul; God almighty appreciates wis-

---

[2] Roman goddess of the hearth, whose sacred fire was attended by virgin priestesses.

dom more than age! And as for your gods, whose anger you're trying to spare me, let them be angry. Let them tell me in their own words how they want to be worshipped. They won't, of course—so do what you want with me now."

"I'm giving you a choice, Agnes," said Sympronian, the prefect. "Either serve the goddess Vesta with the other virgins, or join the prostitutes, far from those Christian witches who have made you bold enough to come so shamelessly to this wretched state. This is my sentence: either sacrifice to Vesta, to your family's honor, or—may the gods help me—your noble birth will be degraded by your humiliation in a whorehouse!"

Inspired by grace and strengthened by the holy spirit, the blessed Agnes answered the prefect thus: "If you knew who my God is, wretch, you'd think better and not talk like this. But because I know both the supreme grace and the workings of our lord God, blessed Jesus, I scorn your threats, fully trusting in his goodness. I'll neither sacrifice to idols nor be defiled by sinners: there! I want you to know this for certain—and not only you, but everyone who's standing around: my body is guarded by an angel of the lord, who diligently protects me and helps me in every need, who makes me too bold to fear you. Furthermore, God's son, begotten only of his father's substance, immutable, and eternal—the one you're damnable for not knowing—is an impenetrable wall, a watchman who will never sleep, a defender who will never fail. Your gods, however, as any intelligent person knows, are either made of brass, which would have been better used for cauldrons or pots or pans or other useful things—they can't do anything!—or else they're made of stones, which would have been better off left in a swamp, where they'd at least be safe from filth! As reason proves, divinity, which is immortal, can't be found in stone or in brass or other metal, but in heaven. Therefore, you and those who worship as you do will surely come to eternal pain! As we all know, your 'gods' look the way they do because they were shaped by a hot fire; accordingly, their servants will also be treated by hellfire (and because of their misdeeds, they'll never be cooled down!) in eternal damnation."

Upon hearing her words, the judge nearly went mad. He commanded her to be stripped shamefully and led to the brothel, and he had a crier proclaim, "Agnes, this witch, who impudently scorned our gods, is consigned to a brothel for her blasphemy." But as soon as she was stripped, her hair bands slid from her hair, and by grace of God it was made so thick that it covered her on all sides, hiding her nakedness. In fact, her hair seemed to conceal her even better than her clothes had done.

When Agnes, thus devoutly clothed, entered the filthy place—the brothel, I mean—she found an angel, who promptly enveloped her in such bright light that no man could either see or touch her. This glorious brightness so illuminated her cell that the sun, even at the height of its celestial journey, never shone as brilliantly as this house did through divine grace. Whoever dared to look at it felt a sharp pang in his eye. When Agnes saw this brightness sent by God, she prostrated herself to him. Immediately a white stole appeared before her. She put it on, then said, "Thanks be to you, lord, for all the kindness and grace and comfort and goodness you have shown me now and always, in so many ways. Thanks be to you, God, who, numbering me among your handmaids, just sent me this new, white garment from heaven." When Agnes put this garment on, which was white as snow or as a lily, it conformed itself so perfectly to her body that it seemed to have been made for her. Indeed, no one who saw it dared doubt that it had been made by angels.

Look at this wonderful transformation: a brothel has become a special house of prayer! Whoever entered left worshipping God wholeheartedly, by God's grace cleaner when he came out than when he went in.

The prefect's son was delighted to hear that Agnes was in the whorehouse. He rushed to the place with a crowd of young fellows, expecting to satisfy his foul lust with her. When he arrived at the brothel and saw many young men who had gone there full of lust leaving full of reverence, he jeered at them, calling them wretches and saying, "Damn you, useless cowards!" With these taunts, he went right to the place where Agnes lay in prayer. And when he impudently and irreverently presumed to enter the light surrounding her, he fell flat on his face, and a devil strangled him on the spot. When his companions, who were waiting outside, saw that he was gone such a long time, they assumed that he had overcome her somehow and was busy sinning. One of them ran inside to celebrate the victory. When he saw him lying there dead, he ran right out again, tearing his clothes like a madman and crying, "Oh noble Romans, kill this witch who has killed the prefect's son through her witchcraft!" When the news of the young man's death had spread through the city, everyone ran to the brothel to witness the unfortunate accident. When they had seen it, they shouted loudly, some calling her a witch and some calling her innocent.

When the prefect learned of his son's death, he rushed like a madman to the scene, and when he saw his son lying there stone dead, he looked at Agnes and cried, "Cruelest of women, why have you worked your witchcraft so viciously and relentlessly against my son? Why? Tell me why!"

When he had repeated his question over and over, she demurely answered, "Don't blame me for your son's death, for I'm innocent, sir. The devil whose will he was about to do took his life—and rightfully. As to why those who came before him escaped unharmed, here is my answer: in his goodness, God sent this great light and, as everyone can see, he had his angel clothe me in this white garment. The men who came first thanked God humbly and didn't dare touch me. Therefore, they left unharmed. Not your son, though. He came in shamelessly, intending to satisfy his foul fleshly lusts, and didn't respect the light that enveloped me. When he presumed to approach me, an angel of God protected me by driving him to this death, as you see."

"Agnes," said the prefect, "only one thing will convince me that you don't operate by witchcraft, and that is if you ask your angel to restore my dead son to life."

Agnes replied, "Although your faith doesn't deserve the favor you ask, it's time to show the power of our lord Jesus to this crowd. Leave me, now, so that I can return to my prayer."

When all the people had left, Agnes fell flat on her face. She tearfully beseeched God, in his singular grace, to show a sign of mercy and pity in that place by causing the young man to rise again. While she was praying and crying, an angel appeared. Lifting her up, he comforted her, saying that her request was granted. Immediately the young man rose and shouted, "There is just one God—the Christian God—in heaven, on earth, and in the sea. All the temples raised to the gods are futile, as are the gods worshipped within them, for they can help neither themselves nor others."

Upon hearing these words, the witches and bishops of the temple cried loudly, "Seize this witch and put her to death, for she's converting people!" Upon hearing their words, the people agitated more than ever before.

The prefect was stunned. He was afraid of being censured for defending Agnes and thus acting against the bishops of the temple. To appease the people, he promptly appointed a deputy and went home, deeply regretting that he couldn't save Agnes from torment, since she had, as he'd seen, raised his son from the dead.

Bowing to the people's will, the prefect's deputy, Aspasius, had a great fire made and put Agnes in the middle of it. Immediately the flames divided, killing people on either side of Agnes but not touching her. Ascribing the miracle to sorcery rather than to God's power, the angry people cursed and yelled. Agnes, standing amidst the flames, spread her hands demurely and prayed wholeheartedly: "Praise be to you, most virtuous almighty God, worthy of fear and honor, father of our lord Jesus Christ. Through your son, I have escaped the threats of these wicked people, and by your grace I have trodden a clean path through the devil's filth. I see now, lord, that through your spirit I am bathed with heavenly dew. The fire right next to me dies; the miraculously divided flames come nowhere near me, but by your will, they burn those who intended to burn me. Bless you, father, worthiest to be preached and praised in all countries. Through your grace, you most kindly made me unafraid among the fiery flames, and you make me come happily to you through the torments others wish to inflict on me. I see now, lord, what I have believed; may your blessed grace be thanked forever. What I have thirsted for is given to me; what I have coveted I now embrace, much to my spiritual comfort. Therefore, with lips and heart, I will acknowledge and desire you wholly, lord, forever. See how I come to you, living and true almighty God, who equally with Jesus your son and with the holy ghost now live and reign eternally, in one substance, as I well know, forever and ever. Amen."

When she had finished praying in this vein, as devoutly as she could—and much better than I am able to express here—the fire was extinguished. Fire and heat were gone, as if they had never been. Upon seeing that, Aspasius, the prefect's deputy, to appease the seditious people, commanded that a sharp bright sword be thrust deep into her throat. Thus, Christ married this holy, innocent maiden, so cruelly martyred for his sake.

Being Christians themselves, her father and mother were not grieved by her death. They took her body joyfully and buried it outside the city walls, in one of their properties by the Nomentan highway (so called because it runs right through the city of Nomentum). There they and others devoutly kept a vigil at her tomb for many nights, as the custom was then. Exactly at midnight, they saw a great company of maidens clothed in garments of gold come toward them, preceded by a brilliant light.

Among those maidens, they saw their daughter, Agnes, freshly clothed in lovely and shining garments, just like the rest. To her right, a darling lamb, whiter than snow, walked at her feet. They thought it a marvelous sight.

Then Agnes asked her companions to stop awhile, and she said to her friends, "Don't grieve as if I were dead, but rejoice in my promotion, for with this blessed and glorious company I have entered the bright kingdom of heaven. What's more, I'm perpetually joined in heaven to him who was my only love on earth, the one I loved more than anything." When Agnes had said these words, all the maidens vanished in a twinkling of an eye. There was no trace of them.

When news of this vision, which grew greater and greater by the minute, spread through castles and towns, some people who heard of it told Lady Constance, daughter of the emperor Constantine.[3] This Constance was a glorious queen and a prudent maiden, we read, but she had an onerous disease: from head to foot, she was covered with sores. Because no medicine could cure or even alleviate her great distress, she was advised to visit the tomb of the pure virgin Agnes, hoping and trusting to recover her health. She did so, and when she arrived, she prayed devoutly, even though she was a heathen. As Constance lay in prayer, she fell asleep, and blessed Agnes appeared to her, saying, "Constance, believe devoutly and faithfully that Christ, God's son, is your true savior, and he will cure your ailment completely." Upon hearing this voice, Lady Constance awoke, as whole and healthy as could be. She could see no trace of infirmity on her body. She immediately went home and told her father and brothers exactly what had happened. The entire city gathered together in joy and wondered at the news. The faithlessness of the heathen was confounded and the faith and high virtue of Jesus Christ proclaimed.

In Rome and throughout the empire, people started believing that whoever devoutly visited Agnes's tomb would be cured of any infirmity. (No one doubts that Christ continues to grant cures, even to this day.) In the meantime, Constance asked her father and brothers to build a church over Agnes's tomb and beside it a place where she could live in black clothes and serve Saint Agnes, the pure virgin, for the rest of her

---

[3] Roman emperor whose Edict of Tolerance ended, in 313, state-sponsored persecution of Christianity. The prose *Life of Saint Katherine* details Constantine's career.

life. She asked them to do this for her sake. The emperor's daughter, blessed Constance, whom Agnes cured of all infirmity, persevered in perfect virginity. Through her, many Roman maidens of all classes were consecrated there with a holy veil to God and to blessed Agnes. And because faith is not damaged through death, many of the young Roman virgins, who followed Agnes with devotion as if she were alive, took example from her great deeds and persevered, hoping to gain thereby the glorious palm of perpetual victory.

There now: I've finished Agnes's life, I suppose, just as I promised in the prologue. I followed the account of Saint Ambrose, but not word for word—for that, Jerome[4] says, is impossible to do in any translation. Instead, I translated loosely, sentence by sentence. Even so, it is certainly hard to adhere to him, for of all the Church Fathers, his writing is the strangest and most alien. Whoever doesn't believe me can look at his books!

Praise to you, Ambrose, holy theologian, who had such affection for Saint Agnes that, for the edification of virgins, you undertook the blessed labor of writing her life, which you found tucked away in a corner of oblivion and feared lest it be lost through neglect.

Praise to you, too, oh blessed virgin and martyr, most gracious Agnes, who were good enough to incline your ears to the prayer I made in my introduction. Praise to you, lady, for now I have finished. As my reward, lady, let me see you in bliss after this wretched life.

Amen. Praise Jesus.

Saint Dorothy

When Christianity was a new religion, young and still not fully and firmly rooted, many a tyrant tried hard to stamp it out. Among the cruelest of those tyrants was Diocletian, who raged against it with his vicious cohort, Maximian.[5]

At the time, a worthy man lived in Rome, descended from the high and noble blood of senators. His name, as the story goes, was Dorotheus. He had a wife called Theodora, who was as distinguished as he.

---

[4] Influential theologian, Bible translator, and theorist of translation (d. 420).

[5] The Roman emperor Diocletian made Maximian co-regent in 285; they ruled together until Diocletian's retirement in 305.

This Dorotheus, being a Christian, and seeing the accelerating persecution of his faith, abandoned Rome with his lovely wife, Theodora, and their two daughters, Christen and Calisten. He left all his possessions behind—fields, vineyards, and stately house—and fled to the kingdom of Cappadocia, arriving by chance in the city of Caesaria.[6] There he and his wife had a daughter, whom they called Dorothy. Bishop Apollinaris baptized her in a secret ceremony.

This Dorothy, filled with the grace of the holy spirit from her youth, grew ever greater in virtue and goodness. Her single desire was to keep her body from physical corruption; and as far as physical beauty went, she was the loveliest maiden in the land. But the devil, ever resentful of purity, made the prefect of Caesaria, Fabricius, ache with desire for the glorious Dorothy. He sent for her and offered her plenty of treasures and honors; he proposed to wed her with a ring. Dorothy, her spirit rooted in grace, despised these worldly treasures. Indifferent to temporal wealth, she stood before him and fearlessly declared that she was Christ's spouse.

Furious at this reply, Fabricius ordered her thrown into a vat of blazing hot oil, but she, trusting in her spouse, Jesus, was as happy as if she were being anointed with sweet balm. Many a pagan who saw this miracle privately converted to Christ. Fabricius, however, ascribed it to witchcraft. He ordered her promptly led to prison, where she was left for nine whole days without food. During that time, angels fed her with heavenly sustenance.

At the end of the nine days, she was brought before the judge. Her beauty had not diminished a bit; in fact, it had increased greatly. All who saw her were baffled at how, after being deprived of food for so long, she could grow so much lovelier. But Fabricius, blinded by madness, thought nothing of this miracle. He told her, "Unless you meekly worship my gods—and I mean now—I'll have you dangling from a gibbet!"

"I'll worship God, not devils," she replied, "and not idols—which your gods are!"

With that, she fell to the ground, and gazing devoutly toward heaven, she prayed, "Lord, in your mercy, reveal your power here; show by some heavenly sign that you—and only you—are God."

Suddenly a tall pillar, which Fabricius had erected there with a foul and ugly idol on top, was shaken so violently by a multitude of heavenly

---

[6] Cappadocia lay in present-day central Turkey; Caesaria is now called Kayseri.

angels that by the time Dorothy had finished her prayer, neither the pillar nor the idol remained. Up in the air, the voices of devils could be heard, crying, "Why can't you leave us alone, Dorothy, you tender young maiden?" By those signs, many a pagan was converted and martyred for Christ's sake in that place.

But Dorothy was cruelly hanged by her feet from a gibbet, her body beaten with rods and scourges, her flesh ripped savagely with iron hooks, her breasts mercilessly burned with firebrands. Then she was taken down, half dead, and locked in prison.

The next morning, when she was brought before the judge, neither a bruise nor a gash could be seen on her body. Astonished, Fabricius said to her, "Oh noble and pretty maiden, repent, I tell you, for you have surely been punished enough!"

Then he sent her sisters to her—Christen and Calisten—who had renounced Christ for fear of being tortured. He was sure that they would easily convert her, too. But the exact opposite of what he expected took place, for Dorothy returned both sisters to the Christian faith.

Upon hearing this, Fabricius nearly lost his mind. In his madness, he devised a new torment: he had the sisters bound back to back with a heavy chain and thrown into a fire to burn together. Then he turned his pale face to glorious Dorothy and began threatening her: "How long will you continue to provoke us with your witchcraft? Now both of your sisters are dead. If you wish, though, you can still live. Sacrifice immediately to my gods, and I'll pardon you. Otherwise I'll have your head cut off."

Dorothy replied meekly, "I'm ready to suffer whatever you want for Jesus, my lord and spouse. Indeed, I have been since I first knew him. I'll gather roses and apples in his garden and be happy with him forever."

At this, the furious tyrant commanded his torturers to beat her lovely face to a pulp with bats and staves. And when she was beaten beyond recognition, they locked her in a dark cell for the night. But early the next morning, when she was brought before the judge Fabricius, she looked as if she hadn't been beaten at all. Utterly bewildered, Fabricius was at a loss for what to do next, so he ordered her beheaded without delay.

When she came outside the city walls, a certain Theophilus, protonotary of Cappadocia, sarcastically asked her to send him some roses from her spouse's garden. She promised faithfully to do so, even though it was very cold that winter.

When she was brought to the place where she was to be beheaded, she earnestly prayed that most gracious God save from every tribulation those who remembered her passion—especially from shame, hateful poverty, and slander. She also asked that God grant her devotees at their death true contrition and full remission of all their sins. She asked that he grant prompt relief to pregnant women who remembered her. Finally, she asked that no house containing an account of her passion should be harmed by fire or lightning. As soon as she had made this prayer, a voice replied, "Come, my love, my spouse; be happy, for all your requests are granted, and all those you wish to be saved shall be."

As she bowed her head to the executioner, a child dressed in lovely purple appeared. He was barefooted and had curly hair; golden stars beamed from his clothes. He was carrying a little basket with three roses and three apples. Kneeling down, he offered the basket to Dorothy. She humbly asked him to take it to Theophilus the scribe and to tell him that she had sent the present she'd promised him. Off he went. Dorothy accepted the stroke of death fearlessly and meekly, and her soul ascended to heaven.

This blessed Dorothy was cruelly martyred by the prefect Fabricius on February 16, A.D. 288, during the reign of the emperors Diocletian and Maximian.

The curly-haired child appeared to Theophilus at the palace. Taking him by the hand, he led him politely aside and said, "My dear sister sent you these roses and apples from her husband's garden." Then he vanished.

Theophilus immediately began to praise and glorify Dorothy's God, Christ, who could send roses and apples in February, when frost and cold grip the earth and not a leaf can be seen on the trees. Blessed be his name forever! Theophilus's credible testimony and earnest preaching soon converted everyone in the city.

Fabricius was so baffled by these events that he scarcely knew where he was. And when he saw the converted Theophilus preaching so devoutly, his heart nearly stopped. After torturing him even more than he tormented Dorothy, he chopped his body into tiny bits, which he threw to the beasts and the birds.

But first this Theophilus was baptized and devoutly received the Eucharist. Then, after suffering the cruel torments I just mentioned, he followed his mistress, Dorothy, to Christ's heavenly kingdom. Through their merits, may Christ bring us there too. Amen.

Now, blessed virgin Dorothy, who are glorified in heaven above, let John Hunt prove his friendship, as he wishes, before he dies—and his wife, Isabel, who loves you too. At their request and humble entreaty this life was translated. Jesus have mercy. Amen.

Saint Katherine

Anonymous, ca. 1420

A ruler and scholar, Katherine of Alexandria is a most unusual virgin martyr. She was often designated as God's favorite saint, second only to the Virgin Mary, and more lives were written of her than of any other virgin martyr. Indeed, with Christ's mother and Mary Magdalene, she is one of the three best-represented female saints in medieval art and literature throughout Europe.

The legend of Katherine of Alexandria underwent intriguing permutations during the late Middle Ages. Virgin martyr legends usually confine themselves to the saint's passion. In the thirteenth century, however, first on the Continent and later in England, numerous stories were told about Katherine's life before her confrontation with the emperor Maxentius. The plots of these stories are variegated. For example, sometimes Maxentius originally makes his trip to Alexandria as Katherine's suitor rather than as a persecutor of Christians. Again, Katherine's mother is sometimes her daughter's adversary and sometimes a devout Christian who initiates her daughter's conversion. One common element, though, is the story of Katherine's mystical marriage with Jesus, which literalizes the ancient metaphor of the virgin martyr as Christ's bride.

The prose life of Saint Katherine which follows bears all the hallmarks of fifteenth-century virgin martyr legends. The saint displays many qualities that would make her a model for devout fifteenth-century laypeople, including courtesy, grace, tact, and eloquence. She performs her social and political responsibilities as best she can without subordinating her spiritual pursuits to them. Although the author clearly commends Katherine's piety, he in no way intimates that social expectations are wrong, nor does he vilify her mother and subjects for trying to persuade her to marry.

The devotional and didactic emphases that marked the narratives of Lydgate and Bokenham are even more conspicuous here. The language of the mystical and contemplative treatises that were popular in fifteenth-century England pervades the narrative. Indeed, Katherine's pursuit of God through study and meditation exemplifies methods outlined in contemporary tracts that aimed to bring readers into a more intimate relationship with Christ.

This prose life is one of two Middle English legends supplying a detailed account of events preceding Katherine's passion. (The other is John Capgrave's ca. 1445 legend in rhyme royal.) I have translated what appears to be the oldest surviving manuscript of the prose legend, which dates from around 1420: MS Richardson 44, Houghton Library, Harvard University. This version of Katherine's life was widely disseminated. Medieval editors reworked it in various ways, often substituting Jacobus de Voragine's version of Katherine's passion for the longer account found here. It was incorporated into the earliest prose collection of saints' legends, the 1438 *Golden Legend*, and later into Caxton's better-known printed legendary of the same name.

Editions: *The Life and Martyrdom of St. Katherine of Alexandria.* Ed. Henry Hucks Gibbs. London: Nichols, 1884.

St. Katherine of Alexandria: The Late Middle English Prose Legend in Southwell Minster MS 7. Ed. Saara Nevanlinna and Irma Taavitsainen. Cambridge: D. S. Brewer, 1993. A later, shorter version of the life translated here.

Lewis, Katherine J. "Model Girls? Virgin Martyrs and the Training of Young Women in Late Medieval England." In *Young Medieval Women,* ed. Noël James Menuge, Katherine J. Lewis, and Kim M. Phillips, 25–46. Stroud, Gloucestershire: Sutton Publishing, 1999.

———. "Pilgrimage and the Cult of Saint Katherine of Alexandria in Late Medieval England." In *Pilgrimage Explored,* ed. Jennie Stopford, 145–60. Woodbridge, Suffolk: Boydell and Brewer, 1999.

———. *The Cult of St. Katherine of Alexandria in Late Medieval England.* Woodbridge, Suffolk: Boydell and Brewer, 2000.

Winstead, Karen A. *Virgin Martyrs: Legends of Sainthood in Late Medieval England,* 147–80. Ithaca: Cornell University Press, 1997.

Fig. 6. Saint Katherine. (Courtesy of the Pierpont Morgan Library, New York. MS M. 451, fol. 126v.)

Saint Katherine

A short prologue to the life and martyrdom of Saint Katherine, virgin and martyr

After I had translated the martyrdom of the holy virgin martyr Saint Katherine from Latin into English, as it is recorded in complete legends, I obtained a quire containing an English translation recounting not only her martyrdom but also her birth and life before her conversion, as well as her conversion and marriage to our lord Jesus Christ. But since the virgin's martyrdom was no clearer there than in my own translation, to honor our lord and his holy mother and hers, I have combined the two translations into one, dividing the text into chapters and adding somewhat, here and there, for clarity. The resulting text should stir Christians to love and honor this blessed virgin and to desire to know all about her life and passion; it should also encourage them to reflect on the charity she showed at the hour of her death, when she prayed that whoever remembered her life and passion and called on her for help should receive prompt relief. (Our lord heard and granted that prayer, as will be shown in Chapter 28.)

It should be known, moreover, that the noble and worthy theologian Athanasius wrote the life of this glorious virgin Saint Katherine.[1] He knew all about her birth, her family, and her habits; he was one of the teachers of her youth, before she was converted to the true faith. After her conversion, she converted him with her holy teaching and through the marvels that our lord worked in her. Made bishop of Alexandria after her martyrdom, he was a mighty pillar of the Church, by the grace of our lord and the holy merit of Katherine. He is the same Athanasius who wrote "Quicunque vult," which is sung in church at prime.[2] Having suffered great persecution for the faith, he is now honored by the Church and is a holy saint in heaven.

[Chapter summary omitted.]

---

[1] The Greek bishop of Alexandria lived 293–372; the conventional claim that he authored Katherine's life is spurious.

[2] "Quicunque vult" ("Whoever wishes [to be saved]") is better known as the Athanasian Creed; "prime," which took place at approximately 6 A.M., was one of eight periods of ritual prayer that structured monastic life in the Middle Ages.

Chapter 1: Of Katherine's forebears and how she was related to the Roman emperors

This excellent and glorious virgin, Saint Katherine, was related to the emperors of Rome on her father's side, for the emperor Constantine and King Costus, Saint Katherine's father, had the same father (though not the same mother, as will be explained shortly).

It is well known and documented that the Romans subjected nearly the entire world to their empire through their great wisdom and manliness. At that time, the Britons (we call them Welsh now), descendants of the Trojans and cousins of the Romans, ruled England, then called Britain. (Later it was called the greater Britain to distinguish it from the lesser Britain across the sea.) These Britons were conquered by the emperor Julius Caesar and remained subject to Rome for many years.

But during the time of the emperors Diocletian and Maximian, such cruel tyranny was inflicted on the world—on Christians and pagans alike—that many Roman tributaries cast off the yoke of servitude and openly rebelled. Of them, Armenia most staunchly withheld the tribute owed to Rome. A Roman senator of great dignity and judgment called Constance (or Constantine) was chosen to quell the uprising, for he was not only the manliest in arms but very prudent and virtuous as well. When this lord arrived in Armenia, he subdued the rebellion through his manly and virtuous behavior in such a way that he earned and won his enemies' love. Indeed, the king and all his people wanted Constance to marry his daughter and heir. Some time after the marriage, the king of Armenia fell ill, and Constance was crowned king of the land. He and his wife the queen had a son, whom he called Costus. Soon afterward, his wife the queen died and was greatly lamented by all her people.

After the queen's death, King Constance left his son, Costus, in charge of the country and returned to Rome to visit the emperor and see how his holdings in the region were being governed. He was received with great honor in Rome. The emperor Diocletian made him caesar, along with a man called Galerius, whom he also made caesar (in other words, Diocletian made Constance and Galerius co-rulers of the empire). In the meantime, news reached Rome that the greater Britain (now called England, as mentioned earlier) had rebelled against Rome.

King Constance was unanimously chosen to put down the rebellion. He accepted the commission and hastened to those parts. When he arrived, the Britons, not daring to fight him on account of his reputation, asked to negotiate. He conducted himself with such discretion, virtue, and judgment that they returned amicably to the empire; furthermore, King Coel and the inhabitants of Britain thought so highly of him that the people unanimously demanded that the king give Constance his daughter and heir in marriage. Coel's daughter was Helen, now known as Saint Helen, who later discovered the holy cross. Both kings approving, a solemn marriage was performed.

About a month after the wedding, King Coel died and Constance was crowned king of Britain. He and Helen had a son, whom he called Constantine, who was later emperor of Rome, as shall be told. At that time, the emperors Diocletian and Maximian freely resigned their title, and the said King Constance and his partner Galerius divided the empire between them, with Galerius ruling the east and Constance the west (that is to say, Italy, France, Spain, England, etc.). But Constance gave up much of his empire and contented himself with France, Spain, and England. He died and was buried in England at York. His son Constantine ruled England and France after him, not only as king of England by right of his mother but as emperor of both realms by right of his father. His expansion of the empire shall be told, in part, in Chapter 10. This is the same noble Constantine who was baptized by the holy pope Saint Silvester and cured of an incurable leprosy.[3] He is the same worthy Constantine who overcame his enemies by virtue of the cross and later sent his mother, Saint Helen, to find the cross at Jerusalem. This same Constantine, after persecuting Christians for a long time, built churches and first endowed the Church with possessions. It would take a long time to relay all his virtues and the generous, holy deeds for which he is venerated as a saint in the East, as chronicles tell. This noble emperor Constantine was Saint Katherine's uncle on her father's side, for he and King Costus were brothers, as stated earlier. After Constance died, Costus, his first son, was crowned king of Armenia. He married the daughter and heir of the king of Cyprus, whom he succeeded as king. The two of them begot Saint Katherine, who, as you see, was thus of imperial blood.

[3] A version of this apocryphal story can be found in *Golden Legend* 1:64–65.

Chapter 2: Of the birth and life and education of Saint Katherine until she was fourteen years old

Two hundred years after the incarnation of our lord Jesus Christ, a noble and prudent king called Costus ruled the land of Cyprus. He was the handsomest and richest and most virtuous of men. He had a queen as virtuous as himself, with whom he lived a most blessed life, by worldly standards, except that he and his wife were pagans and worshipped idols. To spread his reputation throughout the world, this king built a city, where he raised a temple to honor the false gods that the blind world then worshipped. He named the city Costi, which, as time passed and the language changed, was renamed *Fama Costi*[4] to preserve the king's reputation. He and his queen lived happily in that city.

Just as the fair and sweet rose blossoms among thorns, Jesus Christ's precious spouse, the holy virgin Saint Katherine, sprang from these pagans. When this holy child was born, she was so fair of face and so shapely that everyone marveled at her; by the age of seven, she had grown so beautiful and fine that everyone who saw her expected her to become the joy and treasure of Cyprus. After seven years had passed, and she had grown strong in body, she was put to school, where she performed better than anyone her age. She absorbed the art and knowledge of all seven sciences[5]—and no wonder she drank deeply from the well of wisdom, for she was destined to became a teacher and purveyor of eternal wisdom. King Costus, her father, was so delighted with his daughter's wisdom that he set aside a tower in his palace for her, full of studies and rooms, so that she would be distracted from her books only when she wished to be. He appointed the seven best and loftiest scholars in that part of the world to attend her. And when these masters had been with this young lady Katherine for a while, she grew so wonderfully wise that the very scholars who had come to teach her were happy to become her disciples.

Chapter 3: How Saint Katherine was crowned queen after her father's death and required by her parliament to take a husband

A few years later, when this glorious virgin was fourteen years old, her father, King Costus, died, leaving her queen and heir to the realm. And

---

[4] This city in eastern Cyprus is now known as Famagusta.
[5] The seven liberal arts: grammar, logic, rhetoric, arithmetic, geometry, music, and astronomy.

when the days of mourning had passed, the lords and dignitaries of her land came to this young queen and requested that a parliament be summoned at which she could be crowned and receive the allegiance of her subjects and establish the kind of rule and government that would ensure peace and prosperity in her realms. The young queen thanked them graciously and granted their request. Some time later, the parliament began and the young queen was crowned with great pomp in a royal feast, much to her people's delight.

One day, after the coronation ceremony, when the queen sat in parliament, her mother beside her and all her lords around her, a representative of her mother and all her lords and commons stepped forward. Kneeling before the queen, that lord said, "High and mighty princess, our most sovereign lady on earth, if it please your sovereign nobility, your mother and all your lords and commons have commanded me to ask your highness to allow them to choose some noble king or prince to rule you and your lands and all of us in peace and security, just as the noble king your father did before you. In making this request, we are also thinking of your gracious progeny, which is now our greatest desire and which will be our greatest delight, without which we live in sorrow and heaviness. I beseech your royal excellence to heed our desire and grant us, in your high grace, a gracious answer."

This request of her mother and all her lords greatly troubled this young queen. She wondered how to answer so as both to appease her mother and lords and to preserve her chastity, for all her joy had been in keeping her body and soul from all corruption; indeed, she cherished her chastity so completely that she would rather die than blemish it in any way. But thinking it unwise to reveal her intention now, she answered the lord with a serious look and steady voice: "Cousin, I thank my lady mother and all my lords and commons for their great love and for their tenderness toward me and my realm. But I honestly believe that there is no hurry in this matter of my marriage. There is no danger, considering the great wisdom of my lady mother and of you all, and given the kindness and loyalty that you have shown—and, I fully expect, will continue to show—toward myself and my realm. We do not need to seek a foreign lord to rule us and our lands, for, with your loyalty and wisdom, we are confident that we can govern our realms and you in the same peace and stability as my lord father the king left you. Therefore, I ask you to leave this matter for the time being and speak of matters more conducive to and necessary for the good government of our realms." When the queen had finished speaking, her lords and her mother the queen were dumbfounded, for they concluded from her words that she had no intention of marrying.

Chapter 4: How she described the man she would marry, if she married anyone

Then a duke of her land, her uncle, stood up and knelt reverently before her and said, "My own sovereign lady, with due respect for your high and noble discretion, this answer weighs heavily on my lady your mother and on all us liege men. We ask that, in your noble and discreet heart, you reconsider. Let me remind you of four notable things that great God has endowed you with above all known creatures, which must make you take a lord and husband, so that those abundant gifts of nature and grace may pass, as is proper, to future generations, whose fruit will bring infinite joy and gladness to your people and whose fruitlessness will fill them with misery."

"Now, dear uncle," the young queen said, "what are those four things you praise us highly for?"

The duke replied, "Madam, if your highness please, I will tell you at once."

"Please proceed, uncle," she said. "I am listening."

Then the duke said with great reverence, "Madam, this is the first notable point: that we know you are descended from the worthiest blood on earth. The second is that you are the greatest woman alive. The third is that you surpass all others in knowledge and wisdom. The fourth is that your equal in form and beauty has never been seen. In our opinion, madam, these four points require you to grant our wishes."

The young queen regarded him gravely and said, "Now, uncle, since God and nature have worked such wonders in us, we are especially bound to love and please him; indeed, we humbly thank him for all his great gifts. As for our marriage, we will describe a lord and husband that befits your description of us, and if you can find him, we will gladly marry him. Whoever will be lord of our heart and my husband shall be so endowed with these four things that all creatures will depend on him and he will depend on no one. Any lord of mine must be must be of such noble blood that all kings honor him. It follows, then, that he must be such a great lord that I would never presume to think that I made him king. He must be richer than anyone else and so beautiful that angels rejoice at the sight of him. He must be so pure that his mother is a virgin and so meek and kind that he can gladly forgive all wrongs done to him. Now I have described the lord and husband I desire. Go look for him; if you find him, we will be his wife with all our heart—provided he agrees—and if you don't, we will never marry anyone. That is my final answer." With those words, she lowered her eyes meekly and held her peace.

When the queen mother and all Katherine's lords had heard this, they were most distressed, for they knew there was no changing her mind. Then her mother said angrily, "Alas, daughter! Is this the wisdom that everyone talks about? You're bound to bring much grief to me and to all your family and people. Alas! Whoever saw a woman concoct a husband with words—the man you've devised never lived and never will! Abandon this foolishness, dear daughter, and do as your worthy elders have always done."

Then this young lady sighed mournfully to her mother, "Madam, reason convinces me that there is one better that I can imagine, if only one had the grace to find him. Unless he finds me through his grace, rest assured, I will never be happy. Reason tells me that there is a true way and that we are far from it. Therefore, we are in darkness, and until the light of grace comes, we cannot see the true way. And when that light comes, it will disperse the dark clouds of ignorance and show me the one my heart so passionately desires and loves. And even if he doesn't wish me to find him, reason dictates that I do my best to find him. Therefore, my lady and mother, I humbly beg that neither you nor anyone else broach this matter, for upon my life I will never have any but the one I described, and I will remain true to him."

With this, she and her mother and all her lords rose from the parliament and sadly said good-bye and went their ways. The young queen went to her palace so consumed with this husband she described that she could do nothing but think about him and long for him. Though she constantly studied and pondered how she might find him, she made no progress, for she lacked the means. Nonetheless, he was very close to her heart, for he had kindled within her heart a burning fire of love, which, as her glorious passion attests, could never be quenched by any pain or tribulation.

But now I will leave this young queen awhile, sitting in her palace, worrying about how to find this new spouse with many tears and much long-ing—and with many sad sighs for her blind ignorance. And I will de-scribe—grace permitting—how our lord miraculously summoned her to baptism in a manner that was never heard of before or after, and how he then openly married her, showing her the highest tokens of his special love that had never been shown—and would never be shown—to any other living person except our lady, his most blessed mother.

Chapter 5: How our lady appeared to a hermit in the desert and sent him to fetch Saint Katherine to marry her son

Some miles outside Alexandria, a holy father had been leading a life of great penance in the desert for thirty years. One day, as he walked outside his cell, consumed with pious thoughts, he was approached by the most magnificent woman ever seen. Her splendor and her supernat-ural beauty so astonished and frightened him that he fell down as if he were dead. Perceiving his dread, this blessed lady called his name kindly and said, "Don't be afraid, brother Adrian, for I am here only for your honor and profit." With that, she raised him gently and reassured him, saying, "Adrian, you must take a message from me to the young queen in her palace at Alexandria. Tell her that you bring greetings from the woman whose son she chose for her husband when she was seated in parliament, surrounded by her mother and her lords, and engaged in a great struggle to preserve her virginity. Tell her that the lord she chose is my son, that I am a virgin, and that my son values her chastity above that of all the virgins on earth. Tell her that she must come here alone, with-out delay, and she will put on new clothes and see him and have him as her everlasting spouse."

Hearing all this, the hermit replied anxiously, "Oh my, blessed lady! How can I convey this message, for I know neither the city nor the way? And even if I did, who am I to take a message to a queen? Her people wouldn't let me near her, and if they did, she wouldn't believe me. I'd be arrested as an impostor!"

"Don't be afraid, Adrian," said this blessed lady, "for what my son has begun in her must be completed. Rest assured that she has been chosen above all living women as a special vessel of grace. Don't hesitate and don't worry, for you will know the way to the city and to her palace and no one will notice you. When you enter her palace, watch which doors open before you and go through them boldly until you come to this young queen, whom you will find alone in her study struggling to comprehend what cannot be understood through study. Therefore, my son has taken pity on her and will reward her effort with a grace that sets her apart from everyone but me, his own chosen mother. So hurry, Adrian, and bring me my dear daughter, whom I love with all my heart."

Upon hearing this message, Adrian prostrated himself before this sovereign lady, saying, "All honor and joy to my sovereign lord God, your blessed son, and to you. May your wills be fulfilled; I go at your command."

Chapter 6: How the hermit completed his mission and brought Saint Katherine with him to the desert

Then Adrian arose, hastened to the city, and went into the palace as he was instructed. Passing through the doors he found open before him, he went from room to room until he came to Katherine's private study. When he entered the door, he saw the fairest and most splendid person ever seen. And she was so caught up in her studies that she didn't hear him until he kneeled down beside her and began his message: "Madam, may the limitless might of the father almighty, the wisdom of his most wise son, and the goodness of the holy ghost, three persons and one God, be with you now in your study."

When this young queen heard a man's voice beside her and saw a hairy old man in her study dressed in the worn cloak of a pilgrim, she was astounded. Sure that she had shut her doors behind her, she said uncertainly, "Who are you that so marvelously enters my study, where no man comes? Did you come by magic?"

"No, madam," he said, "I come as a messenger."

"And, good sir," she said, "who was bold enough to send such a simple person to our private study?"

"Madam," this old father said, "the queen of queens and lady of ladies and most bountiful and beautiful of all women."

"Good sir," she said, "where does this lady you praise so highly live, for we have never heard of her."

"Madam," he said, "her home is in her son's kingdom where everlasting joy reigns."

"And, good sir," she said, "who is her son?"

"Madam," he said, "the king of bliss."

"How surprising," she said, "that a such a splendid woman with a son as mighty as you claim would send such a simple messenger as yourself!"

"Madam," he said, "that lady most values those who deprive themselves of all earthly things for the love of her son. That is why she sent me to you. She welcomes you as her daughter on the grounds that when you sat in parliament, your mother and lords around you, to keep your virginity you stipulated a husband that greatly distressed your mother and all your lords. Because you were so staunch in that conflict that you refused all earthly kings, she tells you that you shall have a heavenly king, who was born of a pure virgin and is king of all kings and lord of all lordships, whose command is obeyed by heaven and earth and all that is within. This lord is her own dearest son, whom she conceived by the power of the holy ghost and bore without blemishing her virginity, with such honor and joy that no woman has ever experienced, nor ever will. She sent me to tell you that you should come alone with me to my cell, and there you will see that blessed lord and that blessed lady, who eagerly await your arrival."

When this young queen heard him speak so clearly of the one that she had sought with such diligence and passion, she was so inflamed with desire that she was speechless. Forgetting her rank and her people, she arose and, meek as a lamb, followed old Adrian out of her palace, through the city of Alexandria, and on into the desert. And as she walked, she asked many serious questions, which he answered to her satisfaction, and he instructed her on all matters of faith, and she wholeheartedly received his instruction and understood him marvelously.

So this old man Adrian and this young queen wandered through the desert without knowing where they were going. Realizing that he was completely lost and unable to find his cell, Adrian was understandably upset and said unhappily to himself, "What! Have I been fooled? Was my vision just an illusion? Oh no! Shall this young queen die here among the wild beasts? Help me, blessed lady, for I'm about to give up. I'm only thinking of this young lady, who so meekly left all she had to obey your command." Perceiving his distress, the young queen asked what was wrong. He replied, "Truly, lady, my fears are all for you, for on my life I can't find my cell; I don't know where I've brought you or what I should do. I just don't know!"

"Don't worry, father," she said, "for surely such a good lady would not have sent us to die in the desert. Father," she said, "what's that splendid minster over there?"

Adrian looked up and said, "Where?"

"Over there in the east," she said.

He wiped his eyes and saw the most glorious minster ever seen. Overjoyed at the sight, he said, "You are truly blessed, whom God has given such perfect faith, for there is the place where you will receive more honor and joy than anyone but the queen of all queens."

Chapter 7: How virgins and martyrs welcomed her and brought her to our lady, and how she was baptized

Walking quickly, they soon approached that glorious place. When they arrived at the gate, a glorious company of virgins with white garlands of lilies on their heads met them. Katherine and Adrian were so ravished with their beauty that they swooned in dread. Then the most excellent of the company said to the young queen, "Stand up, dear sister. We welcome you with all our hearts, for through your meekness and pure chastity our honor and joy will be greatly increased. Therefore, rejoice in our lord, for all virgins shall honor you. Come with us to that sovereign lord, who will perform marvelous works of love in you." They proceeded joyfully and solemnly to a second gate. When they passed through it, they were greeted by an even more glorious company—the incomparable company of martyrs, dressed in purple with red roses on their heads. When the young queen saw them, she fell down before them in terror and reverence, and they reassured her kindly, saying, "Don't be afraid, dear sister, for no one was ever more welcome to our sovereign lord than you are. Therefore, rejoice in our lord, for you shall receive our clothing and crown with such honor and joy that all the saints will rejoice in you. Come quickly, for the lord of joy awaits you eagerly."

Trembling with joy, this young queen humbly accompanied them, and she was so rapt with joy and wonder that she could not respond to anything that was said to her. When they entered the church, she heard a marvelous melody of indescribable sweetness and saw a splendid queen surrounded by a multitude of angels and saints. This queen's beauty and splendor were too great for the mind to think or the pen to write, for they surpassed human imagination. Then the martyrs and virgins who accompanied this young queen fell before the empress and with the utmost reverence said, "Most sovereign lady, queen of heaven, lady of the world, empress of hell, mother of our sovereign lord, the king of bliss, whose command is obeyed by all creatures in heaven and on earth: know, blessed lady, that at your command we present our dear sister, whose name has been so specially inscribed in the book of everlasting life. We beseech your most benign grace to receive her as your servant and chosen daughter and complete the work that you and our sovereign lord, almighty God, your blessed son, have so wonderfully begun in her."

With that, that glorious empress looked at them with gladness and respect and said, "Bring me my beloved daughter, so that I can speak with her." And when this young queen Katherine heard the most sovereign queen's words, she was so full of joy that she lay for a long time as if she were dead. Then this holy company raised her gently and brought her to the queen of bliss, who said to her, "Welcome, my dear daughter. Be strong and confident, for you have been chosen above all women to be honored with the love of my son. Katherine, daughter, do you remember how you described a husband when you were sitting in parliament, when you had to struggle so greatly to defend your virginity?"

Then this young queen, with the utmost reverence and dread, said, "Oh, most blessed lady, you are indeed blessed among all women. I remember how I chose a lord then who was far from my knowledge. But now, good lady, by his mighty mercy and your special grace, he has opened the eyes of my blind ignorance so that I perceive the clear path of truth. Therefore, most blessed lady, I ask with all my heart that you have mercy and grace and give me the one you have promised me, the one whom my heart loves and desires above everything, without whom I cannot live." With these words, her senses left her so suddenly that she lay as if she were dead.

This noble queen of grace reassured her with sweet words, saying, "Don't be afraid, dear daughter, for you shall have your wish. You lack only one thing that you must have before coming into the presence of my son, that is, you must be clothed with the sacrament of baptism. Therefore, come, for everything is ready." There was a font in the church, adorned with all the necessary provisions. Then this queen of joy summoned Adrian, the old father, and said to him, "Brother, this work is for you, a priest, to perform. Baptize my daughter, but don't change her name, for she will continue to be called Katherine. I myself will stand as her godmother." Then Adrian baptized her as our lady had commanded him.

Chapter 8: *How our lady led Katherine to her son and how she was espoused and married to him*

When this blessed Katherine had been baptized and clothed again as she should be, the glorious queen of heaven said to her, "My own daughter, be glad and joyful, for now you lack nothing that a heavenly spouse ought to have. Come with me now, for I shall bring you to my lord and son, who joyfully awaits you." Then this young queen Katherine was filled with inexpressible sweetness. She accompanied this queen of heaven to the choir, where an incomprehensible sweetness enveloped them. Then she saw the handsomest young king standing at the altar, crowned with a rich crown, and surrounded by a multitude of angels and saints. And when his blessed mother saw him, she prostrated herself before him and removed the crown from her head and said with the utmost reverence, "The highest honor and joy be yours, king of bliss, my lord, my God, and my son. If your holiness please, I have brought, according to your will, your humble servant and handmaid Katherine. For your love, she has forsaken all earthly wealth and has come here alone with old Adrian, at my bidding, forgetting all earthly possessions and rank and trusting entirely in my promise. Therefore I humbly beseech you, my sovereign lord God and dearest son: in your endless goodness, fulfill my promise."

When this sovereign king had heard his mother, he raised her graciously and said to her, "My dear mother, you know very well that your desire is my wish entirely, and I have desired her to be bound to me in marriage above all living virgins. Therefore, Katherine, come here." And when she heard him name her, she was consumed with such sweetness that she fell down before him as if she were dead. With that, he gave her a supernatural strength and said to her in a friendly fashion, "Katherine, daughter, can you find it in your heart to love me above everything?"

And she, seeing the beloved face that angels rejoice to see continually, said, "Oh, sweetest and most blessed lord, I have loved you, and I shall love and live for you alone the rest of my life."

Then this blessed king said, "Katherine, give me your hand." When she most joyfully did so, the glorious king said, "Here I take you as my wedded wife, promising never to forsake you as long as you live, and after your present life I shall bring you to everlasting life, where you shall live with me in endless bliss. As a token of this I put this ring upon your finger, a wedding ring for you to keep in remembrance of me. And now, my dear spouse, be glad and hardy, for you must do great things for my sake and suffer much torment and pain and a great stroke on your neck. But don't be afraid, my dear spouse, for I will never leave you but always comfort and strengthen you."

Then his humble spouse said, "Oh most blessed lord, I thank you for your great mercy with all my heart and beseech you, my sovereign lord, to make me worthy to join you, who suffered so much for me. If only I may be somewhat like you, whom my heart loves and desires above all else!"

Then this glorious king told Adrian to put on his vestments and conduct Mass, performing the wedding service in the usual manner. And that sovereign lord of bliss knelt before Adrian for the entire Mass, holding his spouse's hand. Oh lord, the joy and bliss that blessed virgin experienced in her soul was never experienced by anyone before or after, with the exception of the one who conceived that sovereign joy, namely, his most blessed mother. All the spirits of heaven rejoiced in this marriage, and to an unimaginably beautiful melody they sang "Sponsus amat sponsam, salvator visitat illam," that is, "The husband loves his wife, the savior visits her."[6]

Chapter 9: How our lord left her and she returned home and how she behaved in her palace

Because such a solemn and singular marriage had never taken place on earth, this glorious virgin deserves to be loved and honored more than any living virgin. At the end of Mass, the heavenly king said to her, "Now, my dear spouse, it is time for me to return from where I came. I have done your will, and I am ready to do whatever more you might ask of me. After my departure, you will stay here ten days, until you have been instructed perfectly in my laws and wishes. When you come home, you will find your mother dead, but don't worry, for during all this time you were not missed, for I put someone in your place whom everyone thought was you, and when you return, she will disappear. Farewell, now, my dearest spouse."

---

[6] A liturgical chant sung on Saint Katherine's feast.

With that, she cried out pitifully, "Oh, my sovereign lord God and my soul's delight, remember me!"

Then he blessed her and disappeared, and Katherine swooned in sorrow and lay a good hour without any sign of life. Adrian was then an unhappy man. It was indeed a pity to see and hear how he wept and cried over her! At last she awoke and opened her eyes and saw nothing around her but a small, old cell and Adrian weeping beside her. Everything that had been there before was gone—the minster and the palace, the comforting visions, and especially he who was the source of all her joy and comfort. Her heart was so sad that she could do nothing but weep and sigh until she saw the ring that our lord had placed on her finger. Then she swooned again and kissed it a hundred times with many a sad tear. And Adrian comforted her as best he could with many holy exhortations. She accepted his reassurances meekly, obeyed him as her father, and lived with him for the appointed time, until she learned all she needed to know.

When the time came, she returned to her palace, and as soon as she could, she had her entire household baptized. She governed her household and palace in a Christian manner for four years, and all her joy was to speak or think about her lord and husband; she thought of nothing other than his honor and praise. During this time, she converted many people to him. Never idle, she was ever charitable, and always happy to bring people to him. She governed the realm she inherited with great care, not because she craved sovereignty, but because she thought it would be a sin to keep her father's income to herself and to leave her people needy just because she had decided to have nothing to do with the world. Therefore, she kept just a little of her father's income and gave all the rest—along with his treasures—to the poor. She did not care for plays, or jokes, or idle words, or secular songs, but instead devoted herself entirely to the study of holy scripture. Moreover, she did so with great diligence, for since her childhood her father had set her to study the liberal arts, as related before, and she was too well taught to be deceived with specious arguments. Though many scholars tested her with clever questions and objections, they only proved her invincible and themselves fools. She diligently preserved the purity of her virginity, and so she lived in her father's palace full of the virtues and graces appropriate to the dear and special spouse of almighty God.

Chapter 10: Here begins the martyrdom of the most glorious virgin, Saint Katherine of Alexandria: first, how the emperor Maxentius was overcome by the emperor Constantine and came to Alexandria and ordered a solemn sacrifice in honor of his false gods

After the death of King Constance (Constantine's father, as mentioned in Chapter 1), some Roman knights chose Maximian's son Maxentius to be emperor. After his election, Maxentius ruled the empire with such cruelty that many knights and other people fled his jurisdiction to Constantine, who was then worthily and manfully governing England and France, as stated earlier. These knights and others urged Constantine to consider his own right to the empire and the wrongs done to them by the tyrant Maxentius. They thus incited him to action in both his own interest and theirs, holding out every expectation of good fortune should he do their will. At last Constantine assented. Arriving in Rome with a strong force, he expelled Maxentius and occupied the empire.

Maxentius fled Rome for the eastern parts of the empire and came to Alexandria. When he heard that Constantine, distracted by various wars, had ceased pursuing him, he was driven by a sudden madness to pursue Christ's Church and either entice or force Christians to practice the cursed rites of idolatry. Therefore, in the thirty-fifth year of his reign, he issued from the city of Alexandria a cruel decree to all the provinces that Christians should either sacrifice to his gods or suffer the most terrible death. And when everyone had gathered at his palace the next day, he sat in judgment and commanded everyone to come to the temple of his gods. When the priests had placed incense on the altars and the emperor had solemnly sacrificed to the gods, everybody else was to follow suit, each according to his means. The rich were to offer bulls and sheep, the poor live birds.

Then the emperor, in royal array, surrounded by a multitude of knights, offered one hundred and thirty bulls. After him, kings and princes and masters of knights, then mayors and provosts and other nobles, offered fair animals they thought would most please the tyrant. Those who could obtain no animals brought sparrows and other birds. Then the cacophony of animal voices resounded throughout the city, and the ground overflowed with sheep's blood. The earth—either in joy or in indignation—seemed to quake with the noise of songs and melodies.

Chapter 11: How Saint Katherine went to the temple and denounced the emperor for his illegal sacrifice

At the time, the blessed young queen Katherine was eighteen years old and lived in her palace, surrounded by wealth and servants. As she sat in her study, contemplating her dearest lord and truest spouse, she was surprised to hear the roar of animals and the din of trumpets and organs and many other noises. She sent a man to find the source of the racket, and when the messenger told her, she agonized over the disrespect being shown to her lord and spouse. Then she stood up and, forgetting her personal safety and worldly position, she gathered a few attendants and went to the temple. There she saw professed Christians weeping and wailing because they were being forced to perform cursed sacrifices to avoid being killed. Deeply offended, this holy maiden resolved to condemn that unlawful sacrifice with her noble authority and to denounce the tyrant's cruel ordinance. After pausing silently to pray and marking herself with the sign of the cross, she went boldly to where the emperor presided over that disgusting sacrifice.

The people who saw her marveled at her beauty. Many of them abandoned their sacrifice to follow her and watch. When she came to the emperor, she studied him gravely and said, "Reason and respect for your rank should make us salute you, oh emperor, if you served your creator rather than devils, if you realized that he alone is to be worshipped, by whom kings reign and princes are governed and through whom all things take their beginning and their being—who doesn't rejoice in the slaughter of animals, but rather in faith and adherence to his just commandments. Nothing offends him more than when man, a creature of reason, worships unreasoning creatures as gods and honors visible creatures as he should honor only God's invisible majesty. The inventor of evil, the devil, is never more cunning and deadly than when he incites us to give what we know we owe our creator to worldly elements like the sun and moon. You give these elements the names and honors of a god and worship them simply because they seem eternal. But truly, God made them all from nothing and set them in the world, where they endure only because of him. Therefore, they are not everlasting with God, because something created in time cannot coexist with its timeless maker. Only he who began all things is without beginning. Therefore divinity should not be attributed to things that are disposed of by God rather than by their own free will, things that exist only at God's pleasure.

There is only one God who has made everything alive and disposes of his creation as he pleases.

"Think of it this way, emperor: you're a man—and therefore mortal—and, as the sovereign of an earthly empire, you're placed above many thousands of men. If any of them—great or small—gave to another the honor they owed you and returned your favors by serving another, wouldn't you cast him down for wronging your earthly majesty and give his honors to someone more loyal and dedicated to your service?

"God's amazing patience should make you tremble with fear, for he's promoted you to such a lofty position, and you respond by offering to unreasoning creatures what you should dedicate to his majesty. Aren't you ashamed of your blindness? You wonder at this manmade temple and admire precious ornaments that will become no more than dust in the wind. If you were rational, you would marvel at the earth and seas and everything in them. You should be marveling at the ornaments of heaven—the sun and moon and stars. You should marvel at their obedience, how they cross the world, night and day, without tiring. And when you have contemplated this, you should wonder who was mighty enough to create it all. When through his power you have found him—and you can find nothing like him—then honor him alone and praise him, for he alone is God and he alone is king of kings and lord of lords and of all creatures."

Chapter 12: How the emperor answered, saying that the service done to his gods was good and commendable but that Christianity was useless and senseless

As Katherine spoke, the emperor stared at her clear complexion and listened to her grave words. At last he broke out, "Your claims, maiden, would be fine if they were only reasonable! We know that all the heathen sects, their rites, customs, and observances, are grounded in reason. The Roman princes, who surpass all mortals in devotion and righteousness, have subjected the whole world to heathen laws. It isn't unreasonable to observe the religious practices of so many lands and to follow our forebears as piously as they followed theirs.

"But your religion is so ridiculous that no one in his right mind adheres to it! What can be more outrageous than to say that Jesus, whom the Jews crucified, should be the son of God, conceived without sexual intercourse, born without rupturing the womb? Imagine that one betrayed by his disciple, hanged on the cross, and buried for three days should come to life and rise from the dead! These things are too silly to be believed by any intelligent person. And not satisfied with believing such foul errors, you stupidly presume to damn the sun and moon, our eternal gods, whose favors all mortals enjoy. We can't stop worshipping them as gods without giving great offense! What part of heaven is so far away, what country on earth is so isolated, that it doesn't worship the great god, the sun? What people are so strange that they don't duly honor heaven's moon?"

Chapter 13: How Saint Katherine answered, showing that there is only one God who governs all things

Smiling slightly, the maiden said to the tyrant, "It's obvious that all your arguments are erroneous, for you worship the sun and moon and other natural phenomena as if they were gods, never considering that divinity is not *in* them but rather far *above* them. Divinity is self-sufficient; it needs no help. God is the incorporeal and invisible and unchangeable being at whose command all the elements of the world serve their maker—just as he ordained them to do. And according to his command, for man's benefit, they give the air of life or of corruption to mortals. Therefore, there cannot be any divinity in them, for they act not according to their own will but according to the will of the one who made them. Consider the course of the sun and the phases of the moon and their daily rising and setting. When night falls, the sun ceases to shine; indeed, it doesn't even shine during the day when clouds block it. The moon waxes and wanes at the Creator's will. Consider, too, the various movements of the stars and the ebbing and flowing of the sea, which is calm in fair weather and troubled in storms. The earth is in turn softened with rain, hardened with frost, and dried with heat. When God looks at it, it quakes in recognition of his sovereignty. Evil exhalations corrupt the air, and when corruption increases, pestilence ensues. Prayer can overcome both deluge and drought. See, then, how the elements are guided by their creator and, through his grace, subject to man. These are the things you worship as god, without understanding that you're wronging their maker and yours, that you're inviting your own damnation unless you turn to the one, unchanging God, self-sufficient and unfailing, whose mighty divinity acts upon all things without ever being acted upon. Stop asserting things that can't be proved by reason." Then she told him about the incarnation and about the marvelous goodness of the son of God. And everyone who saw her wondered at her great wisdom and peerless beauty, for she seemed lovelier than any other living woman. Then the people who were being forced to sacrifice on pain of death took such comfort from her gravity and her ethereal beauty that they chose to die rather than forsake their faith.

Chapter 14: How the emperor had the virgin led to his palace and how he sent private letters summoning scholars to debate her; how she exposed his false gods

Astonished by her wisdom and eloquence, the emperor said, "If your words are any indication, had you been educated in the schools of our philosophers from your youth, no one would surpass you in wisdom—and, if that were the case, you would not deny our gods' divinity. Wait while we complete our sacrifice and accompany us to our palace. There you'll be honored with great gifts if you do our bidding."

After ordering Katherine closely guarded, the emperor privately dispatched a messenger with letters, sealed with his royal ring, ordering all the rhetoricians, grammarians, and scholars in neighboring countries to come to him immediately in Alexandria. He promised them great honor and a distinguished place in the imperial council if they could persuade this maiden that she was only hurting herself by blaspheming the gods. "It seems reasonable," he said, "that she first be shown up by the learning she's so proud of. If she still refuses to honor our gods, she shall be tortured to death." The messenger set out.

After the emperor had completed his detestable sacrifice, he had the virgin conducted to his palace. First he treated her politely, saying, "Tell me your name, virgin. I don't know your family or your teachers in the liberal arts, but your loveliness attests that you are descended from noble blood, and if you did not reprove our almighty gods, your wisdom would reflect well on your teachers."

The maiden answered the tyrant, "It is written that one should neither praise nor disparage oneself, for that is what pompous fools do. I will answer you not in pride but in meekness and honesty. My name is Katherine, daughter of King Costus. I was born and raised in purple and well educated in worldly knowledge, for I had excellent teachers and doctors of the liberal arts. But because I learned nothing from them that would lead me to everlasting life, I have put them out of mind and consigned them to silence. Later I was bathed in the light of a holier doctrine, and I left the darkness of erroneous teaching. I heard the blessed gospel of my lord Jesus Christ, to whom I have pledged myself as spouse and handmaid. His spirit inspired the prophet to cry out long ago, 'Perdam sapientiam sapientium et intellectum intelligentium reprobabo,' that is, 'I will confound the wisdom of the wise and challenge the understanding of those who understand.' I also heard that another prophet said, 'Our God is in heaven and he has made and done everything he wishes. The gold and silver idols of heathens are manmade. They have mouths but do not speak, eyes but do not see, ears but do not hear.' And the same prophet says, 'The heathen gods are devils.' If they aren't, you should show some evidence of their power, you who call these manmade things almighty gods and worship them prostrate in the street and urge me to worship them too! Though man's skill can form brass or wood or stone into the likeness of a living human being, it cannot make their mouths speak, eyes see, ears hear, hands feel, or anything else appropriate to a real human. It is a futile religion—indeed, an insanity—to worship things that can neither reward their worshippers nor avenge themselves against their offenders. In fact, they don't know they exist, since they're insensible matter; they can't rejoice at being shapely or recoil at being deformed. It doesn't matter to them whether they sit in a marble temple or lie in a dirty privy. What praiseworthy gods they are whose worship elicits no kindness and whose neglect provokes no anger! How blessed are the devotees of those gods: they are neither helped in their tribulation nor protected from perils!"

Then the emperor said, "If what you say is true, then all the rest of the world is mistaken. Yet all truths should be attested by two or three witnesses, not just one. Even if you were an angel or a heavenly virtue, you wouldn't be credible in and of yourself—so much the less so, since you're actually just a weak woman."

The holy virgin answered, "Please don't let anger and madness overcome you, emperor, for they have no place in the heart of a wise man. Indeed, the poet says, 'If you are governed by reason, you are a king; if you are governed by the flesh, you are a slave.' But I see that you want to ensnare us with venomous subtleties, which can neither help you nor hurt us. If you will only become a meek disciple of truth, I will teach you how you can know your God and maker and reign eternally, not just as a temporal king."

Chapter 15: How, when they arrived, the scholars blamed the emperor for putting them to such trouble for a mere girl

In the meantime, the king's messenger went though all the countries and returned to Alexandria with fifty men who claimed to surpass all mortals in worldly wisdom and in their knowledge of the liberal arts. When they were brought before the emperor, he began to ask about their learning and wisdom. They replied that in wisdom they reigned supreme. "But emperor," they said, "you should tell us why you had us leave our seats of learning and come here. What great and noble thing do you wish us to accomplish?"

He answered, "We have with us a maiden, young in years but well endowed with words and wit. She seems amazingly wise, for whoever argues with her is left speechless. Worst of all, she claims not only that worshiping our gods is vain but also that our gods themselves are devilish counterfeits. Of course, I could use my imperial power to compel her to sacrifice, or I could slay her with terrible torments, but it seems better to have you bring her to the path of reason by confounding her arguments and thoroughly embarrassing her. If she remains obstinate, I'll torture her to death. But if you can overcome her, I'll send you home with great gifts or, if you prefer, make you preeminent among my counselors."

Upon hearing the emperor's words, one of the scholars grew indignant and said bitterly, "Oh the great wisdom of an emperor! What wisdom to summon from such a distance the world's wisest men to contend with a girl, when one of our disciples would have sufficed for the task. There was no need to bother so many scholars on account of a single maiden! Well, whoever she is, bring her in, and she'll soon know that she's never seen or heard wisdom until this day!"

Chapter 16: How the holy maiden Saint Katherine, hearing that fifty great scholars had come to debate her, commended herself to God, and how the archangel Michael came to comfort her

In the meantime, the holy maiden who was to fight all alone against fifty opponents was in prison. When a messenger from the king's council told her about the battle she was to face the next day, Christ's holy servant was unperturbed. Fearlessly she commended her chivalrous undertaking to our lord, saying, "Oh dear Jesus, you promised the wisdom and power of almighty God the father when you comforted your knights, telling them neither to fear the world's tribulations nor to be troubled by their enemies' threats. On that occasion you said, 'Dum steteritis ante reges et presides' etc., that is, 'When you stand before kings and judges, don't worry about how you speak or what you say, for I will give you such wisdom that your adversaries will be left speechless.'[7] Dear lord, stay with me, your servant, and have me speak so that those who are gathered together to refute you do not prevail against me. Let them be overcome, let their wits grow so dull and so confounded by your word that they either keep quiet or convert and give glory to you, who alone are glorious, with the father and holy ghost forever. Amen."

Before the maiden had finished speaking, the angel of God appeared to her, illuminating the room with his marvelous brightness. The virgin was nearly overcome with awe. Then the angel said, "Don't be afraid, maiden of God. Proceed confidently and staunchly, for God, in whose honor you have engaged this battle, is with you. He will release from your mouth such a flood of eloquence that your enemies not only will capitulate but will be stunned into conversion. After receiving the crown of martyrdom, they will enter the gate of life and will encourage others through their example. Soon afterward, you will end your battle with a glorious death and be received among the illustrious company of virgins and joined forever to your immortal spouse. I am the archangel Michael, sent from God to tell you these tidings." When he had finished speaking, he left her. Through this, God's holy virgin took heart and awaited her summons to battle.

Chapter 17: How Saint Katherine and the scholars were brought before the emperor and began to debate

The emperor, acting in his royal capacity as judge, sent for the clerks and ordered that the maiden should also be brought before him. Signing herself with the cross, Katherine went fearlessly into the palace. People came from all over the city to hear the debate. On one side the scholars stood, swelled with pride; on the other side the maid stood, trusting in God. They scornfully noted her youth, and she quietly prayed for help.

[7] Matthew 10:18–29, Mark 13:11, Luke 12:11.

When the emperor complained that they were wasting the day in silence, the maiden said, "Emperor, you've arranged an uneven battle, pitting fifty great scholars against a girl. What's more, you've promised them kingly rewards in return for victory, but you've offered me nothing at all. I'm not worried about being cheated out of my reward, for the one in whose name I have entered this battlefield will be my reward, that is, my lord Jesus Christ, the hope and crown of all his soldiers. But I do ask for one thing, which you cannot rightly deny me: if I happen to win this conflict, honor and believe in my God immediately."

To this, the tyrant retorted, "You're in no position to make demands of me! My faith is none of your business! Do what you have to do, and we'll see if your God gives you victory."

Then the maiden turned to the scholars and said, "Since you are elders spurred by the promise of reward to debate here, and since all these people are waiting to hear, how shameful it would be to lose the crown of your profession by keeping silent. If any of you have eloquence and reason and the knowledge of Latin, speak!"

One who seemed to be older and more learned than the others answered, "You should speak first, since we undertook this exhausting journey on your account!"

She said, "As a young girl, after I had set aside the heathen error and became a Christian, I cast aside the pompous deceits that I see you ready to use against me. I've rejected Homer's philosophy and Aristotle's crafty subtleties, the discoveries of Aesculapius and Galen, and the famous books of Philistion, Plato, and other authors. And though I was so well informed in these things that I have yet to find my peer, I tell you they're all useless and far from true blessedness. I present myself to you as knowing only him who is true knowledge and everlasting life to true believers, that is, my lord Jesus Christ, who said through the prophet, 'I will confound the wisdom of the wise and challenge the understanding of those who understand.' He's the one who in previous generations revealed the way and the teachings of righteousness, thereby exciting his worshippers to pursue the rewards of eternal life. Grieving that mankind was denied the pleasures of paradise by the devil's deceits, he—that is, invisible God—took flesh and blood through a virgin. In so doing, he became visible and gave us his presence. Through the miracles he performed and the things he suffered on earth, he showed us that he was both true God and man. This is our God; this is my philosophy; he is my victory. In his name I will overcome all my adversaries, for it is just as easy for him to protect his followers from many enemies as from a few."

The virgin had barely finished speaking when one angry scholar burst out laughing. Filling the king's court with his blasphemies, he said, "Citizens of the most noble Roman Empire, how long will these Christians be allowed to wrong our gods with their presumption and folly? We are indeed ungrateful for the gifts our gods have given us if we allow this girl's errors and scorn to go unpunished. The emperor made such a big fuss about her by summoning us—the wise men of the earth—that we expected to hear something great. But no! She begins by speaking of that Jesus, whom Christian fables purport to be God! The one who was betrayed by a disciple and condemned to a death he could not escape! His disciples stole his body by night and lied to the people, saying he overcame death and rose on the third day. To crown their lies, they said he ascended into heaven!"

To this the virgin replied, "I certainly did begin by talking about the one who is the beginning of everything, the well and spring of all good, through whom God the father made this world from nothing as well as everything in it, including me and you. In short, he is the one of whom, by whom, and in whom are all things visible and invisible."

Then the scholar said, "If, as you claim, he's God—or God's son—how could he die? If he's a man, how could he *not* die? Nature and reason make it impossible for a mortal man to overcome death. We might grant that he could be God *or* man, but not both at once."

Chapter 18: How Saint Katherine proved that Christ is God and man, how he died in his manhood, not in his divinity, and why he preferred to redeem man himself than send an angel

The holy virgin answered, "I see that your strategy is to take apart what you don't believe in order to destroy the whole. You say that while he is God he cannot be man, as though it were impossible for almighty God who created everything from nothing to assume man's form so that he who is invisible might be seen and he who is immortal might die! If you will only distinguish the truth of God's law from the pride of false wisdom and become a disciple, you will understand his marvelous works and his power, and you won't despise the human weakness he assumed voluntarily. Though God's wealth surpasses human imagination, his majesty was most evident when, to call people to the true faith, he gave life to the dead and sight to the blind. Most amazing, he did not have to use witchcraft, but through sheer divine power he summoned the spirits of the dead back to their bodies; his mighty power alone cured lepers and enabled the lame to walk. If you don't believe that he did these things, I can assure you that others performed the same miracles in his name. If he weren't God, he couldn't give life to the dead; if he weren't man, he couldn't have died. Thus, the same Christ is both God who suffered death in his manhood and man who defeated death through his divinity. The same son of God, who in his divinity could not die, died in his manhood, and immortal God assumed that manhood. Thus God's son, Christ, who died in his body, rose because he never shed the immortality of his divinity. Death did not slay Christ, but rather Christ slew death within him. Therefore, our faith is not so poor and needy that it requires outside witnesses to defend it.

"If you're so far gone in your error that you doubt this, listen to how the foul spirits of fiends who you think are divine break down at the mere sound of God's name.[8] Not daring to deny Christ, the son of God, they're like thieves under torture, forced to speak the truth regardless of what they want. So if you deny our beliefs, at least believe your own gods; or deny—if you can do so without shame, you men—what the devils acknowledge. Since I've cited the vain sayings of demons, you'll accuse me of taking the changing words of fickle spirits as witnesses to my faith. I don't say these things because Christ *needs* the testimony of foul spirits, but because that testimony should not be taken lightly: were they not under invisible duress, those spirits would rather speak for than against themselves.

"I can't believe that such knowledgeable men as yourselves would not only deny that Christ is God but also consider his majesty tarnished through death. You know very well that books written by your own authors bear witness both to his divinity and to the cross you scorn. I'll cite two examples. You claim that Plato was the wisest and most knowledgeable of men, and when Plato speaks of Christ's worthy majesty, he says that a god would come whose sign would be known and wor-

[8] The extensive discussion of the spiritual authority of demons and of people possessed by demons may reflect what Barbara Newman characterizes as "a sudden upsurge of interest in demoniacs" in the later Middle Ages, in "Possessed by the Spirit: Devout Women, Demoniacs, and the Apostolic Life in the Thirteenth Century," *Speculum* 73 (1998): 733–70.

shipped everywhere.[9] The sayings of Sibyl, which you so esteem, associate his name with his divinity.[10] In them, she names both his divinity and the cross, saying, 'Felix ille deus ligno qui pendet ab alto,' that is, 'blessed is that god who hangs on high from the tree.' These testimonies clearly reveal that God will come and be seen as a man. Sibyl called him blessed because she foresaw his divine power in a man's frailty and his manhood's victory over death. These authorities aren't to be followed indiscriminately, though: a vision allowed them to speak this particular truth, not because heathens deserved to receive the prophecy of God, but so that your authors should attest that Christ is God and the son of God.

"I could cite many more examples. If Christ's miracles don't incline you to believe, at least pay attention to the involuntary confession of the fiends. And if you don't believe them, at least trust your own authors! And you shouldn't blame me for proving Christianity's truth through your own authorities or the testimony of the devils you worship as gods. I could give you a thousand examples of testimony from holy scripture, but victory is more convincing when an adversary is caught in his own traps and overcome by the testimony of his own authors. Besides, as unbelievers you will set little store by the testimony of scripture and saints.

"There now: I've defended myself through my faith. If your gods have ears and hear me speak, let them stop me if they can. Otherwise, you speak for them and I'll answer."

Then the scholar replied, "If God in his manhood did the miracles you claim he did, why should he have suffered the humiliation of the cross? Why didn't he escape death, since he was saving others from death? How could he help others if he couldn't help himself? By saving himself, he would have given others the hope of salvation."

The maiden replied, "You're mistaken here, too, in that you think that God in his divinity suffered the agony of death through crucifixion.

---

[9] Late antique and medieval theologians read Plato, in particular *Timaeus*, as prefiguring Christian concepts of Christ, the Trinity, and so on.

[10] Sibyls were ancient Greek, Roman, or Jewish seers. Beginning around the end of the second century, Christians reinterpreted or revised their prophecies to contain references to Christ. The allusion here is to the so-called Tiburtine Sibyl, whose pronouncement is quoted in Jacobus de Voragine's *Golden Legend* 2:170.

The fragile manhood God assumed—not his divinity—endured the wrong of crucifixion. God, who is free from all suffering, could never suffer or be restrained except in triumphing over the devil by the manhood he assumed when he put his flesh upon the tree. As a man, without harming his divinity, he overcame the offense against God that had brought man to sin. Thus man, not God, was nailed to the cross, and he who sinned through the tree was nailed to the tree. This is the chief reason God became man: so that the sin done by man should be undone by man and so that the promise of resurrection should begin with him who most deserves to rise. If he'd wanted to, God could have overthrown the devil and delivered man through an angel or by some other heavenly means. But God, who always acts rationally, arranged it so that he who overcame man should be overcome by man."

Chapter 19: How all the scholars, astonished by her words, accepted Christianity and suffered martyrdom by fire

The virgin's words stunned the scholar. Indeed, all the scholars were so disturbed and embarrassed by the raw power of God that, not knowing what to respond, they looked at one another silently. Then the indignant emperor raged at them, "What imbeciles you are! Has a woman's power tamed you and turned you into weaklings? Wouldn't it have been degrading enough if fifty women—or more—had outargued one of you? But now—what humiliation—fifty scholars chosen from the farthest reaches of the world have been stunned into silence by the words of a single girl!"

Then one of them, whom the others called master and leader, answered the tyrant: "I tell you one thing, emperor: all the scholars of the East can attest that until this day there was no one bold enough to debate us with words and worldly wisdom. And if anyone presumed to challenge us, he was scotched and sent on his way in disgrace. But this maiden tells the truth because no living person speaks in her but rather the spirit of God, which has left us so stunned that we can say nothing against the Christ she speaks of. As soon as we heard her speak the name of Christ and the power of his divinity and the mystery of his cross, our stomachs churned and our hearts throbbed and our wits left us. Lord emperor, we won't prevaricate: unless you show us a more stable religion than the one we followed up to now, we are converted to Christ. We acknowledge that he is the true God, who gives so many great benefits to mortals, just as this maiden has said."

When the tyrant heard this, he flew into a frenzy. He made a great fire in the middle of the city and ordered the scholars bound hand and foot and burned to death in the painful flames. As they were being taken to the fire, one of them said to the others, "My companions and knights, what shall we do? God has taken pity on us and called us to his grace after our long lives of error; now we aren't dying ignorant of his holy name and faith. Shouldn't we be renewed in the holy well of baptism before our death?"

When he had said this, the others all entreated the holy virgin that they might be baptized. She answered, "Don't be afraid, strong knights of Christ. Be firm in your faith and don't worry about baptism, for the shedding of your blood will count as a worthy baptism; the fire of your martyrdom will bring you to the comforting fire of the holy ghost."

Then the servants came and, at the emperor's command, bound God's holy martyrs hand and foot and cast them into the fire. Amidst the flames, they made the sign of the cross on themselves and acknowledged Christ and his faith. So they were crowned with holy martyrdom on the thirteenth of November, and Christians took their bodies and buried them with great devotion. And this wonderful miracle occurred: the fire harmed neither the martyrs' clothes nor the hair on their heads. Their faces shone bright as roses; indeed, you would think they were asleep rather than dead. Through this miracle many were converted to Christianity and then were martyred and went to heaven.

Chapter 20: How the emperor tried to overcome the maiden by fair promises, all of which she refused and proved despicable by force of reason

When the tyrant saw that the holy virgin was persevering in her faith, undaunted by flames or threats, he made fine promises to entice her to perform the unlawful sacrifice. He said, "Oh most gentle and beautiful maiden, worthy of being decked in imperial purple, consider how sorry I am for you and how worried I am about your welfare. I'm devastated that you not only scorn to worship our immortal gods but also claim that the malice of unclean spirits is within them, using subtle tricks to lead worshippers to hell. You need to abandon your presumption, lest the gods, who have been patient for a long time, avenge themselves by tormenting you as you deserve! Consider your youth and sacrifice to the gods. If you do, you'll rank second only to our wife the queen in the palace. You'll be able to determine all the affairs of our realm. People you consider worthy of honor will be decked with royal favor, and people you don't will have to remain dishonorably in their houses. You can bring into and exclude from my kingdom whomever you wish. The queen will differ from you in just one respect: the lawful knot of matrimony will not be severed. But in all policies and precepts, you will be prince and governor.

"What's more, I'll have a statue of you bearing a queen's scepter set up in the middle of the city to be honored by everyone. Whoever passes it without honoring it will be guilty of treason. Anyone guilty of an offense—no matter how great—will be forgiven if he venerates it. And to make you still more hallowed, I'll make you a marble temple among the goddesses."

The virgin smiled a little and said to the tyrant, "How blessed I must be to deserve a statue in my honor! Now, how blessed would I have to be to be made of gold? Not that I would be badly served if I were made of silver. But, my, how the jewelers will fight over my price, weight, and value!

"Let's suppose that it's done, though: I get made of metal or marble and am honored by everyone who passes. May I ask, emperor, what wonderful substance will give my likeness life and understanding, so that the eyes can see, the ears hear, the tongue speak, and the other parts function appropriately? After all, if I can't appreciate the honors being heaped upon me, what will I care whether the image is shaped like a fair woman or a foul ape? You say, 'What a noble memorial you will have, when people see the image and say, "This is that noble virgin Katherine, who by abandoning her God has so blessedly kept her memory alive forever." ' But how blessed will I be when scoundrels honor me with irreverent jingles? And even if the emperor's threats scare off the scoundrels and make people respect me, who will scare away the birds, when the buzzard and crow land on me and shit on my face? What about the children, who don't know any better? Won't they soil me with their pranks? What about the dogs who come and piss on my image? My, what honor and beauty and privileges the emperor promises me for abandoning Christ and worshipping devils!

"What do you say, emperor? Will this statue be set up during my life or afterward? If during my life, will it make my time happier, my life longer, or my health better? Will it make me a smarter, better person? And if that fine image is set up after my death, will it keep my body from rotting and being eaten by worms? And what heavenly reward will my soul receive for this fair image? Will it be kept in a special region of heaven to receive the immortal rewards of eternity?

"Hush, emperor! Stop talking about things that are sinful to think about. You're foolish to invest so much effort where you cannot profit! Christ has chosen me for his spouse and I have married myself to him with a knot that shall never be undone. He is my happiness, my nobility, my love, my sweetness, and my delight. Now that I am bound to him, neither pleasure nor pain can drive me from his faith and love."

Chapter 21: How the holy virgin prophesied that many of the emperor's own household would convert to Christ, and how he had her beaten with iron scourges

Then the emperor Maxentius said, "I intended to give you some sound advice, thinking of your youth. Now I see you're so stubborn that you not only despise the honors I offer but also care nothing for your physical well-being. Since that's the case, I'll give you a more straightforward, starker, choice: sacrifice to the gods or suffer a cruel death."

The maiden answered, "Since, for my sake, the king of heaven himself, my lord, did not try to escape being tempted by the devil, seized by the Jews, and condemned to death by a wicked judge, it is appropriate that I suffer not only pain but also death, if I must. Since he offered himself as a sacrifice to God the father for me, I am delighted to be able to offer myself to him. You rejoice in your power over me and over other servants of God. Well, sometime soon when the devil claims his mastery over you, you'll endure forever the torments you now inflict on Christ's servants. But I will please Christ all the more for having suffered so many torments in his name. You're trying to condemn me alone with your unjust sentence, but I'll have you know that I won't go to Christ alone, for throughout your palace many, many people have given themselves to Christ."

Then the tyrant went crazy with anger. He told his servants to seize the blessed virgin, pull off her clothes, beat her with cruel scourges, and lock her up in a dark prison. When the virgin was led forward, she said to the tyrant, "I'm happy to be scourged and to suffer the horror of a dark prison in the name of him who let his body be scourged for me, who, though he held the whole world in his hand, let himself be enclosed in the narrow cloister of the virgin's womb. You cast me into darkness now, but I'll have you know that everlasting light has been ordained for me, and eternal darkness for you."

Then the torturers ripped Katherine's tender body with iron scourges, beating her most cruelly. And when some grew tired, others joined in to help. But despite the beatings, the virgin never ceased praising and thanking God. When the tyrant asked whether she was ready to obey his orders and stop the pain, the holy virgin, being stronger than they who beat her and better than he who ordered her beating, answered gravely, "You shameless dog! Do whatever your most wicked heart can devise. Through pain, I offer myself to the one who through pain redeemed me. Thanks to these torments, you will someday see me in eternal bliss, while you, in everlasting torment, will regret that you ever did such things and that you ever had power over me or over other servants of Christ."

Chapter 22: How Saint Katherine was put in a dark prison for twelve days without food or drink; how she was comforted by angels; and how the emperor's wife was inspired to visit her

At the emperor's command, the virgin was imprisoned for twelve days in a pitch-dark cell without food and drink and light. But Christ did not fail his servant, for angels comforted her, illuminating the darkness with such light that the jailers grew frightened. Yet none of them dared tell the emperor, for fear of his rage.

It happened that business called the tyrant away to distant parts of his realm. While he was gone, the queen was told about her husband's cruelty. She learned how he had made Katherine debate the scholars, and how they, overcome by the maiden's words, had converted to Christianity and left this world through a glorious martyrdom. She learned how her angry husband had had the virgin beaten for refusing to sacrifice to the gods and how he kept her under strict guard, without food or drink, in a dark prison.

Though a heathen, the queen was so kindhearted that she pitied the girl who was so cruelly treated by her husband's maniacal dictates. She was anxious to see and speak to the virgin, but she was afraid that her husband would find out. Pondering the dilemma, she paced the king's hall alone and—what good fortune!—happened upon that prince of chivalry, a certain Porphirius, a noble man, by worldly standards, and a prudent one, too, who gave good advice and knew how to keep a secret. The queen called him over and confided her desires, asking him either to get rid of the prison guards or to bribe them so that she could see and speak to the virgin. "Porphirius," she said, "I'll tell you what's on my mind. A vision tonight has revealed amazing things to me. Whether for good or ill, I know what I saw will come to pass. I saw this maid we're talking about sitting in a house, bathed in unspeakable light and attended by men dressed in white whose faces were so bright I couldn't even look at them. Porphirius, I want you to find some means for me to see this maiden."

Porphirius answered, "Lady empress, I'm yours to command, and I'm ready to undertake this assignment, even though I know that, if the emperor finds out, I won't escape his anger. He's treated the maiden you speak of most cruelly. I was there when he summoned wise men from the farthest ends of the world to debate her, promising great gifts if they should defeat her. And despite those promises they failed, and within the hour were publicly proclaiming this maiden's God. Then the emperor became indignant and had them burned. I myself saw that, miraculously, the fire harmed neither the hair on their heads nor the threads of their clothing. I admit, queen, that from that day forward, the maiden's reproof of our gods has stirred my heart, convincing me that all our religious observances are vain and useless. Were Christianity not illegal, I might easily have been converted. And now, since you are of the same mind, I think we should go and bribe the jailers to keep our secret."

Chapter 23: How the empress and Porphirius visited Katherine in prison and were converted to Christianity; and how Porphirius then converted all his knights

Without any delay, Porphirius got the guards to agree, and in the first watch of the night, the queen and he went to the prison. When they entered, they were prostrated by an unimaginable and unspeakable sweetness which permeated the cell. Then the holy maiden said to them, "Arise and don't be afraid, for Christ calls you to receive a royal reward."

They arose and saw the maiden sitting while angels of God anointed her wounds and bruises with a sweet ointment that made her flesh wonderfully fair. They also saw elders sitting around her, whose faces shone with an unspeakably fair light. Then Christ's virgin took from one of them beside her a shining gold crown. Placing it on the queen's head, she said to the elders, "This is my lord's queen, whom I told you about—the one I asked God to allow into our knighthood and crown as my companion. The knight with her will also have been written among our number."

They replied, "Oh precious pearl of Christ, he for whom you are willing to endure beating and horrible imprisonment has heard your prayers. What's more, he has promised to help anyone on whose behalf you entreat his majesty. These visitors are written among the first fruits of your labor, for the kingdom of heaven shall receive them, crowned with victorious martyrdom, even before you. Then, after you have done chivalrous battle, your immortal spouse will take you into the gates of eternity, where the sweetest notes of heavenly organs will greet you, and where the purest company of virgins, shining among the lilies and carrying roses, follow the lamb wherever he goes."

Then the holy virgin began to comfort the queen, saying, "Now, queen, be brave, for in three days you'll join God. Don't dread the short pains of this life, for all the pains and agonies that can be endured on earth for Christ's love can't match the eternal happiness they will buy you. Don't be afraid of the temporal king, your mortal husband, who revels in his power today but will be filth and worms tomorrow. I tell you, don't be afraid of rejecting his company for the everlasting king and immortal spouse, our lord Jesus Christ, who will repay you with endless rewards. In exchange for ephemeral goods, he will give you eternal goods."

Hearing these words, Porphirius—who, thanks to the emperor's favor, had acquired many earthly goods—asked how exactly Christ would repay his knights for giving up their temporal wealth. "Listen carefully, Porphirius," the maiden replied. "No mortal man—no matter how rich, how healthy, or how important he may be—will enjoy his current situation forever. Think of how short life is. See how easily worldly riches laboriously accumulated over a long time slip away. What are lawsuits and battles about, if not the seizing and withholding of property? Are cities now of the same quality as they were when they were built? Now consider the rewards Christ gives his servants in exchange for these transitory things. If fleeting, failing, worldly things should be desired, shouldn't durable, heavenly things be desired all the more? After all, unlike the worldly things we cannot keep, these heavenly things, once obtained, can never be lost. This world is like a dark prison, where no one who is born can escape death. That heavenly land for which men despise the world is like a city that needs no sun, that is never troubled by adversity, need, sadness, or unrest, but remains forever happy. You wonder what's there. There is such great happiness that I can only say that good is where it is and evil is where it is not. You ask, what good? The good that has never been seen or heard or even imagined by man, the good that God ordained for those who love him. A rich person desiring this bliss once said, 'How long, lord God, will you keep me in this prison? How long will you keep the soul imprisoned by flesh? How much longer will I live here?' In the land that person desires, there is no wailing or crying or sorrowing, for God wipes all tears from the eyes of his holy servants. One of his chosen says, 'I will be fulfilled when your glory and happiness are revealed.' But what I say is nothing compared to what you will experience if you persevere to the end."

Then the queen and Porphirius, rejoicing at the sight of the angels and the words of the blessed virgin, left the prison, ready to suffer in Christ's name whatever the mad tormentor inflicted upon them.

Porphirius's knights asked where he had been with the queen. Porphirius replied, "Never mind about that, but whoever takes my advice will profit greatly, for I've been in the presence of heavenly, not earthly, things. I've found out how to live and have received knowledge of God himself. Therefore, if you're my knights and wish to share my joy, forsake the vain gods that we've worshipped up to now, and worship the one God who created everything, including us. He is lord and God of the entire world. The entire world at his command, he rewards the faithful with unending happiness and damns unbelievers to unending torment. This lord God, who so long tolerated our error, has revealed himself to us through the blessed Katherine, whom the emperor Maxentius in his madness has locked in prison."

More than two hundred knights heard Porphirius's words. All of them immediately forsook their vain idols and converted to Christianity.

Chapter 24: How for seven days a white dove fed Saint Katherine in prison and our lord Jesus Christ appeared to her with a multitude of virgins; how she prophesied the emperor's death and comforted those who grieved when she was tormented

In the meantime, Christ's holy maiden was kept in prison by the emperor's command. And because the tyrant ordered that she should remain without food or drink for twelve days, he who fed the prophet Daniel in the lion pit kept feeding this innocent maiden with a dove sent from heaven. After twelve days, our lord Jesus Christ appeared to her, followed by a multitude of angels and an innumerable company of virgins. Our lord said to her, "Know your creator, daughter, in whose name you have entered this arduous battle. Stand firm and don't be afraid; I am with you and will not leave you. Not a few people will believe and worship me on your account!" Having said this, he returned to heaven. The maiden gazed after him for a long time.

When the emperor had dealt with the affairs that had taken him out of town, he returned to Alexandria. The next day, he sat on his throne, surrounded by his princes and lords, and ordered his servants, "Fetch that presumptuous fool, so that we will find out whether hunger has inclined her to worship our gods!" But when Katherine stood before him, her face, which he had expected to be discolored from so many days of starvation, was brighter and more beautiful than ever. Concluding that someone had slipped her food and drink, he was gripped with fury. He ordered the guards tortured unless they told who had sustained the maiden in prison.

Christ's holy maiden, seeing that the innocent guards were about to be tortured, was forced to reveal what she would have preferred to keep secret: "Emperor, your office authorizes you to punish the guilty, not torture the innocent! It's clear that you're not worthy to be a judge, since you illegally order innocent people harmed. Nobody has given me food, but he who will not abandon his knights to hunger and tribulation has had his angel sustain his handmaid with spiritual food. He is my God, my lover, my father, and my only husband."

Worried that he might be accused of wickedness and injustice, he replied, "I'm sorry to see that you who are born of kings' blood should be so depraved by witchcraft and so untrue to your noble progenitors that you not only abhor the worship of our immortal gods but also denounce them with insults, deceiving people into believing that they're unclean spirits. Still, I'd rather save than kill you, so tell me what you've decided during the reprieve we gave you. You have two choices: sacrifice to our gods and live, or have your tender body tortured to death."

Katherine answered calmly, "I desire to live only for Christ. Therefore, I'm not afraid to die for him; indeed, I welcome the opportunity, for I trust that by dying for him I will win eternal life. Even if you rip me to pieces with torture, my lord Jesus Christ will replace my mortal body with an immortal body. And though nature allows you to abuse my body and put me to death, you have no power over my soul. All you can do by destroying my body is set my soul free to seek its maker. Don't delay, tyrant: bring on all the awful torture machines you can devise! My lord Jesus calls me, and I long to offer him not roaring bulls, not innocent sheep, but my own body and blood in sacrifice. After all, he offered himself to God the father for my sake.

"Nonetheless, I'll tell you one thing—and I speak the truth: the day of retribution will not be long in coming. My lord Jesus Christ will raise up against you an adversary who upholds the faith you impugn. With his wrathful sword, he will strike your cursed head from your detestable body. And your gods, the devils of hell, will enjoy the sacrifice of your most sinful blood. You can escape this judgment if you listen to my advice: abandon your vain idols and accept the Christian faith."

At these words, the tyrant gnashed his teeth and roared like a lion: "Why are we putting up with these outrages? How long will we allow this witch to slander our gods? We should have her body torn limb from limb as an example to other Christians who might presume to blaspheme against our gods. Everyone who ought to abhor the insults to our gods, take this witch and torture her to death! Let her get the God she so boasts of to help her!"

As the holy maiden was taken off to be tortured, some regretted that such a beautiful virgin should suffer such an unworthy death. They urged her to obey the emperor and avoid dying at the peak of her youth. "Oh," they said, "what virginal beauty, what radiant whiteness! What obstinacy could drive such a noble maiden to choose a quick death over wealth and honor? Oh most worthy virgin, consider your blossoming youth, and don't let your beauty die a sudden death."

The worthy maiden replied, "Stop your weeping and wailing and complaints! The body you think is blossoming is like a blade of grass, which wilts and fades as soon as the spirit is gone. Eaten by worms, it becomes the dust it came from. Therefore, don't cry over my death, for this punishment does not mean my death but rather my life—my passage to bliss! Save your wailing and sorrow for yourselves, for eternal damnation rather than salvation awaits you." Some of them were moved to reject the worship of idols and the emperor's friendship—but not openly, for they feared the emperor. These people were very curious to see how the virgin's passion should end.

Chapter 25: How four painful wheels devised to slay Saint Katherine were smashed to pieces by an angel of God, killing four thousand heathens

In the meantime, Cursates, the mayor of the city, came to the emperor. Seeing him so angry, he egged Maxentius on to new levels of madness in his zeal to heap torments upon torments. He said, "Oh great emperor, aren't you ashamed to be spending so much time on an obstinate woman? Lord emperor, Katherine hasn't yet seen a torment frightening enough to make her do your will and sacrifice to our great gods. Over the next three days, have four great wheels made according to my specifications. Have both the outer and inner circles of each wheel lined with sharp, hooked nails and the spokes set thickly with sharp saws. The horror of these turning wheels will scare her into honoring our gods to save her life. Otherwise, she will be cast into that dreadful machine and torn to pieces by hooks on the one side and saws on the other. Then she'll be killed by a sword, an example to terrorize all Christians."

The tyrant lost no time in ordering the construction of the wheels. On the third day, the tyrant called for the awful machine and ordered the maiden bound among the wheels so that her tender body would be completely torn if she did not do his will. The wheels were brought forth and set in the middle of the court, striking dread into all who saw them. The wheels were arranged so that two turned in one direction and the other two in the opposite direction; thus, some were tearing downward and the others upward. Christ's maiden was to be set amidst them so that the rotating saws and hooks would rip her limb from limb and bring her to an amazingly painful death. Seeing all this, Christ's maiden raised her eyes to heaven and prayed silently to God, saying, "Almighty God, you never fail those who call on you in peril and distress; hear me, lord, crying out in need. Let a stroke of heavenly thunder and lightning destroy this excruciating machine so that all around can see your raw power and worship your holy name, blessed forever. Lord, you know that I'm not asking this because I fear pain; you know that no matter how I die, I long to come to you. But those around me will take heart from your help and be more resolved to acknowledge your holy name." She hadn't finished speaking when an angel of God, descending from heaven, struck the machine with such force that the wheels broke and their fragments fell on the people so hard that they killed four thousand heathens at once. What more is there to say? The heathens were devastated, the Christians overjoyed. The tyrant gnashed his teeth and agonized over what to do.

Chapter 26: How the empress came and rebuked the emperor; he ordered her teats torn from her breasts and her head struck off

All this time, the queen was above, watching the marvelous signs of God's vengeance. Though fear of her husband had made her discreet up to this point, she now boldly made her way into that wild beast's presence and said, "Wretched man! How much longer are you going to fight God? What madness incites you to wage war on your maker? Do you really think you'll triumph in your battle against God and his servants? This deed should at least make you acknowledge how powerful the Christian God is and realize how mightily he shall damn you, given that he has just slain so many thousands with a single stroke. As you can hear, many—heathen and others—having seen the great marvels of God, have turned to Christ, proclaiming, 'How great is the Christian God! From this day on, we will become his servants, for your gods are just vain idols who can help neither themselves nor their worshippers.' "

When the tyrant heard this, he railed at everyone, especially the empress. "What are you saying, queen?" he demanded. "Has some Christian bewitched you into forsaking our almighty gods, the gods by whom we rule this empire? What evil chance has overtaken me, that while I make others honor the gods, the deadly venom of deceit has crept far enough into my own home to poison the only companion of my bed? Yet if the fondness of marriage were to keep me from punishing this crime, I would be insulting our gods. Besides, other Roman matrons would surely follow your example and persuade their husbands to abandon the gods. Our entire kingdom would bow to the lies and follies of Christians. Therefore, queen, I swear by our gods' great empire, unless you come to your senses and sacrifice to our gods, I will have your head struck from your neck and throw your body out to be mangled and eaten by animals and birds. And don't expect to enjoy a quick death, for I'll prolong your agony by tearing off your teats!"

Then the cruel tyrant told his servants to take the queen and tear the teats from her breasts with iron hooks. And when they led the queen away to be tortured, she looked at the blessed Katherine and said, "Most venerable virgin of Christ, pray for me to the God for whose sake I've engaged this battle. Ask him to strengthen me so that in the heat of torture my frail flesh won't cause my heart to fail. Don't let fear make me lose the crown you told me that Christ has promised his knights!"

The precious virgin answered, "Don't be afraid, honorable and beloved queen. Be bold, for this day you'll exchange an earthly kingdom for an everlasting one, an earthly husband for an everlasting spouse. Today, for a little pain you will receive endless rest, for a brief death eternal life."

These words strengthened the queen's resolve and she urged the tormenters to carry out the tyrant's sentence without delay. They led her outside the city and attached iron hooks to her royal teats. Suspending her in the air, they cruelly tore her teats from her breasts. Then they cut off her head. Thus, with blessed martyrdom she went to God on Wednesday, November 23.

Chapter 27: How Porphirius buried the empress's body and the following day was martyred with all his knights

That same night, Porphirius, accompanied by some trusted companions, took the queen's body, anointed it with sweet spices and ointments, and buried it. The next day, an interrogation was undertaken to find out who had taken the queen's body away. When he saw that many people were going to be tortured in the process, Porphirius manfully confronted the emperor, saying, "What are you doing, emperor? Why have you ordered innocent men punished as if they had committed sacrilege? If nature had taught you that human bodies should be kept from animals and birds, you would be defending these people! You are clearly possessed by a mad spirit in not granting burials to human corpses. But rather than let the innocent perish if you find them guilty of burying Christ's martyr, I'll tell you—damn me, if you dare, for I don't fear your condemnation—that I defied you by burying Christ's servant. Moreover, I profess and acknowledge Christ."

As if pierced with a deep wound, the tyrant roared so loudly that his voice resounded through the palace. He said, "Oh me, wretched me, most wretched of all people! Why did Mother Nature give me life only to take away everything I need to govern? Porphirius, guardian of my life, solace of my labor, my special helper—he brought me relief from care and toil. What fiendish temptation led him to deceive me and despise our religion? It's as if he's gone out of his mind: he proclaims that Jesus, whom the crazy Christians worship as God! He must have been the one who deceived the queen into betraying her love and her gods. We need look no further for the mischief maker who instilled such craziness in our queen. But even though he lost us our wife, that wrong can't be un-done. I would rather that he abandon his folly, return to the gods, and be my friend, as before, than suffer a harsh sentence." Having said this, he ordered Porphirius's knights brought before him, and taking them aside, he asked how Porphirius was converted. They answered with one voice that they were themselves Christians and that no fear of death would make them abandon Christ's faith or Porphirius's friendship. Hoping to undermine their resolve, the tyrant ordered them tortured. But when Porphirius saw them brought to the place of torture, he wor-ried that the fear of pain would shake them and said to the tyrant, "What do you mean, tyrant, by sparing me, their prince and head, and pursu-ing those who are only my limbs? Unless you defeat me first, you're wast-ing your efforts on them. If you have anything to ask them, I'm here to answer for them." The tyrant answered, "As you say, you're their head and prince. Therefore, you should be their example. Either be the first to reject this folly and live gloriously with us or be the first to have your head struck off." He immediately ordered that Porphirius and all his knights should be taken outside the city and beheaded; their bodies were to be left unburied, to be eaten by dogs. So it was done. Their mar-tyrdom took place on Thursday, November 24.

Chapter 28: How judgment was passed on Saint Katherine and how she comforted virgins and matrons who grieved for her death; how she asked God to help all who honor her; how after her beheading milk flowed instead of blood; how she was buried at Mount Sinai

The next day, the ravenous tyrant, who had still not killed enough Christians, sat in ceremony and ordered the holy virgin brought before him. He said, "Though you are guilty of the deaths of all those you corrupted with witchcraft, if you renounce your error and sacrifice to our almighty gods, you may still live and reign with us in joy and bliss and be called the first and worthiest of our realm. Therefore, don't delay, but choose one of these two things: either sacrifice, or your head will be struck from your neck today and displayed as a pitiful spectacle to all who see it."

The virgin answered, "It's no pitiful spectacle when such a glorious rising follows a fall, when immortality follows death, when everlasting pleasure follows sadness, and when endless joy follows a little suffering. Therefore, I don't want to keep you from your purpose. You'll see me ready to suffer anything you inflict on me and thereby deserve to see my king and to be among the choirs of virgins who follow the lamb at the gate of the celestial city."

On her way to the place of execution, she saw a great crowd of men and women following her and weeping, the virgins and noble matrons crying hardest of all. The holy virgin turned to them and said, "Oh gentle matrons and most pure virgins, don't lament my passion. Instead of pitying me, rejoice with me, for I see Christ, the honor of saints and crown of virgins, beckoning me. Save your weeping for yourselves, so that your last day won't find you in the heathen error that will condemn you to eternal sorrow."

After saying this, she asked her executioner to allow her space and time to pray. When he agreed, she raised her eyes to heaven and said, "Oh Jesus, honor and health of all believers, hope and joy of virgins, thank you for numbering me among your handmaidens. I beg you this mercy: help all those who remember my passion when they worship and praise you—whether it be at the point of death or in some other anguish. Let disease and starvation and tempests and all other bad weather flee far from them. Let the air of their countries be fresh, the harvests plentiful. Oh lord Jesus Christ, my battle is over and I await my executioner. Let him not take my soul but rather order it carried by the hands of holy angels to the seat of eternal rest, to be nurtured with the other holy virgins."

She hadn't finished speaking when a voice resounded from a high cloud, saying, "Come my love, my fair one, my spouse. Look—the gate of bliss is open before you and the home of everlasting rest awaits your arrival. The choir of virgins and saints comes to welcome you with joyful hearts, bearing the crown of honor, your reward. Come, then, and don't worry about your requests. Those who devoutly honor your passion and call on you in their needs and troubles will receive, I promise, prompt relief from heaven."

After the voice had spoken, Christ's virgin stretched out her fair and precious neck and said to the executioner, "My lord Jesus Christ calls me. Don't be slow in fulfilling the tyrant's command." He immediately struck off her head.

At that, two memorable wonders occurred. First, in testimony of her virginal purity, milk rather than blood flowed from her neck onto the earth. Second, angels lifted her body into the air and carried it to Mount Sinai—more than a twenty-day journey from there—and gave it an honorable burial.

Not long afterward, the tyrant Maxentius was killed in battle with the emperor Constantine, just as the holy virgin Saint Katherine had predicted.

Chapter 29: How her body was discovered a hundred years after her burial; concerning the oil that flows from her tomb

After this most glorious virgin's holy body was carried away by angels and buried on Mount Sinai, the place of her burial was concealed from Christians for one hundred and thirty years. Then, when our lord wanted to show his abundant mercy, he revealed it in this way. In the desert surrounding Mount Sinai, there lived many Christian hermits who were consumed with devotion for Katherine. Together they established a chapel for the continual worship of that holy virgin spouse of Jesus Christ. This chapel, by God's providence, was not far from where the bush grew in which God had appeared to Moses.[11] These holy hermits lived a life of great abstinence and devotion in that chapel. Therefore, the angel of God appeared to them, saying, "God has watched your devotion from heaven and has decided to allow you the privilege of finding, to his great honor, the holy body of the glorious virgin Saint Katherine. Therefore, get up and follow me. Though you may lose sight of me, the shadow of the palm I'm carrying will always be visible." These hermits followed the angel to a place that could hardly be entered because it was so narrow and there were so many sharp rocks. When they reached

---

[11] I.e., the famous burning bush of Exodus 3.

the hilltop, they could not see the angel but so clearly saw the shadow of the palm that they came to the rock where the holy lady had lain for one hundred and thirty years. Time had withered her flesh, but her bones were so well preserved they seemed to have been cared for by angels. With great joy and reverence, they took her holy body back with them to their chapel. This could not have been accomplished without a great miracle, for the place she had rested was unimaginably narrow and perilous. When Katherine's holy body was solemnly brought into the chapel, they proclaimed it the feast of the finding of the holy virgin, and that finding is observed by devout Christians in that region around the feast day of the finding of the holy cross.

Our lord honored this holy place with a great miracle, for, from the holy bones that had been drying out on the top of the hill for a hundred years, oil flowed like a river, running abundantly out of her tomb. That oil is so powerful that it heals all sicknesses, as many devout pilgrims to that holy place know. And oil never ceases to seep from the bone fragments that come out with the oil—no matter where they're carried. Bodies of the sick are anointed with it.

So blessed Katherine suffered martyrdom around the year of our lord 309, on the twenty-fifth of November. She suffered around midday on Friday, keeping the day and hour that our lord Jesus Christ suffered his passion for the world's redemption. Honor and praise and glory and power to him forever. Amen.

Chapter 30: Of two miracles and five prerogatives of Saint Katherine[12]

A monk from the city of Rouen in Normandy went to Mount Sinai, where he lived and served Saint Katherine most devoutly for seven years. Then he asked her to give him some of her holy body. Suddenly a joint of her finger sprang from her hand, which he happily took as a precious gift from God and brought home to his monastery.

There was a man who was especially devoted to Saint Katherine and called on her for help in all his needs. In time, however, he grew careless and stopped calling on her. Once, as he was praying, he saw a great multitude of virgins pass before him, and among them was one who seemed

---

[12] It was not uncommon for a saint's life to conclude with accounts of miracles that occurred after her death. Cf. Mirk's "Saint Winifred."

fairer and brighter than any other. But when she drew near him, she hid her face before moving on. Puzzled at why such a wonderfully beautiful woman should shun him, he asked who she was. One of the virgins answered, "That is Katherine, whom you once knew but have apparently now forgotten. That's why she passes by you with her face covered." Then he grieved, asked for mercy, and afterward was more attentive in his service.

This glorious virgin Saint Katherine was excellent and marvelous in five respects. The first is wisdom, for she understood the seven sciences more thoroughly than anyone in her time—a remarkable achievement for such a young maiden. She also was wise in governing herself, her household, and the peoples and lands under her care. She also had wisdom with respect to God, through her heavenly contemplation and knowledge of the mysteries of the faith, which she proclaimed without error. She also had the wisdom to recognize the wretchedness of the world and the flesh, and therefore she despised all worldly wealth and subjected her body to torture and death for the love of everlasting life, which is God himself. The second of her virtues is eloquence—not only the beauty of her language, but also the effective arguments she used to confound the emperor, overcome the fifty great scholars, and convert the queen and Porphirius to the true faith. The third is her stability, for neither promises nor threats could move her from her purpose. Therefore, when the emperor promised to make her second in command of the empire and promised her own devotional statue in the city, she not only declined his promises but scorned them. And when he threatened her with torments, she told him to do his worst, declaring herself ready to suffer anything he could devise. Her fourth virtue is her chastity and purity. Indeed, she preserved her virginity under the most adverse circumstances. For one, as queen and heir of all her father's estate, she was very wealthy; second, she was young; third, she was lovely; fourth, she was able to do as she wished. Wealth, youth, beauty, and freedom are all enemies of chastity, yet Katherine kept her virginity intact despite them. Katherine's fifth virtue is the special privileges she enjoys. God gave gifts to various saints upon their death. Our lord Jesus Christ visited some of them, as he did John the Evangelist and others. Others, like Saint Paul, had milk rather than blood rush from their wounds. Others, like Saint Nicholas, had oil run from their tombs. Some, like Saint Clement, had their graves adorned by angels. But this glorious virgin Saint Katherine received all these favors, as her legend has shown. That makes her pre-eminent in terms of privileges. Thus, we can see that she was so distin-guished on earth that she ranks high in the blessed sight of her spouse, the lord Jesus Christ, in heaven. Through her holy prayers, she can gain for us such grace during our lives in this sorrowful and declining world that we might sometime come to see and know and feel the joy she now experiences. Amen.

So ends the life and martyrdom and miracles of the virgin martyr Saint Katherine

This life and passion of the virgin martyr Saint Katherine teaches all virgins and maidens to despise and flee all worldly vanity and greatly and truly to love our lord Jesus Christ. It teaches you to persevere in his love to the death, trusting in that comfort and reward he gives all his lovers. It teaches all you Christians to be strong and stable in the faith of Christ and to love Saint Katherine, and to know how she may help you if you honor and serve her faithfully. Amen.

Saint Ursula and the
Eleven Thousand Virgins

Anonymous, ca. 1485

The mass martyrdom of the British princess Ursula and her eleven thousand female companions provides ample occasion for depicting an orgy of violence. Surprisingly, however, it is among the least violent martyr legends. Artists tended to depict the saint protectively enfolding her companions in her cloak, and writers were more concerned to detail the pedigrees of Ursula's companions than their eventual slaughter. This prose version is typical, except in one detail: the writer tells us that, immediately following her martyrdom, Ursula was married to the king of England in the presence of the king of heaven—a startling variation on the usual marriage to Christ. Ursula's heavenly union with her earthly suitor is a most striking example of fifteenth-century mitigation of the unequivocal denunciation of worldly relationships and institutions that had formerly characterized the genre. Indeed, in its portrayal of Ursula's dealings with her father and her suitor, this legend contrasts sharply with the legend of Juliana which opened this volume.

Eleven thousand is an extraordinary number of martyrs. The usual, and most probable, explanation of this figure is that it derives from the misinterpretation of the abbreviation "XI M V" in some early version as "XI M virgines" (eleven thousand virgins) rather than the intended "XI martyres et virgines" (eleven virgin martyrs). The misreading required that Ursula and her ten companions each be supplied with a thousand attendants, as they are in the text that follows. The story of the eleven thousand virgin martyrs was well known by the early eleventh century.

Fig. 7. Saint Ursula and the eleven thousand virgins. (Courtesy of the Pierpont Morgan Library, New York. MS M. 349, fol. 181v.)

Midcentury, Urusula's cult burgeoned, when a mass burial discovered outside Cologne was assumed to be the remains of Ursula and her companions, despite the presence of men's and children's skeletons. Shortly thereafter, the nun Elizabeth of Schönau recounted a series of visions in which the slain men and women identified themselves to her and explained their presence in the company. Ursula's story was thus expanded to include the fictional Pope Cyriac, her betrothed, and other pious men who chose to share the virgins' martyrdom.

The Ursula legend translated here was written in ponderous Middle English prose. It survives in two manuscripts: MS HM 140, Huntington Library, a miscellany containing, among other things, works by Chaucer and Lydgate; and MS Southwell Cathedral VII, where it occurs with a version of the prose *Life of Saint Katherine.*

Edition: Garmonsway, G. N., and R. R. Raymo. "A Middle English Prose Life of St. Ursula." *Review of English Studies* 9, n.s. (1958): 353–61.

Görlach, Manfred. "A Second Version of the Huntington Prose Legend of St. Ursula." *Review of English Studies* 24, n.s. (1973): 450–51.
Staley, Lynn. "Huntington 140: Chaucer, Lydgate, and the Politics of Retelling." In *Retelling Tales: Essays in Honor of Russell Peck*, ed. Thomas Hahn and Alan Lupack, 293–320. Woodbridge, Suffolk: D. S. Brewer, 1997.

Saint Ursula and the Eleven Thousand Virgins

In Britain there lived a king, a most Christian prince, whose name was Nothus, or Maurus. This king had a daughter named Ursula, a virgin whom God had endowed with such piety and beauty that her name and good reputation were known in many lands; and among those it reached was the mighty king of England, who had brought many nations under his rule. When he heard of this gracious virgin's worthiness, he decided that he would like his son and heir to marry her. His son agreed wholeheartedly. Official messages were therefore dispatched to the king of Britain, promising many pleasant things if he would consent to the marriage and threatening dire consequences if he would not.

This Christian prince and king of Britain was terribly shaken by these messages for three reasons in particular: first, he deemed it unworthy and inappropriate to give his baptized daughter to an unbaptized prince such as the king's son; second, he was sure that his daughter, Ursula, would not consent to the match; and third, he was terrified of the king of England and his fierce threats. Nevertheless, the blessed virgin Ursula comforted her father as best she could. Inspired by God, she advised him to grant the English king's petition on these conditions: that he and the king of England would, for her solace and comfort, appoint the ten fairest and worthiest virgins that could be found; that they would assign to her and to each of the other ten virgins a thousand other virgins; and that the marriage would be delayed for three years so that they would have time to prepare themselves to be formally dedicated to virginity. In the meantime, the king's son was to be baptized and instructed in the Christian faith of Holy Church. Ursula made these stipulations with great wisdom and discretion: if the severity of the conditions did not cause the English king and his son to abandon their desire, she would at least be able to dedicate many holy virgins to God.

When the English king's son heard all this, he was not at all discouraged but immediately insisted that his father accept the conditions. He himself was christened right away in holy baptism and ordered everything done just as Ursula wished. But first the king of Britain appointed worthy companions for his beloved daughter, to encourage and strengthen her good behavior. These virgins, chosen from diverse realms, came together in Britain. From them, the ten worthiest ladies' daughters were assigned to Ursula, and to each of these eleven a thousand virgins, as mentioned before. At last, when Ursula had converted all the virgins who were not yet Christians, they began to gather in public worship in a marvelous way, as God inspired them to do, to such an extent that many countries and kingdoms wondered greatly at their solemn and marvelous purpose. Many worthy lords and ladies, both spiritual and temporal, came to England and Britain to see that new spiritual chivalry. And many of them, when they learned their blessed purpose, resolved to accompany the eleven thousand virgins and to live and die with them in God's cause.

At last, when all necessary preparation was made for the journey, as God ordained, this multitude set out by water to the city of Cologne. There an angel informed Saint Ursula in a vision that they should all go to Rome and that everyone would return safely to Cologne, where they would endure martyrdom for Christ's sake.

Rejoicing at these good tidings, they sailed from Cologne to Basel. The bishop of Basel, Pantulus, went with them, intending to join them in martyrdom. So did Gerasina, Queen of Sicily, with her son and four daughters, who were Ursula's close relatives. Then, leaving their ship at Basel, they journeyed to Rome on foot. Pope Cyriac, who was born in Britain and had many relatives among the virgins, was delighted at their arrival, and received them with honor at his court. That night, he learned in a vision that he would be martyred along with the company. He kept that revelation secret for a while, until he had baptized many of those who had not previously been baptized. And when he found an opportunity, he declared his intent to the College of Cardinals and immediately resigned the dignity and office of pope.

At that time, two wicked pagan princes, Maximus and Africanus, ruled in Rome. Considering the multitude of virgins and of those who flocked to them, they feared that, if unchecked, Christianity would increase greatly throughout their lands. When these princes saw that the company was returning to Cologne, they sent messengers to their relative Julius, who was the pagan prince in that region, requesting him to slay the Christians when they arrived.

Shortly afterward, our holy father the pope, Cyriac, departed from Rome for Cologne, along with a cardinal, an archbishop, four other bishops, the daughter of the king of Constantinople, the eleven thousand virgins with all their attendants, and all the other people that had flocked to them before. No one but God knows how many there were in all.

In the meantime, as they were coming from Rome, Ethereus, the son of the king of England, who was to marry Saint Ursula, was told by an angel of God that he should exhort his mother the queen to be anointed in holy baptism, then hurry himself to meet Ursula, his betrothed, at Cologne, there to suffer martyrdom with her. Since his father the king had died the year he was baptized, Ethereus was now king of England.

When his mother was baptized, he set forth with his mother, his sister, a bishop named Clement, and many other English people. When at last the parties met at Cologne, they found the worthy city besieged by a large host of aforesaid pagans who had been sent there by the two princes. As soon as they saw two large parties of Christians coming together, they fell upon them with a horrible outcry and cruelty, as wolves upon sheep. They slew them all, both men and women, offering heavenly God a precious and abundant present—though they received little or no thanks for their efforts.

But when Julius, the prince of the pagans, saw that holy lady and virgin Ursula, he was stunned by her ravishing beauty and wanted to make her his wife. Because she would in no way consent but rather scorned him, he took an arrow and pierced her through the body. And so she was married that day to the king of England in full glory before the king of heaven. May she and all her companions bring us there through their virtues, merits, and prayers.

As the holy multitude was patiently enduring martyrdom for the Christian faith, a certain virgin of the eleven thousand, whose name was Cordelia, stole away and hid in a ship all night for fear of death. But the next day, she offered herself freely to martyrdom, as her companions had done, and she got her desire. After her death, she appeared to a certain anchoress, telling her that her own feast day should be celebrated the day after the feast of the eleven thousand virgins, who, with their companions, suffered martyrdom in the year of our lord Jesus Christ 238.

APPENDICES

These appendices contain transcriptions of the legends of Justine and Barbara from the *South English Legendary*, which have never been edited, and of the first portion (the vita) of the *Life of Saint Katherine of Alexandria*, which is available only in a rare edition. The Middle English thorn and yogh have been replaced with their modern equivalents. Abbreviations have been expanded, and modern conventions of punctuation, capitalization, and word division have been adhered to.

Appendix A

Lives of Saints
Justine and Barbara:
The South English Legendary

Saint Justine[1]

Seint Justine of heighe men in Antioche com.
Wel yong heo lovede Jesu Crist and tok to Cristendom.
An heigh mannes sone ther biside that het Cyprian,
Ar he were feve yer old bicom the develes man;

5   As we beth at oure cristendom Jesu Crist bitake,
Also he tok him the devel, oure lord to vorsake.
Tho he was eldore that he ought of monnes witte couthe,
Wonder he dude thorw the devel mid dede and mid mouthe,
Thorw him he hedde so gret mighte that he mighte ofte torne

10   Men into fourme of best, ne mighte him no mon werne.
This luthere man in fole love lovede Seint Justine
That ar he hadde the love of hir he nolde is thonkes fine.
Aboute he was thorw is power this maide to winne,
Ac heo wuste hire thorw godes grace that he ne com hire withinne.

15   Tho he ne mighte spede in none wise, the devel he gan conjure,
Yif he mighte withinne hire come is soule he gaf to hure.
The devel seide, "Ich overcom Adam in parays,
And thorw sunne is joie him binom, vor he nas nought wys.
Ich made that Caym, is ferste sone, Abel, is brother, slow.

20   Whi ne scholde I not winne a comion wenche? Power ichabbe inow!"
The devel wende forth bi nighte this holi maide to fonde
And in the fol thought broughte hir neigh; ac tho gan heo understonde
That fondinge it was of the devel, the signe of the crois heo made.

---

[1] Reprinted from Ms. Egerton 1993 (fols. 203v.–206r); British Library.

The devel les is mighte anon, overcomen was the tade.
25 "Certes," he seide to Cyprian, "mi mighte is me binome,
Vor thorw a signe of the crois anon ic was overcome!"
"Yif thu ne might," quoth Cyprian, "mi wille of hire do,
Ichulle conjure a strengore devel, that he com me to."
Tho the other devel to him com, he het him don is wille.
30 He wende to fonde this holi maide, ac he ne spedde worth a fille,
Vor he was sone iserved so as is brother er was.
Cyprian he tolde anon that is power nought nas.
"Ye beth nought worth," quoth Cyprian, "awei sithe ffame!
Ichulle conjure oure herte maister; he schal ende this game!"
35 Tho the maister was up icome, "How geth this?" he sede.
"Schal a wenche us overcom? Nolle ye non other rede?"
"Let me iworth," quoth the devel, "ne dred the of no pointe—
Ar midnight heo schal come, ne beo heo never so quainte!"
In forme of a vair maide the devel to hir wende.
40 "Justine," he seide, "Wel ichot that God to the me sende
Vor ichabbe yut mi lif herto in clannesse inome;
And thow art clene maide also to the ich am icome,
Mi soule here mid the in clannesse to bede.
And natheles, ich bidde, tel thu me what schal beo oure mede."
45 "Certes," quoth this maide tho, "oure mede worth angles ifere.
Therfore ther nis non so worthi thing as clene maide to beo here."
"Wel me thinketh," the devel seide, "thu ne gabbest the of nought.
Ac o word that oure lord seide me bringeth ofte in thought—
That tho he made Adam and Eve, vurst he gaf hem lif,
50 Suthe he spousede hem togadere as man to is wif;
He het to ware here tho and to eche an erthe here kinnde.
Gret harm deth me thulke biheste whanne it cometh in mi minnde,
Vor other is heste is for nought, as we here iseth,
Other hi that nulle is heste do in dedliche sunne beth!
55 And the vurste hod, as thu wel wost, that oure lord made alive
That was spoushod in paradis bitwene man and is wive.
Go we vonde awhile how us may best rede
To volfulle oure lordes heste withoute ani misdede."
Welle schrewe (wo him beo!) felliche he gan thenche
60 To mak is valse argument to bitraye that seli wenche!
That reson putteth this foles forth to lecherie al day:
We mai here iseo whos men hi beth, and who hem techeth here play!
Hii siggeth hit is godes heste oure kinnde on erthe to eche;
Hi schullen do here maistires lore and the gudd of helle seche!
65 So neigh hadde this devel this maide in sunne ibrought
That heo wende vorth with him and changede al hir thought.
As sone as god hire gaf the grace of the devel heo hedde fere
Heo ne gede nought fer ar heo bigan godes baner to arere;

Heo made the signe of the crois and blew on hire ifere
70 Hire wommone forme melt awey, snow as thei it were!
Heo nuste whar heo was bicome; this maide hire understod
That hit was the devel hire to schende and turnde anon hire mod.
As this maide alone another time in hire chambre lay,
In a fair yong mannes forme the devel com aday.
75 He clupte hire and custe anon, this maide undernom
And made the signe of the crois, tho nuste heo whare he bicom.
Now the schrewe—wo him beo!—wel fol he was of gile.
Ate laste nas it worth a sire vor he les al is while.
Sore was the schrewe of schamed that he ne com hire withinne.
80 He thoughte he ne spedde nought quointe loker biginne.
With is power he wende forth that was alto strong,
And in strong fevere broughte hire that was hard and long,
So that this maide was neigh to dethe ibrought.
Ac ever heo huld in clannesse to Jhesu Crist hir thought.
85 Tho wende the devel forth anon with is luther power
And broughte qualm among men orf aboute fer and ner
So that orf into al the lond deyede alto grounde.
Al aboute that qualm eode that fewe ther were ifounde.
Gret deol into al the lond was and gret serwe and care,
90 That men nuste whare mide libbe tho here orf was so forfare.
The devel com to the herte men that were in the londe
And seide that the luther qualm was thorw godes sonde.
Thorw love that Cyprian hadde to the fol womman Justine,
That ar hii were togadere wedded that qualm ne scholde fine.
95 And that hii sondede vor here god that hi were togadere ido,
Other al here orf scholde deiye and suthe hemself also.
Gret deol was in Antioche of the luther cas.
That lond was neigh ibrought to nought that er so riche was.
Me mai seo here the develes mighte how he sent ofte winne,
100 In bothe richesse and poverte to bringe men in sunne.
To Seint Justines nexte frendes wende mani a man
And beden hem that hi anon hire spousede to Cyprian
Other hi hem strengthe wolde do, vor hi nolde it soffre nought
That al that lond for hire folie were to grounde ibrought!
105 Yerne fonded al hire frendes to bringe that dede to ende
Ac nomon mighte hire make enes hire thought to wende.
Heo swor heo wolde rathere tholie that me hire to dethe broughte
Ac gret deol heo made natheles that the lond eode to noughte.
Evere heo bad oure lord vaste that he it scholde amende,
110 That he binome the develes mighte and bote a londe sende.
Oure lord sende is grace anon thorw the maidnes bone
And broughte that lond of this qualm in god point wel sone.
Ac arst hadde the luther qualm ilast feve yer.

To muche mighte the devel hath, isene hit was ther.
115 Sore was the devel aschamed that he ne com hire withinne,
Vor evere he bihet Cyprian that he hire wolde winne.
Vor he nolde beo overcome, his forme he tornde there
In Seint Justines owe forme, hireself as theigh it were.
He com bifore Cyprian and ashte what were is wille
120 He clypte him and custe anon, ac al nas nas worth a fille,
Vor ano as he hadde iseid, "Justine thu art welcome,"
He nuste whar the devel bicom, his art him was binome!
Anon tho the devel herde nempne Seint Justine name
He nadde no power leng abide vorte ssende hire fame.
125 What scholde holiere signe than this holi maide that was clene
That the devel ne mighte soffri nought to heren hire name ene?
Dredfol was to his bihofthe thilke holi name
That made him so flen awey, him likede na game!
Me ne dar nought esche wher Cyprian were tho in grete grame
130 Whan the devel bothe and eke him the maide dude such schame!
So that the devel ne mighte this holi maide wynne,
He thoughte mid enchauntens to come hire withynne.
He tornde himself to a maide thorw is art and gynne
And eode vaire and mildeliche to Seint Justine ynne.
135 Anon tho this maide him seigh his forme was ilore:
He bicom to Cyprian, such as he was bifore.
In alle manere this maide was of holi mighte
Whan heo overcom the develes art thorw a lutel sighte.
"Thow fol," quoth this holi maide, "the were betere beo stille
140 Thu hontest aboute nought; thin art nis worth a fille!"
Bi him and bi the devel ek ofte me seigh there
That oure lordes power is ever above, thegh here to muche were.
Another time this Cyprian bithoughte him wel narwe;
Himselve he tornde, thorw is art, to the forme of a sparwe.
145 Over the maidnes chambre he vleigh in the lifte an heigh
And setlede in an heigh boue, ac the maiden him iseigh.
Ciprian he was as he was er; sparwe nas he namore.
He sat and hovede as an ape, of schamed he was sore,
Vor bote he breke his necke, he ne mighte adoun mid al is lore.
150 Yerne he criede and ofte seide, "Justine now thin ore!"
What wolde this sparewe? Whar were hire fetheren tho?
Hail, ape! What wolde he there? Whoder thoughte go?
A feble cok he was ac colde; whi nolde he adoun fleo?
He mighte sitte and capie there, and is owe schendnesse iseo!
155 "What woste?" this maide sede there. "Whi artow so gret ape?
There me vor schame ther scholde mani man on the cape!"
Vor hire owe godnesse, with a laddre, heo let him adoun wende
And bad him come namore there, himselve vorte schende.

This cominn fol stal awey of schamed swithe sore;
160 The devel he clepede anon and essde whar were is lore:
"Whare is al thi wyt? Thi mighte is the binome!
Thu aughtest beo of schamed sore that a wenche the schal overcome!"
The devel seide, "Wel ichot icham strengore than heo,
Ac a maister heo hath, strengore than ic other thow beo,
165 Vor thoew is strengthe, and nought thorw hire, overcome we beth, iwis!"
"Tel me now," quoth Cyprian, "al therof how it is."
"Swere me an othe," quoth the devel, "that thu nelt not vrom me wende,
And ichul the telle al how it is, vrom gynnynge to then ende."
Tho Cyprian hadde iswore then oth, he seide, "Ichul the telle:
Mid a litte thing he maye overcomen us and alle that beth in helle!
170 Mid the signe of the holi crois that heo hath in hire thoughte,
And thorw strengthe of him that theron was, to grounde us hath
   ibroughte."
"Ek me thinketh," quoth Cyprian, "bi thin tale now,
That hire god on whan heo leveth is strengore than thow."
"The thincketh soth," the devel sede, "That me sore of thinketh,
175 Vor us and alle that oure beth in gret torment he bringeth!"
"Eke," seide Cyprian, "right is ate fyne
That ich bicome anon is man, leste he me bringe in pyne."
"Ow Cyprian," quoth the devel, "is it now so bi the
Nim god yeme of thin oth how thu swore me!"
180 "Sithe othe," seide Cyprian, "that ichabbe bi iswore,
Ich forsake the and thine vrom toppe to the more.
To the heighe God ichul me take that schal save me,
And of the holi crois signe make that schal me wite from the!"
Anon, tho he hadde the crois imad, the devel ne mighte abide
185 Bote wende vorth mid dreri chere, he ne mighte namore chide.
Now luther wey mote he wende bothe top and tayl—
And ne come he nevere a gode stude to geve no fol asayl!
Ta a bissop ther biside, Cyprian the weye nom,
And let him schrive swithe clene and tok Cristendom.
200 He servede oure lord swithe wel, and swithe holi mon he was,
Bischop he was sone imad, as oure lord gaf that cas.
Justine he lovede in clannesse, that hadde er in folie.
Nonne he made hire after awhile in a nonnerie,
And after heo was sone imad of the hous abbesse.
205 Bitwene hire and Cyprian was gret love in clannesse.
And that was wel betere love than himselve for schape
And as a wrecche sparwe to hire fleo and rouki as an ape.
So that the prince of the lond of hem herde speke,
He let hem vette bifore him bothe, here Cristendom to breke.
210 He het hem do to his godes anon sacrifise.
"We ne schulle never," quoth this othere, "that don in none wise!"

The prince was tho wroth inow and sone he let vette
A chetel muche and strong inow and over the fuir sette.
Ivuld it was with pich and war, and grete was the thridde.
215 This holi thinges nom bothe and caste yn al amidde.
The more the chetel boylede, the lasse hii hadde of wowe.
Hi scornede the quelleres, vor hii were so slowe,
And bede hem legge on more wode and there mid belies blowe,
And lerni vorte make here bath that hii scholden in helle owe!
220 A luther preost of thulke lawe sturte vorth vor prute,
Heore torment to make more, ac he bigat wel lute,
Vor agen him the vuir sturte anon and barnde him al to cole!
Ther ne dorste non tho ner hem go, ac drow ech to is hole.
Hii were somdel agaste, tho ac evere lute inow.
225 This holi thinges longe thoughte sethe ar me hem slow.
The prince suththe atenende, tho he ne seigh non other won,
Let hem nime bothe to and smite of here hedes anon.
Heore bodies hi casten in foule stede, vor bestes hem scholde gnawe,
Ac ther nas nouther foul ne best that therto wolde drawe.
230 Imartird hii were to hondred yer and eighten right
After that oure swete lord in is moder was light.
Suthe com vorth Cristene men and here bodies hole founde.
Hi ladden hem to Rome and burieden hem nobliche and sounde.
Now Jhesu vor the swete love of the maide Justine,
235 And vor the love of Seint Cyprian, schilde us vrom helle pine.

Saint Barbara[2]

Whan Maximian ffor alle his tyrandyse
Hadde governaunce of the emperyalte,
He had a cytezeyn, in foly ware and wyse;
His name was Dyoscours of gret degre.
5   He was a man of ful gret pryse,
Of wordly godes gret abundaunce.
He had also, in dyverse wyse,
Of lond and rent ful suffysaunce.
But a pagan for sothe he wase;
10   He belevyd noght on God almyth,
But ydolatrye he usyd in ony place,
Bothe be day and be nygth.

Of the Cristen feyth he had non lygth;
What man it wolde unto hym preche,
15 He wolde enforce with al his mygth,
So this chevynteyn of the lawe hym a peche.
A dowghtter he hadde and no mo;
Hir name was Barbara, of gret bewte.
In fayrnesse al othir sche passyd so
20 That for hir love a towr made he,
Bothen wyde and long and fayre of sykt.
In that towr he thoughtte his doughtter to hyde,
In somere day and wyntere nyght,
So that alle ravyschouris sche myght exclude.
25 And whan this towr was al ymade,
This chast mayden he enclosyd withinne,
Thowgh she were semly and of chere so gladde
Yet that no man hir love schuld wynne.
The gentyles of the cuntray, thei wold not blynne
30 But cam to hir fadir and spek hym to,
Prayed hym hir love that thei myghtte wynne,
And that sche in maryage with on mygtte go.
To that hir fadir thus had undirnome;
With wyse avyse to the tour he gan go,
35 And to hys doughtter he spak ful sone
And prayed hir to tellen hym what sche wold do.
With a mylde herte sche answerd tho,
"Fadir, mekly I yow beseke
That ye ne constrayne me therto,
40 For to abyden thus it doth me lyke."
Hir fadir ansuerd tho the cytezenys ychone
And sayd, "I suppose it wil not be.
Sche cast to lyven thus alone
Tyl beter tyme that sche may se."
45 And whan the cytezenys thus answerd had he,
In his mynde tho he ferkeste
To maken a place of gret honeste
Wherynne he thoughtte hymself to reste.
Than multytude of werkmen he let calle
50 That schulde this towr fully up make,
Summe it to kasten and summe it to walle,
And to hem alle thus he spake:
"Parformyth thys werk for my sake
That ye now have takyn in hande,
55 And every man his mede here itake,
For I most into anothir londe."
And whan hir fadir was forth gon,

Barbara cam doun that werk to se.
Sche salutyd the workmen everychon.
60 "Damysele," thei sayde, "welcom ye be."
And whan sche seyk that hows so fre
And twyne wyndowes in the north sette,
Anon thyse workmen callyd sche
And prayed hem to tellen hir withoutyn ony lette
65 Why tweyne wyndowes wern ther so pygth
And no mo, in no maner wyse.
Thei answerd, "for youre fadir us dyd hygth
To maken it in this same gyse."
Sche prayed hem thenne onys or twyse
70 Anothir wyndowe ther to make
And say it were at hir devyse.
On this wyse tho maysteres alle spake,
"We drede lest youre fadir veniance wolde take
On us if we youre wil fulfylle,
75 An wel lyghtly for youre sake
On byter deth he wolde us spylle."
Hardely sayde Barbara, "Werkes after myn wille,
For my fadyr I wil so plese
And with fayre wordes speke hym untille
80 Therto he schal do yow non dysese."
Unto hir wordes thei acordyd ychon
And anothir wyndowe thei gan arere
And formyd it and made it anon
So alle the wyndowes werin lyke in fere.
85 Whan this werk was endyd in the same yere,
Fro his jorney hir fadir was comyn agayn
And bad his werkmen alle to apeere
Beforn his precense togedir in certayn.
He askid of hym that had the governance
90 Of the werk, how and in what wyse,
The reverse of hys seyde ordinance,
The thrydde wyndow ther dyd avyse.
"Sir, I can yow telle at the best assyse:
You're doughtter therfor to me gan speke,
95 And sche hirself dyd it devyse
And sayde that ye wolde it not awreke."
Than hir fadir his doughtter did calle
And sayde unto hir on this wyse,
"What have ye don and how is it falle
100 That ye thus changyd han al myn devyse?"
"Lord fadir," sayde Barbara, "no thyng yow dysmay,
But take it wel goodly everylk agre,

For in the best wyse that I cowde don or say,
I have to youre werk don as I cowde best se,
105 For thre wyndowes I have ordeynid so
That the blyssidful Trenite it schuld represent,
In that on God schal ben worschepyd and no mo,
Aboven alle creatures with hol entent,
That also lythnyth alle erthly creature,
110 That is comyn in this wordis here for to dwelle.
And for this skyll only, yow I ensure,
I have don playnly thus every dele."
And whan hir fadir had herd hir wordes stylle,
He voyded of wyt and fuly replenyschyd of yre,
115 He with his knyf thought anon hir to kylle,
And that to fulfylle was fully his desyre.
But God that preservyth ever his trewe servytowr,
He ordenynid for hir in swylk degre,
And so he coveryd hir fro perellys with his gracious socowr,
120 That in a hewyn ston enclosyd was sche,
And sodeynly sche was translatyd into a hylle,
The whiche myracle twey herdmen gan espye.
And to on of hem hir fadir gan say untylle,
"Saw ye ony swylk thyng with youre bodely eye?"
125 "Nay," sayde that on, and gan faste to denye,
Covetyng yyf he myght fro perell hir save,
And sayde, "thowgh I schule her anon dye,
Or for that tydyng yowre reme to have."
Than his felawe, ful of cruelte,
130 The contrary dyd aferme: lo, he sayd wher sche is.
Hir fadir answerd, "Sche schal have hir duete,"
And gan to threten hir unmercyfully and almes.
Than this blyssid virgine cursyd that herdman,
And alle his scheep turnyd sodeynly into flyes,
135 Whylke at hir towmbe may sen every man,
Ther as hir blyssid body in schryne lyes.
Hir fadir was angryd and grevyd wel sore.
He drowe hir by the heer and beet hir grevowsly
And sayde sche schuld out of prison no more.
140 To hir peyne were devysyd redly,
And that by the juge of the lawe the whilk is comanded,
That aforn hym schuld ben brouth and had swilk langage:
"Thou that art so semly and with bewte so endwyd,
Why wilt thu parten fro this avantage?
145 For sodeynly thu schalt departen fro this lyf
And of alle erthely joye ben made al nakyd
And yet tormented with myche peyne and stryf

And fynally to crwel deth than ben takyd.
Therfore, I counseyle the to don sacryfyce
150   Unto oure goddes, withoutyn more delayng.
And yif thu wilt not be of swylk devyse,
Peynfully thu schalt ben browght unto thyn endyng."
Than answerde that blyssyd virgyn anon,
"I do sacryfyse to Jhesu Cryst onlye
155   That fro hevyn descendyd and becam man,
And us for to saven on a cros he gan dye,
That made hevyn and erthe and the see,
For othir God verray may non be founde,
But he only—blessyd most he be!—
160   For alle youris ben as is an helle hounde!"
Than the juge was grevyd al wodly.
He comandyd hir to ben made al nakyd
And with a hydowse instrument so crwelly
Hir flesch on pecemele was al makyd.
165   And whan hir body had no creatures lyknesse,
For hir flesch was al totorn and with blod overgon,
In preson sche was put al in derknesse,
Unto he myght bethynk hym werse to don.
But at mydnyght tyde of the nyght,
170   Owre lorde comfort and grace to hir appeyryd,
And to hir he schewed a ful gret lyght,
And of passyng grace hir he ensured,
That hevyn and erthe of hir is wel glad
For hir gloriouse palme of martirdome,
175   And that hir corone of blysse is al redy made
Withoutyn fayle to comen wel sone.
But yit anothir day the juge hath comandyd
That this mayden brought forth schuld be
And bothyn hir sydys with fyre enflawmyd
180   Of brennyng lampys with most crwelte.
And than after hir hed, thowgh it tendir were,
Al to betyn it with dyverse instrument.
And evyn in this peyne sche fel doun in prayere
To God almyghtty with al hir entent:
185   "Thu lord almyghtty, knower of herte,
Thu knowyst wel that for thyn name I thys her suffyr
So bytter peynis, crwel and smerte.
Yet with thyne mentell of mercy thu me covere,
And forsake me not in myn persecusyon,
190   But graunt me grace that am thyn servant,
That hoso in dysese of me make mencyon,
Largely of mercy and grace thu hem graunt.

And, only lord, in the day of myn martyre,
Hoso aske mekly, let hym ben sped,
195 And of thyn mercy let hym ben swere,
And fynaly to blysse thu do hem ben led."
And sodeynly a voyce to hir is makyd,
"Com to me, myn chosyn spowse, into thyn reste,
With hevynly blysse ever to ben gladyd,
200 For to the is ordeynyd a gracyous feste.
And yit thyn askyng is more herd
Of oure gracious lord that alle thyng governyth.
And therfor to dyen be thu not aferd,
For alle the cumpayne in hevyn it confermyth."
205 And in that same place, of hir fadir hand,
Sche was ther behedyd and made hir ende.
Hir body to the grounde mekly bowand,
To God in hevyn hir sowle gan wende,
And as hir fadir descendyd of that hylle,
210 Fyre of hevyn anon cam doun
And hym al to nought gan brene and spylle
That of hym was not be left no bon.
And thanne a nobyl man of good creaunce
Tok that virgyn bodely fygure
215 And a ryal towmbe he dyd enhawnce.
And with gret worschep he dyd that sepulture,
In whylk place is ever renewyd
Goddys myghty power unto hir reverence
In myrakelis werkyng that ther is schewyd
220 To aproven ever thys virgyn excellence.
Now ye that rede this bryef translacyon
Of so simpul rewarde labowr,
Lord in hem encrese thyn dewocyon
And be to hem bothen
225 Scheeld amd socowr.
And pray for me that in Englysch dyd it wryte.
Of youre charite, I beseke that almesse,
And of owre enymyes to sen dyscomfyte,
And ever in grace and mercy God us alle blesse.
AMEN.

Appendix B

The Life of Saint Katherine

A schort proloog into the lyf and martirdom of Seynt Kateryne,
virgyne and martir[1]

After I had drawe the martirdom of the holy virgyn and martir Seynt
Kateryne from Latyn into Englesshe as hit is wryton in legendis that are
compleet, ther was take to me a quayere whereyn was drawe into Englesshe not oonly hire martirdom, but also hir birthe and lyvynge tofore
hir conversion and how sche was converted and spoused to oure lord
Jhesu Christ. Netheles, the martirdam of the saam virgyn was not
allinges so plener in that quayere as hit was drawe by me tofore. And
therfore, to oure lordys wurschip and his holy moders and hyres, I have
sett hem togyder and maad on of bothe, and departed hem in chapitres,
and somwhat addet therto to moor cleer understondyng in som places.
And hit aught muche to sture cristene peple to the love and devocion of
this blessed virgen, and to wylle knowe hir lyf and passione, and ofte to
have hit in mynde the charite that sche schewed in the howre of hir
deeth, whan sche prayed that whosoevere had hir lyf and passion in
mynde and called unto hir in eny neede, he schold fynde and fele hasty
help. Whiche prayere oure lord herde and graunted, as hit is wryte
moore pleynly in the xxviii chapitre folewyng.

Furthermore, hit is to knowe that, as hit is sayde, the noble and worthy

---

[1] Reprinted from MS Richardson 44, by permission of the Houghton Library, Harvard
University.

doctour Atthanasius wrot this lyf of the gloriouse virgyn Seynt Kateryn, for he knewe hir birthe, and hir kynred, and hire holy conversacioun; and also that he was oon of hir maisters in hir tendir age or she was converted to the ryght fayth. And after hir conversion, sche converted hym by hir holy techyng and by merveylous werkes that oure lord wrought in hir. And aftur hir marterdom, he was made Bisshop of Alisaunder in Egipte and was a myghty pyler of holy chirche by grace of oure lorde and by hir holy merites. This saam Athanasius made *quicunque vult,* that is songe at prymys in holy chirche. And moche persecution he suffred for the fayth, and now he is worscheped in holy chirche and is an holy seynt in hevene.

[Chapter Summary Omitted]

Cap. 1: Of the progenitours of Seynt Kateryn and how she was of the emperours blood of Rome

The excellent and ryght gloriouse virgyn seynt Kateryn was of the noble kynrede of the emperours of Rome by hir faders syde, for the Emperour Constantyn and Kyng Cooste, Seynt Kateryns fader, were brotheren bothe of oo fader, but not of oo moder, as schall be declared suyngly aftur.

Hit is wryte in cronicles and openly knowen that the Romayns, by gret wysdom and manhod, made soget to here empire nyghande all the world. That tyme the Brytons (whiche come of the noble blood of Troye and were cosyns to the Romayns, and now by us are called Walsh men) regned in Engelond, that was than named Brytayn (and aftur hyt was named the moor Brytayn, for difference of the lasse Brytayn that is on the tother syde the see). These Britons were first subdewed to the empire of Rome by the emperor that was called Julius Cesar, and so thay abode many dayes and yeeres. Bot in the tyme of the emperours that were called Dioclician and Maximian, so gret and cruel tirantrye was shewde in the world, not oonly to cristen but also to paynems, that many a reme that were soget to Rome put away the yook of here servage and rebelled openly, amongst whiche the reem of Ermanye was oon that moost myghtyly wythstod the tribute that longed to the empire of Rome. Wherfore ther was chose to appese that rebellioun a senatour of Rome whyche was a lord of gret dignite and of the counsaill that hyght Constaunce, or Constantyne, for before alle other he was manly in armys and therto ryght discreet and ful of vertues. This lord, whan he come into Ermanye, he staunged soo by hys manly and vertuouse governaunce that rebellioun that he deserved and had the love of his enemyes. And mooreover the kynge and all the puple desired that he schuld wedde his doughter and heyr of his that lond. This doo, wythynne a whyle aftur, the kyng of Ermanye dyed, and Constaunce was crouned Kynge of that londe and had a sone by his wyf the queene whom he called Coste. Sone aftur this dyed the saam queen, his wyf, for whom was made gret lamentacion of al hir peple. Than, aftur the queenes deeth, Kyng Constaunce lefte his sone Coste governoure of that londe and went hymself ageyn to Rome to see the emperour and also to knowe howe his lordshypes were governed in thoo partyes.

Whan he come ageyn to Rome, he was receyved wyth gret worshep, and the Emperour Dioclician made hym cesar, and another wyth hym that was called Galerius he made cesar also; that is to say, he made hem parteners in cure and governaunce of the empire. In this meenetyme come tydynges to Rome how the moor Britayn (that now ys called Englond, as ys tofore sayde) rebelled agens the empire of Rome. Wherfore, by the avys of al the counsaill, hit was seen needful to require the sayde Kynge Constaunce to take uppon hym to ceese that rebellion, whiche request he graunted goodly, and drow hym in haste toward tho partyes. And in his comynge thider, the Britons, herynge his greet fame, derst not wel werre agenst hym, but sent to trete, and he ageynward by his vertu and prudence reuled hym so discreetly that not oonly wyth pees he subdewed hem ageyn to thempyre, but he was also acceptable to the kynge of Brytayn, that hyght Coel, and to all the peple of the londe, that the peple with o voys required the kynge to geve hym hys doughter and his heyre in mariage, that was named Eleyne, and now is called Seynt Eleyne, whyche afturward fonde the holy crosse. Of this request booth Kynge Coel and the Kyng Constaunce were plesed, and so ther was maad bytwene hem a soleme mariage. Aboute a monthe aftur that mariage, Kynge Coel dyed, and thanne was Kynge Constaunce crouned kynge of Brytayne, whyche begat of hys wyf and quene Elyne a sone, whom he called Constantyn, whiche was aftur emperour of Rome, as hit shal here be declared.

In this tyme, the Enperour Dioclician and Maximian lefte the empire

by here owne wyll, and thanne the sayde Kynge Constaunce and Galerius, his felow, parted the empire bytwene hem so that Galerius had
the enpire in the est party of the world and Constaunce in the west par-
tye, that is to say, uppon Italy and Fraunce and Spayne and Englond and
suche other londes. Bot Constaunce lefte a greet parte therof unto other
and held himself content wyth Fraunce, Spayne, and Engelond. And aftur, wythynne a whyle, the same Constaunce dyed at York in Englond,
and there he was buryed, and the sayd Constantyn his sone regned aftur
hym uppon Englond and Fraunce, not oonly as kyng of Englond, by
ryght of hys moder, bot also as emperour uppon booth reaumes, by
ryght of his fader, and how he encresed further in thempire shal
somwhat be tolde aftirward in the tenthe chapitre. This is that noble
Constantyn that was baptized of the holy pope Seynt Silvestre and cured
of an uncurable lepre. This is that worthy Constantyn that by vertu of the
holy crosse overcome his enemys and afturwarde sent his moder Seynt
Eleyne to seke the same crosse at Jerusalem. This is the same Constantyn
that aftur longe persecucion of Cristen peple bilded and made bilde
chirches and first endowed holy chirche wyth possessions. Hit were
longe to telle here alle his vertues and bounteuous holy dedes, for the
whiche he is worshiped as a seynt in the eest partyes of the world, as
cronicles telle. This noble emperour Constantyn was Seynt Kateryns
uncle on hir faders syde, for Kynge Coste hir fader was his brother, as is
tofore sayd. Therfore after the deth of Kynge Constaunce the said Coste,
his first sone, was crouned kynge of Ermanye, and he wedded the
doughter and heyr of the kynge of Cypres, by whom, after hir faders
deeth, he was crouned kynge of the saam kyngdom of Cypre, and of
hem tweyne was brought forthe Seynt Kateryn, whiche was thus of the
emperours blood, as ye may see by this that is now wryte.

*Cap. 2: Of the birthe and lyf and lernyng of Seynt Kateryn tyl she was aboute
fourtene yeere of age*

After two hondert yeere from the incarnacion of oure lord Jhesu
Criste, ther regned in the lond of Cipre a noble and a prudent kynge
that hyght Coste, whiche of bodyly schap was moost seemly and goodly
above alle other, and in rychesse mooste plenteuous, and in alle good
condicions noon lyke to hym. A queen he had, lyke hymself in al vertu-
ous governaunce, wyth whom he lyved a blessed lyf in as muche as

longeth to the world, except that booth he and his wyf lyved aftur the
ryte of paynemys and worschepid ydolys. This kynge, for he wold have
his name sprad thurgh the world, he made a cyte in whiche he raysed a
temple in worshep of fals goddys that the blynde world worshiped at that
tyme, and he named thys cyte Costy; procedyng than forth, the tyme and
the langage of the peple sumwhat chaunged, they chaunged the name
of the cyte and called hyt *fama costi*, kepynge alwey the fame of the
kynge. In this cyte he and the queen lyved in al worldly prosperite as fer-
forthe as her hertys coude thenke. And ryght as the fayre and swoote
rose spryngeth amonge the thornes, ryght soo amonge these paynems
was brought forthe the preciouse spouse of Jhesu Crist, the holy virgyn
Seynt Kateryn.

 Whan this holy childe was bore, hit was so fayre of visage and soo
shaply of body that alle had mervayl in the beholdynge of hir, and by
that tyme she come to sevene yeere of age, she encresed soo in hye
beaute and stature that alle that sawe hir hoped that in tyme to come she
shulde be the joy and praysynge of the londe of Cypre. Whanne sevene
yeer were passed and that she was wax stronge of body, she was sette to
scole, wheryn she profited soo wonderfully that, above alle tho that
evere were of hir age, she resceyvede merveylously al the crafte and konnynge of alle the vii scyences; and noo wonder though sche dronke plenteuously of the welle of wysdom, for she was ordeyned in tyme to come
to be a techer and an enformer of the everlastynge wysdom. Than Kynge
Coste, hir fader, had so gret joy of the wisdom of his doughter that he
ordeyned hir a toure in his paleys wyth diverse studyes and chambres,
that she myght be at hir owne leyser in hir studye, and noon to lette hire
bot whanne hir liste. And therto he ordeyned to awayte uppon hir sevene the beste and hiest maysteres of konnynge that myght be founde in
the world as in tho partyes. And wythynne a whyle and wythynne a whyle
[*sic*] that these maysters had be wyth this yonge lady Kateryne, she encressed soo merveylously in hir wisdom that tho clerkes that were come
to teche hir were ful glad to become hir disciples and to lerne of hir.

*Cap. 3: How Seynt Kateryn aftir hir faders deeth was crouned queen and
required by hir parlement to take an husband*

 Thus wythynne a fewe yeeres, whan this gloriouse virgyn was xiiii yeer
oolde, hir fadir Kynge Coste dyed, and she was lefte as queen and heyr

aftur hym. And when the dayes of wepynge were passed, the lordes and the states of hir londe come to this yonge queene and besought hir that ther myght be a parlement somned, at the whiche she myght be crouned and receyve hir homage; and that suche rule and governaunce myght be sett in hir yonge begynnynge, that pees and prosperite myght folewe in hir reaumes. And than this yonge queen thonked hem goodly and graunted hem her askynge. The tyme come that this parlement was begonne and this yonge queen crouned wyth gret solempnite wyth a rial feeste and greet joy to alle hir peple.

Whanne the feste of coronacion was ended, as the queen on a day saat in hir parlement, hir moder besydes hir and alle hir lordes aboute hir, a lord aroos by the full avys of hir moder and of alle hir lordes and comons and kneled hym doun before the queen, havyng these wordes: "Ryght hye and myghty princesse and oure mooste soverayn lady here yn erthe, like your soverayn noblesse to wyte that I am coummaunded by youre moder and by alle youre lordes and comyns to require youre hyyenesse to graunte hem that leeve and grace that they myght goo ordeyne unto yow som noble kynge or prince that myght reule you and youre reaumes and us alle in pees and reeste, like as the noble kynge youre fader and oure soverayn lord dyde before yow. And that we myght rejoysse gracious lynage of yow, whyche is oure mooste desyre and shal be oure mooste joye, wythoute whiche joye we lyve in greet sorwe and hevynesse. Besechynge yowre hyye excellence to tendre oure desyr and to graunte us of yowr hyye grace a graciouse answere."

This yonge queen, herynge this request of hir moder and of alle hir lordes, fel in greet trouble of hir sowle how she myght answere to kepe hir moder and hir lordes in reest and to kepe hir chastite, for alle hir joye had be to kepe hir body and hir soule from al corrupcion, and she had so gret and so parfyt a love to that vertu of chastite that she had lever suffre the deeth than for to blemyshe hit in eny wyse. Bot forto uttre hir conceyt so sodeynly hir thought hyt was not for the beste, and therfore wyth a sobyr loke and a debonayre voys she answered in this wyse to this lord: "Cosyn," she sayde, "I thanke my lady my moder and alle my lordes and comyns of the greet love and tendirnesse that they han to me and to myn reaume. But I trust fully that there be no greet haste as touchynge this matiere of my mariage, for ther may be no maner perel, yn considerynge the greet wysdom of my lady my moder and of yow alle, wyth the greet trouthe and kyndenesse that ye have shewde me and my reaumes, trustyng fully of your good contynuaunce. Wherfore we schull not nede to seke a straunge lorde to reule us and oure reaumes, for us thenketh us able ynow wyth youre good trouthe and wysdom to governe us oure reaumes, and yow alle in suche pees and reste as the kyng my lord and fader lefte yow. Wherfore I pray yow alle to cesse of this matiere at this tyme and speketh of suche matieres as ye thenke is moost speedfull and needfull to the good reule and governaunce of oure reaumes." And when this queen had thus ended hir tale, the queen hir moder and alle hir lordes were soo abaysshed of hir wordes that they wist not what to say, for thay considered wel by hir wordes that she was in no wysse to be wedded.

Cap. 4: How she descryved what he sholde be whom she wolde have to hir housbond yf ever she shulde have eny

Than stood there up a duke of here londe that was uncle to hir and kneled unto hir wyth humble reverence and sayde to hir in this wyse, "My ryght soverayn lady, savynge your hyye and noble discretion, this answere is ful hevy to my lady your modir and to us alle your liege men, wythoute ye take bettir avys to youre right noble and discreet hert. Wherfore I schal move yow of foure notable thyngys that the greete God hath endowed yow wyth before alle createures that we knowe, the whiche most nedes cause yow to take a lord and an housbond, that thoo plenteuous gyftes of kynde and of grace myght spryng of yow by succession of ryght lyne into generacions, whiche fruytfull generacions moste cause alle youre lyege puple an infinyt joye and gladnesse, and the contrye ther of gret sorwe and hevynesse."

"Now good uncle," sayde the yonge queene, "whyche be thoo iiii notable thynges that ye prayse us soo greetly of?"

Than sayde the duke, "Madame, yf hyt lyke youre hyye noblesse, I wyl declare hem to yow shortly."

"Uncle," she sayde, "Say what ye lyste; I wyl here yow gladly."

Than sayde the duke with greet reverence, "Madame, the firste notable poynt ys this, that we knowe yow comyn doun of the worthyest blood in erthe. The secunde is that ye be grettest in erthe that lyveth this day of womman. The thrydde is that in konnynge and wysdom ye passe all other. The fourthe is that of bodyly shap and hye beute was never noon seen lyke unto yow. Wherfore, madame, us thynketh that these iiii notable thynges moste nedes constreyne yow to enclyne to oure ententes."

Than this yonge queene, wyth ryght a sad loke, sayde, "Now, uncle, syth God and kynde have wrought these greet werkes in us, we be moche the more bounde to love hym and to plese hym, and we thanke hym humbly of alle his greet gyftes. Bot syth ye desyre in alle ways that we consente to youre entent as of oure mariage, we let yow playnly wyte that, lyke as ye have descryved us, soo we wyl descrive hym that we wil have to our lord and housbond; and yyf ye can gete us suche on, we wyl be his wyf wyth all our hert. For he that schall be lord of oure hert and myn housbond schall have these iiii notable thynges in hym over all mesure so ferforthly that alle creatures schal have neede to hym and he need of noon. For he that schall be my lord moost be of soo noble a blood that alle kynges most worshype hym, and therwyth soo greet a lord that I schal nevere dore thenke I made hym kynge, and so ryche that he passe alle other in rychesse, and soo full of beute that aungels have joye to behoolde hym, and so pure that his moder be a virgyn, and soo meke and benyngne that he kon gladly forgeve alle offenses doon to hym. Now have I descryved hym that I desyre to have to my lord and housbond. Goeth seke hym, and yyf ye may fynde suche oon, we woll be his wyfe wyth all oure hert yyf he wil vouche sauf. And finaly, bot yyf ye gete us suche one, we schal never take noon. And taketh this for a full answere." Wyth this this [*sic*] she kaste hir eyen doun mekely and held hir stille.

And whanne the queene hir moder and alle hir lordes had herde this, ther was greet sorowe and hevynesse, for thay sawe well that ther was noo remedye in that matier. Than sayde hir moder to hir wyth an angry voys, "Allas, doughter, ys this your greet wysdom that is talked of so fer? Muche sorowe be ye lyke to do to me and to alle youres. Allas! Who sawe ever any woman forge hir an husband wyth wordys—suche on as ye have devysed was ther never noon, ne nevere shal be! And therfore, gode doughter, leve this greet folye and do as your noble eldres have doo afore you."

Than sayde this yonge lady to hir moder wyth a pytous syghynge voys, "Madame, I wote wel by verray reson that ther ys oon moche better then I can devise hym, who so had grace to fynde hym, and but he by hys grace fynde me, trusteth fully that I shal never have joye. For I fele by gret reson that ther is a trewe way that we be clene out of. Wherfore we be in derkenesse, and tyl lyght of grace come we may not see the clere way. And whan hym lyste to come, he shal voyde alle the derke cloudes of ignoraunce and shewe hym cleerly to me that myn hert so fervently desyreth and loveth. And yyf so be that hym lyste not that I fynde hym, yeet resoun coumaundeth to kepe hool that is unhurt. Wherfore I beseche humbly yow my lady and my moder that ye ne noon other never meve me of this matier, for I behote yow playnly that, soo to deye ther-fore, I shal nevere have other, but oonly hym that I have descryved, to whom I shall trewely kepe al the pure love of myn hert."

Wyth this, she roos hir up, and hir moder also; and alle hir lordes from the parlement wyth sorowe and lamentacion toke her leve and went on her way. And the yonge queen went to hir paleys, whos hert was soo sette a fyre with thys husbond that she had soo descryved that she coude nothyng doo ne thenke, bot all hir mynde and hir entention was oonly in hym. Wherfore she studyed and mused contynuely how she myght fynde hym. Bot hit wolde not be as yeet, for she had noo menes therto, notwythstondynge that he was ful nyye hir hert, for he hit was that had kynled in hir hert a brennynge fyre of love that shold never be quenched for no peyne ne tribulacion, whyche was wel seen after in hir glorious passioun. Bot now I leve this yonge queene as for a tyme syttyng in hir paleys, contynuely thenkyng and ymagenyng how she myght fynde this newe spouse, wyth many a teere of elongacion and many a soore syghe for hir blynde ygnoraunce. And I wil turne, as my lord wyl geve me grace, how our lord by speciall myracle cleped hir to Baptyme in a syn-gulere manere that never was herde before ne syth, and aftur how he wedded hyr visibly in a glorious maner, schewynge hir soverayn tokens of singuler love that never were shewed before ne syth to noon erthely creature, saaf oonly to oure lady hys moost blessed moder.

Cap. 5: How our lady appered to an hermyte in desert and sent hym to fette Seynt Katryn to be wedded to hir sone

Besydes Alisaunder a certayn space of myles dwelled an holy fader in desert the space of xxx yeere in greet penaunce. And on a day, as he walked afore hys celle in hys holy meditacions, ther come agenst hym the moost reverent lady that ever eny erthly man behelde. Whanne this heremyte behelde hir excellent astat and hyye beaute above kynde, he was so astonyed and adrad that he fel doun as deed. Than this blessed lady, seynge his greet drede, called hym goodly by hys name and sayde, "Brother Adryan, drede you not, for I am not come to you bot for ryght greet worshep and profyt." Wyth that, she toke hym up myldely and counforted hym and sayde in this wyse, "Adrian, ye moost goo on a message from me into the cyte of Alysaundre and into the paleys of the yonge queene. And therfore goth to hir and say hir that thylke lady gretyth hir wel whos sone she chees to hir lord and husbond syttynge in hir parlement wyth hir moder and alle hir lordis aboute hir, where she had a gret conflict and batayle in kepyng of hir virginite. And telle hir that that saam lord that she chees there ys my sone, and that I am a clene virgyn, and he desyreth hire beaute and loveth hir chastite amonge all the virgyns in erthe. And bid hir wythout taryynge that she come allone to this place; and she shall be newe clothed, and thenne shall she see hym and have hym to hir everlastyng spouse."

The heremyte, heryng al thys, answerde dreedfully in this wyse, sayynge, "A, blessed lady, how sholde I do this message, for neyther I knowe the cyte ne the way. And what am I, though I knewe hit, to do a message to the queene? Hir meyne wyl not suffre me to come to hir presence; and though I dyde, she wyl not leeve me of my message, but put me in duresse as though I were a faytour."

"Adrian," sayde this blessed lady, "drede you not, for that my sone hath begonne in hir most nedes be parfourmed; for wyte hit wel that she is a speciall chosen vessel of grace before alle erthly wymmen that now lyven. Wherfore tary not ne drede not, for bothe ye shull knowe the way into the syte and into hir paleys also, and ther schal noo creature take hede of you. And whan ye come in hir paleys, take good heede whiche dores open agenst yow, and entryth yn hardyly tyl ye come to this fayre yonge queene, whom ye shull fynde allone in hir studie, bysieng hir full sore to fynde by hir wyttes that that wyl not be. Wherfore my sone hath compassion on hir labour, and for hir good wylle she shall be soo speciall wyth his grace that there was never noon lyke to hir, out take myn owne persone that am his owen chosen moder. Wherfore, Adrian, hyye you faste, and brynge me my dere doughter that I love wyth all myn hert."

Whanne Adryan had resceyved this message, he layde hym flat doun before this soverayn lady, sayying in this wyse, "Al worshep and joye be to my soverayn lord God, youre blessed sone, and to yow. Youre wylles be fulfylled. I goo at your coumaundement."

Cap. 6: Hou the heremite dyde his erande and brought wyth hym Seynt Katerine in to desert

Than Adrian roos hym up and hyed hym fast toward the cite and soo went forth into the paleys, and as he had lerned so he dyde. He entred yn at the dores that he sawe open and passed from chambre to chambre tyl he come yn to hir secreet study, where no creature used to come bot hirself allone. And whanne he entred yn at the dore, he sawe where sate the fayrest creature and the moost goodly that ever creature beheld; and she was so sadde in hir studye that she herde hym not unto the tyme that he kneled hym doun bysides hir and began his message in this wyse: "Madame, the endeles myght of the fader almyghty, the wisdom of hys sone alwytty, and the goodnesse of the holy gost, thre persones and oo God, be wyth yow now in your studie."

And whanne this yonge queene herde a mannes voys besyde hir and sawe an oold fader al forgrowen in hir studie wyth an oold sklavayn up-pon hym, she was grettly astonyed and aferde, and wondred of this sodeyn caas above mesure, for she knewe well that she had shett hir dores to hir. Wherfore she sayde with a dredfull voys, "What be ye that thus mervelously cometh into my studye where no man useth to come yn? Come ye yn by eny enchauntement?"

"Nay, madame," he sayde, "bot as a messanger that is sent."

"And gode sir," she sayde, "who was so hardy to sende yow so hoomly into oure pryve studye to us?"

"Madame," sayde this oolde fader, "the queene of alle queenes and the lady of alle ladyes, the flour of bounte and of beaute of alle wymmen."

"Goode sir," she sayde, "where dwelleth this lady that ye prayse thus gretly, for we never herde speke of suche oon?"

"Madame," he sayde, "hir dwellyng ys yn hir sones kyngdom, where everelastynge joye regneth."

"And good sir," she sayde, "who ys hir sone?"

"Madame," he sayde, "the kynge of blisse."

"Now this ys to me," she sayde, "a gret mervayl, that she ys so greet in alle dignitees and hir sone so myghty as ye seyen, and sendeth so symple a messanger as ye be."

"Madame," he sayde, "hit ys the propurtee of that lady to love and cherysshe moost thoo that refuse hemself and all erthely thyng for the love of hir sone. And for this cause she sendeth me to yow. She greteth

yow wel as hir doughter by that token that whanne ye saat in youre parlement, your moder and youre lordes aboute yow, in kepyng of youre
virginitee ye discryved yow an husbonde, wherfore your moder and alle
youre lordes were in greet hevynesse. Bot for ye were soo stronge in that
conflycte and batayle that ye refused alle erthely kynges, she sent yow
word that ye shull have an hevenly kynge, the whiche was bore of a clene
virgyn and ys kyng of alle kynges and lord of alle lordshippes, to whos
commaundement obeyeth heven and erthe and all that ys therynne.
This saam lord ys hir owen derest sone whiche she conceyved by the
vertu of the holy gost and bare hym wythoute weem of hir virginite, wyth
soverayn worshep and joye that never was felt of womman ne never shall
aftur. Wherfore she sent yow to say by me that ye shulde come allone to
my celle wyth me, and there shall ye see that blessed lord and that
blessed lady that abyden your comyng wyth greet joy and gladnesse."

Whan this yonge queene herd hym speke so clerly of hym that she had
so bysily sought wyth many a fervent desyr, she was soo brennyngly sette
a fyre wyth the desyr of his presence that she forgat all questions and all
hir astat and meyne, and roos hir up mekely, and as a debonayr lombe
folewed this oold Adrian thurgh hir paleys and the cyte of Alisaundre
and soo thurgh desert. And in hir walkyng, she asked hym many an hye
question, and he answered hir sufficiantly and enformede hir in alle the
poyntes of the feyth, and she receyved plenteuously his doctrine and en-
formacioun and undirstode hym merveylously.

And thus walketh this olde man Adrian and this yonge queene aftur
hym thurghe desert too and froo, they wist not whidere. Therfore
Adrian was a sory man, for he had utterly loost hys celle. He coude in
noo wyse fynde the way thyder, and therfore he was in greet hevynesse,
seyynge by hymself, "Allas whether I be deceyved, whether this vision be
turned to illusion; allas, shall this yonge queen perysshe here amonge
wylde bestes? Now, blessed lady, help now, for I am almoost in dispeyre,
and al my sorwe ys for this yong lady that so mekely hath left and forsake
al that ever she had and obeyed youre commaundement." And as he sor-
wed thus by hymself, this yong queen perceyved hym and asked hym
what hym ayled that he sorowed soo. And he answered to hir and sayde,
"Trewly, lady, hit ys for yow and for nothyng elles, for and I shuld dye, I
cannot fynde my celle, ne I wote neyther whyder I have well brought &
what I schal doo. Allas I wote not."

"Fader," she sayde, "beth of good counfort and haveth trewe fayth, for trusteth fully that that lady that ys soo good sent never for us to perysshe us here in this wyldernesse. Fader," she sayde, "what mynstre ys that whyche I se yonder that ys so ryche and so fayre?"

And Adrian loked up and seyde, "Where see ye that?"

"Yonder in the este," she sayde.

And he wyped his eyen and beheld and sawe the moost glorious mynstre that ever man sawe, and when he had sayen that, he was full of joye and sayd to hir, "Now blessed be ye that God hath visited wyth so parfyt fayth, for there is that place whereyn ye shull receyve soo greet a worshep and joye that there was nevere noon lyke to yow saaf oonly the queen of alle queenes."

Cap. 7: How virgyns & martirs come agenst hir & brought hir to our lady & hou she was baptized

Than, walkyng forth hastyly in her wey, wythynne short tyme thay neyghed to this glorious place; and whan thay caam to the gate, there come agenst hem a glorious company of virginis alle in whyte chapelettys of white lilies uppon her hedes, and ther excellente beute was so greet that neyther this yong queen Kateryn ne Adrian myght beholde hem, bot al ravysshed fille doun before hem wyth greet drede. Than oon that was more excellent than another spake first and sayde to this yonge queen, "Stonde up, oure dere suster, and welcome wyth all our hertys, for by thy gret mekenes and pure chastite oure worship and joye shal be gretly encressed. Wherfore be ye glad in our lord, for alle virgyns shull worshep yow. Come forth wyth us to that soverayn lord that wyl werke in yow mervelous werkes of love." And thus thay passed forth wyth gret joye and solemnite til thay come to the seconde gate, and when they entred yn, there come agenst hem a moche more glorious company wythoute comparisoun that was the company of martirs, clothed all in purpul wyth reed roses uppon here hedes; and whanne this yonge queen sawe hem, she fel doun flat before hem wyth greet drede and reverence; and than [*sic*] benygnly counforted hir and wyth a glad chere sayde to hir in this wyse, "Drede you not oure dere sister, for ther was never noon before yow hertlyer welcome to oure soverayn lord and to us then ye be. And therfore joye ye in our lord, for ye shall receyve ne oure clothyng and oure croune wyth so gret worshep and joye that alle seyntes shall joye in you. Come on now faste, for the lord of joye abydeth you wyth grete desyre of youre presence."

Than this yonge queen wyth tremblyng joye humbly passed forth wyth hem, as she that was ravysshed wyth so gret joye and mervayll that she had noo worde to say to all that was sayde to hir. And when they were entred into the body of the chirche, she herde a merveylous melodye of swetnes which passed alle hertes to descrive, and therwyth she behelde a ryal queen stondynge in astat wyth gret multitude of aungels and sayntes aboute hir. The beute and the rychesse of this queen myght no hert thenke ne penne wryte, for hyt excedith every mannes mynde. Than this noble company of martirs wyth the feleshype of virgyns that ladden this yonge queen bytwene hem fyll doun prostrat before this ryal emperesse, and wyth soverayn reverence sayde in this wyse: "Our moost soverayn lady, queen of hevene, lady of the world, emperesse of helle, moder of oure soverayn lord, kyng of blys, to whos commaundement obeyeth alle hevenly creatures and erthly! Lyke hit to yow to wyte, blessed lady, that at your commaundement we presente here our dere sustir whos name is specially wryten in the boke of everlastyng lyyf, besechynge your most benigne grace to receyve hir as your servaunt and chosen doughter and to make a parfyt ende of that werke that oure soverayn lord, almyghty God, your blessed sone, and ye have mervelously begonne in hir."

Wyth that, that gloriouse emperesse wyth a glad and reverent chere loked uppon hem and sayde, "Brynge my beloved doughter to me, that I may speke wyth hir." And whanne this yong queene Kateryne herd these wordes of that moost soverayn queene, she was so fulfylled wyth hevenly joye that she lay a greet whyle as deed. Than this holy felouship toke hir mekely up and brought hir to thys queene of blys, to whom she sayde, "My deere doughter, ryght welcome to me. Be stronge and of good counfort, for ye be specially chosen amonge alle wommen to be soveraynly worsheped wyth the love of my sone. Kateryne, doughter, have ye mynde how ye descrived you an housbond syttynge in your parlement, wherfore ye had a gret conflyct and batayle to defende youre maydenhed?"

Then this yong queene, wyth moost humble reverence and drede, sayde, "A, moost blessed lady, blessed be ye amonge alle wommen. I have mynde how I chees there that lord that was full fere fro my knowleche. Bot now, good lady, by hys myghty mercy and youre speciall grace, he hath opened the eyen of my blynde ignoraunce that I see the clere way of trouthe. Wherfore, moost blessed lady, I beseche yow with al myn hert that ye doo me mercy and grace, and geve me hym that ye have be-hyght me, that myn hert loveth and desireth above al thyng, wythoute whom I may not lyve." Wyth these wordes, alle hir spirites were shett up soo fast that she lay as deed.

Than this noble queen of grace wyth swet wordes counforted hir and sayde, "Drede not, my dere doughter, for hit shall be ryght as ye desyre. Bot ye lak oo thyng that ye moost have or ye come into the presence of my sone, for ye moost be clothed wyth the sacrament of Baptem. Wherfore, come on, for al thyng ys redy." Ther was a font in the chirche sollempnly arayed wyth al thyng that longeth therto. Thanne this queene of joye called Adrian to hir, the oold fader, and seyde to hym, "Brother, this werke longeth to you that be a prest. Baptize my doughter, and loke that ye chaunge not hir name, for Kateryne shall she hyght forth. And I schal holde hir to yow myself and be hir godmoder." Than Adrian baptized hir as our lady had bode hym.

Cap. 8: How our lady ladde hir unto hir sone & how she was spoused and wedded to hym

Whan this blessed virgyn Seynt Kateryne was thus batized, and aftur clothed ageyn as she sholde be, than the glorious queen of hevene sayde unto hir, "Now, myn owne doughter, be glad and full of joye, for now ye lak noo thyng that longeth to an hevenly spouse. Come now wyth me, for I shal brynge yow to my lord and to my sone that abideth yow wyth gret joye." Thanne was this yong queene Kateryne soo full of joye that noon hert coude expresse [the] swetnesse that she felt. She went forth wyth this queen of joye tyl thay come into the queer, and as thay entred yn, so greet a swetnesse come agenst hem that hit passed alle hertys to thenke hyt. Wyth that, she behelde the semlyest yong kyng stondyng at the auter, crouned wyth a ryche croune, havynge aboute hym multitude of angels and of seyntes, and when his blessed moder sawe hym, she leyde hir doun prostrat and toke the croune of hir heed and seyde to hym wyth humble reverence, "Moost soverayn worshep and joye be to yow, kyng of blys, my lord, my God, and my sone. Lyke youre moost hyynesse to wyte that I have brought yow here, as youre wylle ys, youre humble ser-vaunt and handmayden Kateryne, that for youre love hath refused and forsake al erthly good and ys come allone at my sendyng wyth oold Adrian, forgetyng alle erthly thyngys and astat, trustynge fully to my promys. Wherfor I beseche you humbly, my soverayn lord God and my derrest sone, that ye of youre endeles goodnesse fulfylle my promys."

Whan this soverayn kyng had herde hys moder, he toke hir godely up and seyde to hir, "My dere moder, ye knowe ryght wel that al youre desyr ys my full wylle, and I have desyred hir to be knytte to me in parfyt mariage amonge alle the virgyns that now lyven in erthe. Wherfore, Kateryne, come hyder to me." And whan she herde hym name hir, so gret a swetnesse entred into hir soule that she fel doun as deed lyynge before hym. Wyth that, he yaf hir a noble strengthe that passed kynde and sayde to hir in frendly wyse, "Kateryne, doughter, can ye fynde in your herte to love me best before all thynge?"

And she, beholdynge that blessed visage that angels have contynuely joye to beholde yn, sayde, "A moost swettest and blessed lorde, so have I do and schal whyle I lyve, ne nevere loved I thyng bot oonly yow and for yow."

Than seyde thys blessed kynge, "Kateryn, geve me your honde." And she, wyth soverayn joye, offerde hym hir honde, and thanne that glorious kynge sayde, "Here I take yow to my wedded wyf, behotyng you treuly nevere to forsake you whyl your lyf lasteth; and aftur your present lyyf, I schal brynge yow to endeles lyf, where ye shall dwelle wyth me in blys wythoute ende. In token wherof I sette this ryng uppon your fynger, whiche ye shall kepe in remembraunce of me as your weddynge rynge. And now, my dere spouse, be glad and strong of feyth, for ye most do gret thyngys for my name, and resceyve moche turment and peyne and a greet stroke uppon your nekke. Bot drede you not, my dere spouse, for I schal never departe fro you, bot counfort yow and strenght yow."

Than sayde this humble spouse, "A moost blessed lord, I thonke yow wyth all myn hert of alle your grete mercyes, besechyng yow, my soverayn lord, to make me worthy to be of youre lyverey that suffred so moche for me, and that I may in somthynge be lyke yow that al myn hert loveth and desyreth above al thyng."

Wyth this, this glorious kynge bad Adryan do on his vestimentes and go to Masse, and say the servise over hem as longeth to the custom of weddynge. And that soverayn lord of blys helde his spouse by the honde, knelyng al the Masse tyme before Adrian. A lord, what joye and blys was felt in that blessed virgyns soule al that tyme was never noon suche felt before of noon, out take hir joye and blys that conceyved and bare the soverayn joye, whiche was his moost blessed moder. Alle the spirites of heven joyed of this mariage, so fer forthe that hyt was herde the saam tyme as they kneled togyder how they songe this verse, *Sponsus amat sponsam salvator visitat illam,* and that wyth so gret a melodye that noon hert myght conceyve hit. This verse ys thus moche to say, "The spouse loveth the spousesse, the savyour visiteth hir."

Cap. 9: How our lord departed fro hir and she went hoom ageyn and how she was governyd afterward in hir paleys

This was a solempne and a singlere mariage; there was never noon suche herde of tofore in erthe. Wherfore this glorious virgyn ys worthy greetly to be worshiped and loved among alle the virgyns that ever were in erthe. And whan this masse was doo, this hevenly kyng sayde to hir, "Now, my dere spouse, tyme is come that I most goo ageyn from thens I come. I have fulfilled al your desyr, and yyf ye desyre eny more, I am redy to graunte yow what yow liste to have of me. Aftur my departyng hens, ye shul abyde here ten dayes, tyl ye be parfytly taught alle my lawes and all my wylle. And whanne ye come hoom, ye shull fynde your moder deed; bot drede yow not, for ye were not myste there al this tyme, for I ordeyned oon in your stede that alle wenen that hyt be your owne persone, and whan ye come hoom ageyn she shal voyde. Now farewell, my derrest spouse."

And wyth that she cryed wyth a gret and a pytous voys, "A, my soverayn lord God and all the joye of my soule, have mynde uppon me."

Wyth that, he blessed hir and vanysshed away fro hir sight, and for sorowe of this partynge she fyll doun in a swoun, so that she lay a large hour wythoute spiryt of lyf. Than was Adrian a sory man. He wepte and cryed on hir that hit was pyte to se or to here hit. Soo at last she awoke and held up here eyen, and sawe nothyng aboute hir bot a lytil oold celle and Adrian wepyng besyde hir, for al was goo that there was, bothe mynstre and paleys and alle the counfortable sightes that she had seen, and specialy he that was cause of al hir joye and confort. Now ys hir herte brought in so mornynge that she coude no thyng do bot wepe and syghe, tyl at the laste she beheld the rynge that our lord sette on hir fynger; and thanne she swouned ageyn, and thanne she kyst hit an hondert tymes wyth many a pytous tere. And Adrian counforted hire in his best wyse wyth many a blessed exhortacion; and she toke mekely alle his counfortes, and obeyed hym as hir fader, and dwelled wyth hym the tyme that our lord assigned hir, til she was sufficiantly taught al that was needfull to hir.

And whan hir tyme come, she went home ageyn to hir paleys; and as sone as she myght she made alle hir meyny to resceyve Baptym. And foure yere after this she held hir houshold in hir paleys wyth full cristen governaunce, and al hir joye was ever to speke or to thenke on hir lord and hir spouse; ther was nothyng elles in hir mynde bot his worshep and his praysyng. Many a creature converted she to hym in this menetyme; she was nevver ydel, bot contynuely ocupied in his servyse, full of charite, for all hir joye was to drawe creatures to hym. The puple that was lefte under hir cure by enheritaunce she governed wyth gret entendaunce, not forthy that she delited hir in gret servyce of men and wommen, bot for she thought that she myght not wythoute synne kepe to hirself hir faders lyflode and sufre the puple peryshe for defaute, namely, syth she had caste hir to have ryght nought a doo wyth the world. And therfore of al the substaunce of hir faders lyflode she kept bot a lytell to hirself, and all the remenaunt wyth al hir faders tresour she disposed to the sustenaunce of the pore puple. She loved not to here or see eny playes or japes, or eny veyn or worldly wordes or songes, bot oonly she yaf hir to study of holy scripture—and that wyth gret diligence, for from hir childhode hir fader had sette hir to liberal studyes, as ys tofore sayde, in whiche she was soo sufficiantly taught that she myght not be deceyved wyth no craft of sotilte or of argumentes. For thaugh many grete clerkes assayed hir wyth sotilte of questions and objections, yet they proved hemself bot foles and ydiotes and hir unable to be overcome. Besyly she kept the clennes of hir virgynyte, and in this wyse she dwelled in hir faders paleys, full of alle vertues and graces, as the ryght dere and singlere spouse of almyghty God.

Lightning Source UK Ltd.
Milton Keynes UK
UKHW012343241020
372088UK00014B/273